Mastering SAS Programming
From Basics to Expert Proficiency

Contents

Introduction

SAS (Statistical Analysis System) is a powerful software suite developed by SAS Institute for advanced analytics, business intelligence, data management, and predictive analytics. Since its inception, SAS has been widely adopted by organizations and professionals for its robust capabilities in data analysis and statistical modeling. This book, "Mastering SAS Programming: From Basics to Expert Proficiency," is designed to provide readers with a comprehensive understanding of SAS programming, from fundamental concepts to advanced techniques.

SAS programming is distinguished by its ability to handle large datasets efficiently and perform a wide range of data manipulation and analysis tasks. As data continues to grow in volume and complexity, the skills required to manage and analyze it effectively are more important than ever. This book aims to equip readers with the knowledge and skills necessary to leverage SAS effectively in various scenarios, whether in academic research, business analytics, or data science.

The book is structured into ten chapters, each focused on an essential aspect of SAS programming. Starting with an introduction to the basics of SAS, readers will become familiar with the fundamental building blocks of the language, including data steps, procedures, and macro programming. Each chapter is organized logically, with later sections building on concepts introduced in earlier ones.

In the first chapter, "Introduction to SAS Programming," readers will gain an understanding of the SAS environment, including the installation and setup of SAS software. The chapter covers the various components of the SAS user interface and provides an overview of basic SAS syntax and data types. Additionally, readers will learn how to read and write data, manage SAS libraries, and execute simple SAS programs.

Subsequent chapters delve into more specific aspects of SAS programming. In "Data Step Essentials," the focus is on the data step, which is the core of data manipulation in SAS. Readers will learn various techniques for reading raw data files, creating and modifying variables, and merging datasets. The chapter also covers advanced topics such as the Program Data Vector (PDV) and data step efficiency.

"Creating and Applying Formats" introduces the concept of formats in SAS, which are used to control the appearance of data values. Readers will learn how to apply predefined formats, create custom formats using PROC FORMAT, and manage format catalogs. This chapter also addresses specialized formats for dates, times, and numeric values, and provides guidance on troubleshooting common issues.

The chapter on "Using Functions in SAS" covers a wide range of functions available in SAS for data manipulation and analysis. This includes character functions, numeric functions, date and time functions, and statistical functions. Readers will learn how to apply these functions in the data step and understand their role in efficient data processing.

In "Data Manipulation Techniques," readers will explore various methods for manipulating data in SAS. This includes sorting and filtering data, merging and concatenating datasets, and transforming data structures. The chapter also covers advanced topics such as using arrays for data manipulation and handling missing values.

"Working with SAS Procedures" provides an in-depth look at the different procedures available in SAS for data analysis and reporting. This includes procedures for data summarization, statistical analysis, and data visualization. Readers will learn how to create detailed reports, generate plots and charts, and import and export data using various SAS procedures.

Effective error handling and debugging are crucial skills for any SAS programmer. The chapter on "Error Handling and Debugging" covers the different types of errors that can occur in SAS programs, how to interpret log messages, and techniques for debugging code. Readers will also learn best practices for preventing errors and ensuring robust program execution.

"Data Visualization with SAS" focuses on the powerful graphical capabilities of SAS. This chapter covers various procedures for creating bar charts, pie charts, line plots, scatter plots, and more. Readers will learn how to customize graphs using ODS graphics and create interactive visualizations to enhance data presentation.

For those ready to delve deeper into SAS programming, "Advanced Data Step Techniques" explores sophisticated data manipulation methods. This includes using hash objects, advanced merging techniques, and generating summary statistics within the data step. Readers will also learn about efficient data handling and advanced array processing.

Finally, "Introduction to SAS Macros" introduces the macro facility in SAS, which allows for dynamic code generation and automation. Readers will learn how to create and use macro variables, define macros, and utilize macro functions and expressions. The chapter also covers advanced macro techniques and best practices for writing robust macros.

This book is designed to be accessible and engaging for readers at all levels of SAS proficiency. Whether you are a beginner looking to gain a solid foundation in SAS programming or an experienced user seeking to enhance your skills, "Mastering SAS Programming: From Basics to Expert Proficiency" will serve as a valuable resource on your journey to mastering SAS.

Chapter 1

Introduction to SAS Programming

This chapter provides an essential foundation for working with SAS, including an overview of the software, installation and setup instructions, and an introduction to the SAS user interface and environment. Readers will become familiar with basic SAS syntax, data types, and the processes for reading and writing data. Additionally, the chapter covers the concept of SAS libraries, running SAS programs, and the fundamental data step and proc step constructs, concluding with methods for saving and exporting SAS data.

1.1 Overview of SAS

SAS (Statistical Analysis System) is a powerful software suite used for advanced analytics, business intelligence, data management, and predictive analytics. Developed by SAS Institute Inc., it offers numerous capabilities for managing, analyzing, and interpreting large sets of data. The software comprises a unique combination of procedural and graphical interfaces, which provide users with the flexibility to perform a wide range of tasks, from simple data manipulations to complex analytical procedures.

SAS leverages both macro programming and a robust set of procedures (or procs) to enable sophisticated data processing. At its core, SAS functions using a data-driven approach—every operation revolves around the creation, manipulation, and analysis of data sets.

Procedural Language: SAS is driven by procedures, or procs, which are encapsulated blocks of codes designed to perform specific tasks. Examples include proc means, proc freq, proc reg, among many others.

Data Steps: The data step is a fundamental component used to read, aggregate, and transform data. It plays a crucial role in data manipulation, allowing users to import data from various sources, clean it, and prepare it for analysis.

SAS Libraries: These are collections of SAS data sets that reside either on the user's machine or on a remote server. Libraries facilitate easy management and retrieval of data sets.

SAS operates through a well-defined architecture that includes:

- SAS Software Components: Comprising Base SAS, SAS/STAT, SAS/GRAPH, SAS/ETS, among others, these components allow for comprehensive data manipulation and analysis functionalities.
- SAS Data Sets: These are structured data storage formats used by SAS software. A SAS data set consists of data values organized in rows and columns, similar to a table in a database.
- SAS Programs: Written by users, these programs are sets of instructions executed in the SAS environment to process data and generate output.
- Interactive and Batch Modes: SAS can operate in interactive mode via the SAS interface or in batch mode by running scripts. Interactive mode allows dynamic execution and immediate feedback, whereas batch processing is suited for automated, repetitive tasks.

A typical SAS program structure comprises:

```
data work.example_data;
    input Name $ Age Height Weight;
    datalines;
    Alice 30 64 140
    Bob 25 70 180
```

```
    Carol 35 62 120
    Dave 40 68 200
    ;
run;

proc print data=work.example_data;
run;
```

In the example above, the data step creates a data set named example_data in the work library, which is temporary. The proc print step then submits the data set contents to the output window for review.

SAS scripting allows for advanced data manipulation techniques, including merging data sets, subsetting data, and implementing complex statistical methods. The language encourages users to write modular and reusable code, enhancing productivity.

Additionally, SAS integrates advanced graphical capabilities for visual representation of data. The proc sgplot procedure is often used to create high-quality graphics and visualize data distributions, trends, and statistical relationships.

Key advantages of SAS include its versatility and robustness, extensive documentation, and a large user community that provides peer-support. With ongoing enhancements, SAS remains a preferred choice in various industries, including pharmaceuticals, finance, and academia.

Understanding the overarching structure and capabilities of SAS is crucial in effectively utilizing its diverse features. Leveraging the power of SAS can significantly impact data analysis, providing a robust toolset for data-driven decision-making.

1.2 Installing and Setting Up SAS

SAS, or Statistical Analysis System, is a powerful software suite used for advanced analytics, business intelligence, data management, and predictive analytics. Proper installation and setup are crucial to ensure a smooth workflow and the full functionality of SAS. This section will detail the steps required to install SAS on a personal computer, including system requirements, download instructions, installation procedures, and initial configuration.

System Requirements

Before beginning the installation process, it is necessary to verify that the computer meets the minimum system requirements for running

SAS software efficiently. Typical requirements include:

- **Operating Systems:** Windows 10 (64-bit) or later, or compatible UNIX/Linux distributions.
- **Processor:** Multi-core processor, 2 GHz or faster.
- **RAM:** Minimum 8 GB of RAM, 16 GB or higher recommended.
- **Disk Space:** At least 10 GB of free disk space.
- **Display:** 1024x768 or higher resolution monitor.

These requirements ensure that the software operates efficiently and that the computer can handle large datasets and complex computations.

Downloading SAS

To download SAS, follow these steps:

1. Visit the official SAS website or the academic institution's software distribution center.
2. Log in with the necessary credentials, typically provided by the software distributor or institution.
3. Navigate to the SAS download section and select the appropriate version for your operating system.
4. Download the installer file to your computer. This may take some time depending on the internet connection speed.

Ensure that you have a stable internet connection during the download process to avoid corrupted files. Keep the downloaded installer in a known location for easy access during installation.

Installing SAS

Follow the detailed steps below to install SAS on a Windows operating system. For UNIX/Linux users, refer to the specific installation instructions provided by SAS.

1. Locate the downloaded SAS installer file and double-click to run it.

2. The SAS Deployment Wizard will start. Click Next to proceed.
3. Accept the license agreement and click Next.
4. Choose the products to install. For a complete setup, ensure that all components are selected. Click Next.
5. Choose the installation directory. The default location is typically C:\Program Files\SASHome. If necessary, change the directory and click Next.
6. The installer will now check for system requirements. If any requirement is not met, follow the prompts to rectify the issue.
7. Review the installation summary and click Install.
8. The installation process will begin. This may take several minutes to an hour depending on the system's performance. Monitor the progress bar.
9. Once the installation is completed, a confirmation screen will appear. Click Finish to exit the SAS Deployment Wizard.

Initial Configuration

After installing SAS, it is essential to perform some initial configuration to optimize the environment for data analysis tasks. Follow these steps to configure SAS:

- **Verification:** Launch SAS to verify that the installation was successful. Double-click the SAS icon on the desktop or navigate to it through the Start Menu.
- **Configuration Files:** Configure the sasv9.cfg file located in the SAS home directory. This configuration file allows the user to set system options and other environment settings.
- **Libraries:** Define SAS libraries to easily access datasets. This can be done within the SAS program editor or by modifying the configuration files.
- **Autoexec File:** Edit the autoexec.sas file to include frequently used SAS statements and library definitions. This file executes every time SAS is started, ensuring the environment is set up consistently.

- **Customizing User Interface:** Customize the SAS interface by setting preferences in the 'Tools' menu under 'Options'. Modify the appearance, editor settings, and other user preferences to match personal workflow needs.
- **Updates and Patches:** Regularly check for updates and patches from the SAS website to keep the software up-to-date. Install these updates to ensure compatibility and to benefit from the latest features and bug fixes.

Proper setup and configuration of SAS are critical to enable efficient data management and analysis. Following these detailed steps ensures that users create a stable and optimized environment, facilitating the comprehensive use of SAS capabilities.

1.3 SAS User Interface and Environment

The SAS (Statistical Analysis System) user interface provides various tools and features essential for efficient data analysis, manipulation, and visualization. This section will thoroughly examine the components of the SAS interface, their functionality, and how to navigate the environment. Familiarity with the SAS user interface is crucial for maximizing the software's capabilities.

1. SAS Display Manager System (DMS)

The SAS Display Manager System (DMS) is a comprehensive interface encompassing several key windows: the Editor Window, Log Window, Output Window, and Results Window. These windows work synergistically to allow users to develop, debug, and execute SAS programs.

- **Editor Window:** This window is used for writing and editing SAS programs. It supports syntax highlighting, making it easier to read and distinguish different elements of the SAS code. Users can write Data and Proc steps, macro code, and any other SAS-related syntax in this window.

```
data sample;
    input Name $ Age;
    datalines;
    John 30
    Jane 28
    ;
run;
```

```
proc print data=sample;
run;
```

- **Log Window:** After executing a SAS program, the Log Window displays messages from the SAS system, including notes, warnings, and errors. It is crucial for debugging as it provides detailed information about the execution of each step in the code. Analyzing the Log Window helps in identifying syntax errors or logical issues in the program.

```
NOTE: The data set WORK.SAMPLE has 2 observations and 2 variables.
NOTE: PROCEDURE PRINT used (Total process time):
      real time           0.01 seconds
      cpu time            0.01 seconds
```

- **Output Window:** This window displays the results generated by the execution of SAS procedures (PROC steps). When users run procedures like PROC PRINT, PROC MEANS, etc., the formatted results are shown in the Output Window.

```
Obs   Name   Age
 1    John   30
 2    Jane   28
```

- **Results Window:** The Results Window provides a tree-structured view of all the output produced during the SAS session. This organizational feature enables users to efficiently navigate through multiple output results without overwhelming them with cluttered information.

2. SAS Enterprise Guide

SAS Enterprise Guide (EG) is an integrated development environment (IDE) for SAS that provides a point-and-click interface for users who prefer a more graphical interaction with data. It is particularly useful for those who are less familiar with programming and want to leverage the power of SAS through an interactive and intuitive platform.

- **Project Tree:** The Project Tree is a hierarchical representation of all the tasks, data, and results within a project. It helps in organizing and managing different elements of a project effectively.

- **Task Window:** This window allows users to perform various data manipulation and statistical analysis tasks without writing code. Tasks are grouped into categories like Data, Describe, ANOVA, and Regression, among others.

- **SAS Program Window:** For users who still prefer writing code, the SAS Program Window in Enterprise Guide offers the same functionality as the Editor Window in the Display Manager System, with the additional benefit of a more integrated development experience.

3. SAS Studio

SAS Studio is a web-based interface that allows users to write and run SAS code from any device with a web browser. It is part of the SAS Viya platform and offers a modern, flexible approach to SAS programming.

- **Code Window:** Similar to the Editor Window in DMS, the Code Window in SAS Studio is where users write their SAS programs. It supports features like syntax highlighting, code formatting, and autocompletion.
- **Explorer Pane:** This pane provides access to libraries and datasets, allowing users to easily navigate through their data and perform operations such as viewing or importing data sets.
- **Results Pane:** After executing code, the Results Pane displays outputs, logs, and results in a structured and easily navigable format. This integration streamlines the process of reviewing program execution and output.

4. Navigating the SAS Environment

Navigating the SAS environment efficiently involves understanding how to move between these interfaces and utilize their features:

- To open a new program window in DMS, users can select File → New Program from the menu bar.
- In SAS Enterprise Guide, users can create new projects and add tasks by right-clicking in the Project Tree and selecting the appropriate options.
- In SAS Studio, the Start New Program button quickly opens a new code window for writing SAS programs.

Proficiency in using these interfaces, understanding their specific functionalities, and knowing when to use each can significantly enhance productivity and efficiency in SAS programming. The choice between DMS, Enterprise Guide, and SAS Studio depends on user preference, specific task requirements, and organizational standards.

1.4 Introduction to SAS Syntax

SAS (Statistical Analysis System) syntax forms the foundation of any SAS program. It is crucial to understand the structure and components of SAS syntax to effectively write, read, and debug SAS programs. This section delves into the key elements of SAS syntax, including statements, functions, formats, and the importance of semicolons.

A SAS program consists of a series of steps, each ending with a semicolon. These steps can mainly be categorized as:

- Data steps: used for data manipulation.
- Procedure (proc) steps: used to analyze and report data.

Statements

In SAS, a statement is an instruction that SAS executes. Each statement must end with a semicolon. For example:

```
data mydata;
   set sashelp.class;
run;
```

The above code includes a data step where mydata is being created from the sashelp.class dataset.

Comments

Comments are used to annotate the code and are ignored by the SAS compiler. There are two types of comments in SAS:

- Block comments, wrapped in /* */.
- Single-line comments, prefixed with an asterisk *.

```
/* This is a block comment */
* This is a single-line comment;
```

Data Step Syntax

The data step in SAS is used to create and manipulate data sets. It begins with the data statement and ends with the run statement. Other common statements within a data step include set, input, if-then-else, and merge. Here is an example:

```
data employees;
   input Name $ Age Department $ Salary;
   datalines;
John 28 Sales 50000
Jane 32 IT 60000
Tom 36 HR 55000
;
run;
```

In this example:

- The data statement creates a new dataset named employees.
- The input statement specifies the variables Name, Age, Department, and Salary.
- The datalines statement provides the data for those variables.

Procedure Step Syntax

The proc step performs analysis and reporting. It begins with the proc statement and ends with a run statement. Common procedure steps include proc print, proc means, proc freq, and proc sort. Example:

```
proc print data=employees;
run;
```

This proc print statement displays the contents of the employees dataset.

Functions

SAS functions perform operations on data and return a value. They are used within data steps to manipulate data. Examples of common functions include mean, sum, substr, and length. For instance, to calculate the average salary:

```
data avg_salary;
   set employees;
   AvgSalary = mean(Salary);
run;
```

Here, the mean function computes the average salary for the dataset employees, and the result is stored in the variable AvgSalary.

Formats

SAS formats are used to control the appearance of data values. They are specified using the format statement within a data or proc step. Common formats include date9., comma10., dollar8.2, and percent8.2. Example:

```
data formatted;
  set employees;
  format Salary dollar10.2;
run;
```

This applies the dollar10.2 format to the Salary variable, displaying it as a dollar amount with two decimal places.

Importance of Semicolons

Every statement in SAS must end with a semicolon. Omitting a semicolon can lead to syntax errors and prevent the program from running correctly. For example:

```
data employees
  input Name $ Age;
run;
```

This code will produce an error because the semicolon is missing after the data employees statement.

Understanding and adhering to SAS syntax rules is essential for efficient programming and accurate data analysis. Recognizing the need for exact syntax, while also appreciating the built-in flexibility of SAS, prepares one for more advanced topics, facilitating a robust foundation in SAS programming.

1.5 Basic Data Types in SAS

In SAS, understanding data types is crucial for effective data manipulation and analysis. SAS primarily recognizes two fundamental data types: numeric and character. Each type has distinct properties and methods of handling, which we will explore meticulously.

Numeric data types in SAS are used to store numerical values, enabling arithmetic operations. These include integers, floating-point numbers, and any quantifiable figures. SAS allocates 8 bytes for numeric storage by default, providing ample precision for most applications. It's important to note that missing numeric values are represented by a single period (.), reflecting the absence of data.

Here is an example of assigning a numeric variable in a SAS data step:

```
data example;
    num_var = 100; /* Numeric variable */
    num_missing = .; /* Missing numeric value */
run;
```

The output produced by running the code, displaying the creation of numeric variables, would look like:

```
num_var  num_missing
-------  -----------
  100         .
```

Character data types in SAS, also referred to as strings, are used to store textual information. Variables of character type can hold letters, numbers, and special characters. By default, SAS allocates a length of 8 bytes to character variables unless explicitly defined with a different length using the length statement. Missing character data are represented by a blank.

Below is an example demonstrating the definition and assignment of character variables:

```
data example;
    length char_var $ 15; /* Defining a character variable with length 15 */
    char_var = 'Hello, SAS'; /* Character variable assignment */
    char_missing = ''; /* Missing character value */
run;
```

Upon execution, the following output is generated, showing the creation and assignment of character variables:

```
char_var      char_missing
-----------   ------------
Hello, SAS
```

It is essential to balance the correct use of these data types when processing data. Incorrectly defining numeric data as character, or vice versa, can result in errors or incorrect computations. SAS functions INPUT and PUT are often used to convert variables between numeric and character types. The INPUT function converts characters to numerics, while the PUT function performs the inverse.

For example, converting a character variable to a numeric variable:

```
data convert_example;
    char_num = '1234';
    num_var = input(char_num, 8.); /* Converting character to numeric */
run;
```

The output will be:

```
char_num  num_var
--------  -------
  1234     1234
```

Conversely, converting a numeric variable to a character variable:

```
data convert_example;
    num_var = 1234;
    char_num = put(num_var, 8.); /* Converting numeric to character */
```

```
run;
```

Generating the following output:

```
num_var  char_num
-------  --------
 1234      1234
```

Complex data handling often requires utilization of SAS's functions tailored for specific data types. For numeric data, functions like SUM(), MEAN(), MIN(), and MAX() are instrumental for statistical calculations. For character data, functions such as SUBSTR(), INDEX(), TRIM(), and UPCASE() enable text manipulations and analyses.

For example:

```
data func_example;
    num1 = 10;
    num2 = 20;
    sum_result = sum(num1, num2); /* Using SUM function */

    char_variable = "Hello World!";
    substr_result = substr(char_variable, 1, 5); /* Using SUBSTR function */
run;
```

Resulting in:

```
num1 num2 sum_result char_variable  substr_result
---- ---- ---------- -------------  -------------
 10   20      30       Hello World!     Hello
```

Proficiency in handling these basic data types sets a foundation for mastering more advanced topics in SAS. Properly leveraging numeric and character variable properties ensures data accuracy and efficient processing, critical for any SAS programming endeavor.

1.6 Reading and Writing Data in SAS

Reading and writing data in SAS are fundamental capabilities that significantly influence data analyses. This section delves into the methodologies and syntax required to proficiently handle data input and output within SAS.

To read data into SAS, the DATA step and INFILE statement are paramount. Consider a scenario where the data is stored in a text file named *data.txt*. The following example illustrates how to read this data:

```
DATA mydata;
    INFILE 'path/to/data.txt' FIRSTOBS=2; /* Skips the header row */
    INPUT var1 $ var2 $ var3;
RUN;
```

Here, the INFILE statement points to the location of the file, and the INPUT statement specifies the variable names and their respective types, with a dollar sign denoting character variables. The FIRSTOBS=2 option starts reading data from the second row, presuming the first row contains headers.

For reading more complex datasets like CSV files, the PROC IMPORT procedure offers a streamlined approach:

```
PROC IMPORT DATAFILE='path/to/data.csv'
            OUT=mycsvdata
            DBMS=CSV
            REPLACE;
    GETNAMES=YES; /* Indicates the first row contains variable names */
RUN;
```

The PROC IMPORT procedure imports the CSV file directly, automatically recognizing headers when GETNAMES=YES is specified. The DBMS=CSV option indicates that the input file is a CSV file, and REPLACE option ensures that if mycsvdata already exists, it will be overwritten.

SAS also supports reading Excel files using the PROC IMPORT procedure:

```
PROC IMPORT DATAFILE='path/to/data.xlsx'
            OUT=myexceldata
            DBMS=XLSX
            REPLACE;
    GETNAMES=YES;
RUN;
```

In this instance, DBMS=XLSX denotes that the input file is in Excel format. The remainder of the syntax remains consistent with that of the CSV import.

Writing (or exporting) data in SAS is often facilitated by the DATA step coupled with the FILE and PUT statements for text files. Examine the following example:

```
DATA _NULL_;
    SET mydata;
    FILE 'path/to/output.txt';
    PUT var1 $ var2 $ var3;
RUN;
```

The keyword _NULL_ in the DATA statement specifies that no data set is created; instead, the FILE and PUT statements are employed to write data directly to the specified text file. The PUT statement outputs the data variables, just as described in the input phase.

To write data into CSV or Excel files, SAS provides the PROC EXPORT procedure. The process for exporting to a CSV file is demonstrated below:

```
PROC EXPORT DATA=mydata
        OUTFILE='path/to/output.csv'
        DBMS=CSV
        REPLACE;
RUN;
```

When exporting to Excel, the syntax changes slightly:

```
PROC EXPORT DATA=mydata
        OUTFILE='path/to/output.xlsx'
        DBMS=XLSX
        REPLACE;
RUN;
```

Here, DBMS=XLSX specifies the output file format as Excel, while the REPLACE option ensures that any pre-existing file with the same name is overwritten.

To refine the reading and writing of data within SAS, one must also understand the SAS library references. A SAS library is a collection of one or more SAS files that are referenced and stored as a unit. Libraries are defined using the LIBNAME statement:

```
LIBNAME mylib 'path/to/library';
```

This command assigns the libref mylib to the library directory, enabling all subsequent data read and write operations to utilize this reference conveniently. For example, data read from or written to this library would follow the form:

```
DATA mylib.mydata;
   SET mylib.otherdata;
RUN;
```

This integration of the mylib reference ensures data consistency and simplifies file path management, particularly when dealing with multiple datasets.

Lastly, handling large datasets efficiently often requires the utilization of SAS formats and informats. Formats control the way data is displayed, while informats dictate how raw data should be interpreted during import. Formats and informats are defined as follows:

```
PROC FORMAT;
   VALUE $gender_fmt
```

```
    'M' = 'Male'
    'F' = 'Female';
RUN;

DATA mydata;
   SET mydata;
   FORMAT gender $gender_fmt.;
RUN;
```

The PROC FORMAT procedure creates a custom format $gender_fmt that translates 'M' to 'Male' and 'F' to 'Female'. Applying the custom format is achieved by the FORMAT statement within a DATA step.

By mastering these fundamental techniques for reading and writing data, one can significantly enhance data manipulation and analysis efficiency within the SAS environment.

1.7 Understanding SAS Libraries

SAS libraries are essential components for managing and organizing data sets within SAS. A SAS library is essentially a collection of SAS files that are recognized by a library reference (libref) within the SAS environment. These files can include data sets, catalogs, and other SAS file types. Understanding the structure and utilization of SAS libraries is crucial for effective data management in SAS programming.

A SAS library can be temporary or permanent. Temporary libraries exist only for the duration of the SAS session in which they are created, whereas permanent libraries persist beyond the lifetime of a single session. By default, SAS creates a temporary library named WORK at the start of each session.

To define a SAS library, you utilize a LIBNAME statement. The syntax to assign a library reference is as follows:

```
LIBNAME libref 'path-to-library';
```

In this line of code, libref is the name you assign to the library, which can be used to reference the library in subsequent SAS statements. The 'path-to-library' is the directory path where the SAS files are stored.

For example, to assign a library reference named mylib to a directory located at C:
sasdata, the command would be:

```
LIBNAME mylib 'C:\\sasdata';
```

You can also create libraries that are accessible via SAS metadata servers or database management systems (DBMS) by specifying the appropriate engine name in the LIBNAME statement. For instance, to connect to a PostgreSQL database, you would use:

```
LIBNAME db_lib POSTGRESQL USER=myuser PASSWORD=mypassword
        DATABASE=mydb SCHEMA=myschema;
```

libref names must follow SAS naming conventions: they can be up to 8 characters in length, must start with a letter or underscore, and can only contain letters, digits, and underscores.

To view the contents of a SAS library, the PROC CONTENTS procedure is used. This procedure provides a list of all data sets within the library along with their attributes. Here's how to use PROC CONTENTS to view the contents of the library mylib:

```
PROC CONTENTS DATA=mylib._ALL_ NODS;
RUN;
```

In this command:

- The DATA=mylib._ALL_ statement specifies that the contents of all data sets in the mylib library should be displayed.
- The NODS option suppresses the detailed description of each data set, providing only the list of data set names.

Data sets within a library can be accessed using the libref.data_set_name notation. When referring to a data set, it is essential to specify both the library reference and the data set name separated by a period. For example, to print the contents of a data set named sales within the mylib library, the SAS code would be:

```
PROC PRINT DATA=mylib.sales;
RUN;
```

Temporary libraries, like the WORK library, store data sets only for the duration of the current session. When the session ends, all data in the WORK library is deleted. In contrast, permanent libraries retain data across multiple SAS sessions. To create a data set in a permanent library, specify the desired library reference in the DATA statement:

```
DATA mylib.newdata;
  SET otherlib.olddataset;
RUN;
```

This command creates a new data set named newdata in the mylib library by reading an existing data set olddataset from another library otherlib.

To delete a SAS library, you can use the LIBNAME statement with the CLEAR option, which disassociates the libref and the associated directory path. This action does not delete the files in the directory but only removes the library reference within the current SAS session. For example:

```
LIBNAME mylib CLEAR;
```

The following example demonstrates setting up a permanent SAS library, creating a data set, viewing its contents, and accessing the data set in subsequent steps:

```
/* Define a permanent library */
LIBNAME mylib 'C:\\sasdata';

/* Create a new data set in the library */
DATA mylib.customers;
   INPUT CustomerID $ Name $ Age;
   DATALINES;
   C001 John 30
   C002 Alice 28
   C003 Bob 25
   ;
RUN;

/* View the contents of the library */
PROC CONTENTS DATA=mylib._ALL_ NODS;
RUN;

/* Print the contents of the data set */
PROC PRINT DATA=mylib.customers;
RUN;
```

The above code block illustrates the creation of a permanent SAS library mylib, adding a data set customers to it, and showcasing the steps to view and print the data set's contents.

SAS libraries provide a structured mechanism for organizing data sets and other SAS file types within the SAS environment, enhancing data management efficiency and accessibility.

1.8 Running SAS Programs

Running SAS programs is a fundamental task that encompasses executing the code you have written in the SAS language to carry out various operations on data. Understanding how to efficiently run SAS programs is essential for utilizing the full power of SAS for data analysis, data manipulation, and reporting tasks.

To execute a SAS program, we need to use the SAS System, which interprets and runs SAS code. SAS programs typically involve two major steps: the Data Step and the Proc Step. The Data Step is used to create and manipulate data sets, while the Proc Step is used to analyze and report on the data.

Running a Basic SAS Program

A basic SAS program consists of a sequence of statements that usually include Data Steps and Proc Steps. Here is a simple example of a SAS program that reads data, processes it, and prints the results:

```
DATA mydata;
   INPUT name $ age height weight;
   DATALINES;
John 25 70 180
Mary 28 65 150
Paul 24 68 170
Jane 27 64 140
;
RUN;

PROC PRINT DATA=mydata;
RUN;
```

In this example, the DATA statement defines a new dataset named mydata, and the INPUT statement specifies the variables and their types. The DATALINES statement is used to input the raw data directly within the program. Finally, the RUN statement tells SAS to execute the preceding Data Step. The PROC PRINT procedure then prints the contents of the dataset mydata.

After running the program, the output will display the dataset as shown below:

Obs	name	age	height	weight
1	John	25	70	180
2	Mary	28	65	150
3	Paul	24	68	170
4	Jane	27	64	140

Running SAS Programs in Batch Mode

SAS programs can be run in batch mode, especially useful for large datasets or long-running processes. This involves executing SAS code without interaction, typically using a command-line interface. The following is a sample command to run a SAS program file named program.sas in batch mode:

```
sas program.sas
```

When run in batch mode, the SAS system reads the SAS program file, executes the instructions, and generates output and log files. The log file provides details on program execution, potential errors, and warnings, while the output file contains the results of the executed procedures.

Understanding the SAS Log

The SAS Log is crucial for debugging and understanding how SAS interprets and executes your code. It contains messages about the execution process, including notes, warnings, and errors. Each time a Data Step or Proc Step is run, information is appended to the log.

For example, running the previous Data Step and Proc Step would generate the following log messages:

```
NOTE: The data set WORK.MYDATA has 4 observations and 4 variables.
NOTE: DATA statement used (Total process time):
      real time           0.02 seconds
      cpu time            0.01 seconds

NOTE: There were 4 observations read from the data set WORK.MYDATA.
NOTE: PROCEDURE PRINT used (Total process time):
      real time           0.01 seconds
      cpu time            0.01 seconds
```

These messages confirm that the dataset mydata was successfully created with 4 observations and 4 variables, and that the PROC PRINT procedure executed as expected.

Using SAS Macros

SAS Macros are useful for automating repetitive tasks and enhancing the flexibility of SAS programs. A macro is a piece of SAS code that is stored for later use, which can be invoked multiple times throughout a program. Here's an example of a simple macro:

```
%MACRO PrintData(data_set);
   PROC PRINT DATA=&data_set;
   RUN;
%MEND PrintData;

%PrintData(mydata);
```

In this example, a macro named PrintData is defined to print any dataset passed to it. The %MACRO and %MEND statements are used to define the macro, and the &data_set variable references the argument passed to the macro. The macro is invoked with %PrintData(mydata), causing it to print the mydata dataset.

Error Handling in SAS

Effective error handling ensures that SAS programs run smoothly. It also helps identify and rectify issues promptly. Common errors include syntax errors, data errors, and logic errors. For instance, a syntax error occurs when SAS encounters code that it cannot interpret, such as a missing semicolon:

```
DATA mydata
   INPUT name $ age height weight;
   DATALINES;
John 25 70 180
Mary 28 65 150
;
RUN;
```

This code will generate a syntax error due to the missing semicolon after mydata. SAS will point this out in the log with an error message.

Systematic use of the SAS Log and a methodical approach to writing SAS code can significantly mitigate the occurrence and impact of such errors, thereby ensuring a more productive programming experience.

1.9 Introduction to Data Step and Proc Step

The DATA step and the PROC (procedure) step constitute the backbone of SAS programming. Both are pivotal for data manipulation, analysis, and reporting. Understanding their structures and applications will allow for efficient and effective use of the SAS system.

The DATA step is utilized for data manipulation. It allows you to create, merge, modify, and derive data sets. On the other hand, the PROC step focuses on analyzing and summarizing the data.

DATA Step:

The DATA step begins with a DATA statement and usually ends with a RUN statement. The primary function of a DATA step is to read and manipulate the data. Here is an example:

```
DATA work.sample;
   INPUT Name $ Age Height Weight;
   DATALINES;
John 30 72 180
Mary 25 65 140
Sam 22 68 155
;
RUN;
```

In the example above:

- work.sample specifies the name of the dataset and its storage location (WORK library, which is temporary).
- INPUT statement is used to define the variables (Name, Age, Height, and Weight).
- DATALINES provide inline data for the dataset.
- The RUN statement concludes the DATA step indicating no more statements follow.

The DATA step can also include various programming operations such as loops, conditional statements, and functions. Here is an example demonstrating basic data manipulation:

```
DATA work.modified_sample;
  SET work.sample;
  Age_In_Days = Age * 365;
  Height_In_cm = Height * 2.54;
  IF Weight > 150 THEN Category = 'Heavy';
  ELSE Category = 'Light';
RUN;
```

- SET statement reads in the existing dataset work.sample.
- New variables Age_In_Days and Height_In_cm are created through arithmetic operations.
- IF-ELSE condition is used to derive a categorical variable Category.

PROC Step:

The PROC step starts with a PROC statement, invoking a SAS procedure, and ends with a RUN statement. Commonly used procedures include PROC PRINT, PROC MEANS, PROC FREQ, and PROC SORT. Procedures facilitate various functions such as data summarization, sorting, printing, and statistical analyses. Below are examples illustrating each:

```
PROC PRINT DATA=work.modified_sample;
RUN;
```

- PROC PRINT displays the data from work.modified_sample.

```
PROC MEANS DATA=work.modified_sample;
  VAR Age_In_Days Height_In_cm Weight;
RUN;
```

- PROC MEANS computes summary statistics for specified numeric variables.

```
PROC FREQ DATA=work.modified_sample;
  TABLES Category;
RUN;
```

- PROC FREQ provides frequency counts for the categorical variable Category.

```
PROC SORT DATA=work.modified_sample OUT=work.sorted_sample;
  BY Age;
RUN;
```

- PROC SORT sorts work.modified_sample by the Age variable and stores the result in work.sorted_sample.

These are fundamental illustrations of the power and flexibility of DATA and PROC steps in SAS programming. Their combined use allows for comprehensive data manipulation and analysis, leveraging the full capabilities of the SAS environment. Each step and its components form the building blocks for more sophisticated operations, essential for any proficient SAS programmer.

1.10 Saving and Exporting SAS Data

In the context of SAS programming, saving and exporting data effectively is a critical skill. This section delves into the various methods and best practices associated with saving datasets within SAS and exporting them to external formats to facilitate broader data exchange and analysis.

libname statement enables a user to define a SAS library, a repository where datasets are stored. A primary step in saving data within SAS involves ensuring that these libraries are appropriately defined. Common practices include saving datasets in the Work library (temporary, deletes upon session termination) and defining permanent libraries to store datasets persistently.

To save a dataset to the Work library, you can use the following code:

```
data work.new_dataset;
    set sashelp.cars;
run;
```

To make the dataset permanent, define a library first.

```
libname mylib '/folders/myshortcuts/myfolder';

data mylib.new_dataset;
    set sashelp.cars;
run;
```

Exporting SAS datasets to external file formats such as CSV, Excel, or text files is often required for interoperability with other software environments. SAS provides several procedures (e.g., PROC EXPORT) and utilities for efficient export tasks.

To export a dataset to a CSV file, use PROC EXPORT as shown below:

```
proc export data=mylib.new_dataset
    outfile='/folders/myshortcuts/myfolder/new_dataset.csv'
    dbms=csv
    replace;
run;
```

For exporting to an Excel file:

```
proc export data=mylib.new_dataset
    outfile='/folders/myshortcuts/myfolder/new_dataset.xlsx'
    dbms=xlsx
    replace;
run;
```

It is crucial to specify the dbms option correctly to match the desired output file format (csv for comma-separated values, xlsx for Excel). The replace option ensures that if a file with the specified name already exists, it will be overwritten.

For exporting data to a text file in a tab-delimited format:

```
proc export data=mylib.new_dataset
    outfile='/folders/myshortcuts/myfolder/new_dataset.txt'
    dbms=tab
    replace;
run;
```

Apart from PROC EXPORT, data can also be saved using DATA _NULL_ step to write data to an external file with custom specifications.

```
data _null_;
    set mylib.new_dataset;
    file '/folders/myshortcuts/myfolder/new_dataset.txt';
    put make $ model $ type $;
run;
```

Here, $ denotes that the variables make, model, and type are character variables. The put statement is used to control the format and order in which data are written to the file.

For larger and more complex datasets, especially when precision and specific formats are necessary (e.g., specific number formats), leveraging the flexibility of DATA _NULL_ steps might be advantageous.

Harnessing ODS (Output Delivery System) statements also integrates seamlessly with exporting data, particularly for creating RTF, PDF, or HTML files. For producing an HTML output:

```
ods html file='/folders/myshortcuts/myfolder/new_dataset.html';

proc print data=mylib.new_dataset;
run;

ods html close;
```

The ODS HTML statements open and close HTML output destination, wrapping around the PROC PRINT procedure to produce an HTML file representing the dataset.

Conclusively, understanding these procedures and commands ensures efficient data handling within SAS and across diverse environments, necessitating proper attention to detail and adherence to syntax conventions. The ability to save and export data reliably allows for enhanced data analysis, sharing, and reporting capabilities, reinforcing SAS's role in a data-centric workflow.

Chapter 2

Data Step Essentials

This chapter delves into the core of data manipulation in SAS, covering the data step's fundamental aspects. It explores techniques for reading raw data files and various input methods, including column input, formatted input, and list input. Readers will learn how to create and modify variables, use fundamental programming statements, and employ functions within the data step. The chapter also addresses data concatenation, merging datasets, the RETAIN statement, understanding the Program Data Vector (PDV), and optimizing data step efficiency.

2.1 Introduction to the Data Step

The foundational element of data manipulation in SAS is the DATA step. This step allows the user to construct, read, transform, and output a dataset in a highly structured and efficient manner. Grasping the workings of the DATA step is essential for leveraging the full potential of SAS for data processing and analysis.

A DATA step comprises SAS statements that control data input, modification, and output. The basic syntax to initiate a DATA step involves naming the target dataset and potentially reading from an existing dataset or raw data file. The typical structure is:

```
DATA new_dataset;
    SET existing_dataset; /* if reading from an existing dataset */
    /* Additional Statements */
RUN;
```

In this structure, DATA specifies the beginning of the data step, new_-dataset is the name of the dataset being created, and SET existing_-dataset is used to read an already existing SAS dataset. If reading raw data, the INFILE and INPUT statements will be utilized instead.

Reading Raw Data Files: Raw data can be read into SAS in various formats using the INFILE statement alongside the INPUT statement. An example of reading a CSV file is shown below:

```
DATA work.mydata;
    INFILE 'path/to/datafile.csv' DSD FIRSTOBS=2; /* DSD handles delimiters,
         FIRSTOBS skips header */
    INPUT var1 var2 var3; /* Names of variables corresponding to data columns */
RUN;
```

Here, INFILE 'path/to/datafile.csv' indicates the path to the raw data file. DSD instructs SAS to treat consecutive delimiters as missing values, and FIRSTOBS=2 skips the header row. The INPUT statement lists the variables in the order they appear in the raw data file.

Creating and Modifying Variables: The DATA step also provides the functionality to create new variables and modify existing ones. For instance:

```
DATA work.modified_data;
    SET work.mydata;
    new_var = var1 + var2; /* Creating a new variable from existing ones */
    var3 = var3 * 1.1; /* Modifying an existing variable */
RUN;
```

This script creates a new dataset, work.modified_data, by setting work.mydata and then adding a new variable, new_var, which is the sum of var1 and var2. It also modifies var3 by scaling its values.

Using Conditional Statements: Conditional statements within the DATA step allow for selective processing of data rows. A common conditional construct is the IF-THEN statement, as demonstrated below:

```
DATA work.filtered_data;
    SET work.mydata;
    IF var1 > 100 THEN flag = 1; /* Flagging rows where var1 exceeds 100 */
    ELSE flag = 0;
RUN;
```

Here, the IF-THEN statement checks if var1 is greater than 100 and sets a flag accordingly. The ELSE clause handles the alternative condition.

Looping Constructs: Looping over data, especially arrays, is a typical requirement that can be managed within the DATA step. Using the DO loop construct, one can efficiently perform iterative tasks:

```
DATA work.scores;
    SET work.students;
    ARRAY exams[5] exam1-exam5;
    total_score = 0;
    DO i = 1 TO 5;
        total_score + exams[i];
    END;
RUN;
```

In this example, an array named exams is defined to encompass variables exam1 through exam5. The DO loop iterates over these variables to accumulate their values in total_score.

Efficiency Considerations: Efficiency in the DATA step can significantly impact the runtime and resource utilization. Key practices include:

- **Minimize Variable Length:** Use LENGTH statement to control memory usage.

- **Avoid Unnecessary I/O:** Use WHERE clause instead of IF statements to filter data early.

- **Use Informats and Formats:** Properly utilize INFORMAT and FORMAT statements to streamline data reading and presentation.

An example illustrating the use of the LENGTH statement to optimize memory usage is:

```
DATA work.efficient_data;
    LENGTH var1 $5 var2 8; /* Declaring length of character variable and numeric
        variable */
    SET work.large_data;
RUN;
```

Understanding the intricacies of the DATA step equips the user with powerful tools for comprehensive data manipulation in SAS. The logical progression from reading data, creating, and modifying variables, to efficiently processing and outputting datasets underpins proficient use of the DATA step in any data analytics workflow.

2.2 Reading Raw Data Files

The ability to read raw data files into SAS is a foundational skill for any SAS programmer. SAS provides several methods to input raw data, each with its own strengths and suitable use cases. This section will describe the elementary steps for reading raw data files using the data step, focusing on the different types of input techniques and providing detailed examples.

Raw data files are typically text files that contain data but lack structure or format. Such files can come in various formats like CSV or fixed-width files. Below is an example of a simple raw data file named data.txt:

```
101 John  50000
102 Alice 55000
103 Bob   60000
```

Given the above data, we aim to read these values into a SAS dataset for further analysis. We need to define the variables (e.g., ID, Name, and Salary) and provide the appropriate instructions for reading the data.

To read raw data files efficiently, SAS uses the INFILE statement in conjunction with the INPUT statement within a data step. Below is an example where we read the example raw data file using the simplest of reading methods, list input:

```
data employees;
    infile 'data.txt';
    input ID Name $ Salary;
run;
```

Explanation:

- data employees; initializes a new data step and names the output dataset employees.
- infile 'data.txt'; specifies the location of the raw data file.
- input ID Name $ Salary; defines the variables to read from the file:
- ID is read as a numeric variable.
- Name is read as a character variable; the dollar sign ($) indicates this.

- Salary is read as a numeric variable.
- run; executes the data step.

The above code reads each line of the file sequentially, interpreting values separated by spaces. However, when the data is not well-organized (e.g., columns without consistent spacing), more advanced techniques like formatted input and column input are necessary.

Column Input:

Column input reads data from specific columns in the raw data file. This method is useful when data fields are aligned in fixed positions within each record.

Consider the following raw data file where each field occupies a specific column range:

```
123 Alice   50000
124 Mark    60000
125 Jennifer75000
```

The respective column positions for ID, Name, and Salary are 1-3, 5-11, and 13-17, respectively. Here is how column input can be used:

```
data employees;
    infile 'data_columns.txt';
    input ID 1-3 Name $ 5-11 Salary 13-17;
run;
```

Formatted Input:

Formatted input allows for more flexible and precise reading of data, particularly useful when dealing with complex data formats. Formatted input is managed using informats, which describe how to read the data fields.

Assume data in file formatted as follows, with specific column sizes and formats:

```
00123:Alice:50000
00124:Mark:60000
00125:Jennifer:75000
```

Each value is separated by a colon (:), and ID is zero-padded. The formatted input method would involve informats as shown below:

```
data employees;
    infile 'data_formatted.txt' dlm=':';
    input ID : $w5. Name : $w8. Salary : $w6.;
run;
```

Explanation:

- infile 'data_formatted.txt' dlm=':'; specifies the delimiter as ':'.
- input ID : $w5. Name : $w8. Salary : $w6.; uses informats with fixed column widths to read each variable accurately.

Special considerations when using formatted input include handling missing values, dealing with complex data types (like dates), and specifying appropriate informats.

Datasets may sometimes require reading and filtering only specific rows or applying conditional logic to the incoming data. This can be achieved using the IF statement within the data step to control data flow.

Reading raw data files is a fundamental competency that underpins effective data manipulation in SAS. Understanding the correct methods to read different raw data formats is essential for accurate data representation and subsequent analysis. Mastery of these techniques ensures robust data preparation pipelines and sets the foundation for sophisticated data processing tasks.

2.3 Input Statement and Column Input

The INPUT statement is pivotal in reading raw data files within a DATA step in SAS. Understanding its syntax and the types of input methods is crucial for efficiently importing data. Column input is one of the primary techniques employed for reading data when the positional layout of the data fields within each record is consistent.

The INPUT Statement Syntax

The INPUT statement consists of several components:

- INPUT - The keyword that instructs SAS to read data.
- variable names - The names of the variables that will be created from the data.
- input specifications - Numeric specifications for column positions or formats.

The general syntax for the INPUT statement is as follows:

```
INPUT variable1 $ startcol1-endcol1 variable2 startcol2-endcol2 ...;
```

Where:

- variable1, variable2 - Names of the variables to be created.
- $ - Indicates that the variable is character type.
- startcol1-endcol1 - Specifies the starting and ending columns for variable1.

Example of Column Input

Consider a raw data file named example.txt with the following content:

```
John  45000 34
Jane  51000 28
Doe   50000 40
```

To read this data using column input, the INPUT statement could be defined in a DATA step as follows:

```
DATA employees;
   INFILE 'example.txt';
   INPUT Name $1-5 Salary 7-11 Age 13-14;
RUN;
```

Here, Name occupies columns 1 through 5, Salary occupies columns 7 through 11, and Age occupies columns 13 through 14. The types *character* or *numeric* of the variables are denoted explicitly when required using $ for character variables.

Output Verification

After executing the above DATA step, examine the resulting dataset using the PROC PRINT procedure to validate data import:

```
PROC PRINT DATA=employees;
RUN;
```

This will produce the following output:

```
Obs   Name    Salary   Age

 1    John    45000    34
 2    Jane    51000    28
 3    Doe     50000    40
```

Handling Missing Values with Column Input

If the raw data includes missing values, ensure that the columns are accurately defined in the INPUT statement. Consider the example where the dataset contains missing Age values:

```
John  45000 34
Jane  51000
Doe   50000 40
```

The INPUT statement remains the same, and SAS automatically handles the missing age value for Jane:

```
DATA employees_with_missing_values;
   INFILE 'example_with_missing_values.txt';
   INPUT Name $1-5 Salary 7-11 Age 13-14;
RUN;
```

Upon executing the PROC PRINT procedure, the output will be displayed as follows:

```
Obs   Name    Salary   Age

 1    John    45000    34
 2    Jane    51000     .
 3    Doe     50000    40
```

The dot (.) signifies a missing numeric value.

Best Practices for Using Column Input

- Always ensure column specifications precisely match the column positions in the raw data file.
- For character variables, include the $ symbol in the INPUT statement.
- Utilize the OBS or INFILE options to manage large datasets efficiently.
- Validate the imported data by using procedures such as PROC PRINT to ensure accuracy.

Adhering to these practices guarantees accurate and efficient data import, minimizing errors and ensuring that datasets are correctly structured for subsequent analysis steps. The INPUT statement and column input method are fundamentals that streamline the process of reading organized raw data files in SAS programming.

2.4 Formatted and List Input Techniques

In SAS, reading raw data using formatted and list input techniques enables users to efficiently process diverse data formats and structures.

These methods expand capabilities beyond simple column input, allowing for flexible and precise data handling.

Formatted Input Technique

The formatted input technique leverages SAS informats to read and convert data values from external files into SAS datasets accurately. Informats inform SAS about the structure and type of data, such as numeric, character, or date, and specify how many columns to read for each variable.

To use formatted input, you need an infile statement to identify the raw data file and an appropriate input statement to define the variables and their corresponding informats.

Consider a raw data file rawdata.txt with the following content:

```
123456 John    65000.50 010121
789012 Jane    55000.25 120921
```

We'll process this data using formatted input by specifying informats for each variable:

```
data employees;
   infile 'rawdata.txt';
   input ID $char6. Name $char8. Salary comma7.2 Date mmddyy6.;
run;
```

Explanation of informats used:

- $char6. specifies a character variable of length 6 for ID.
- $char8. specifies a character variable of length 8 for Name.
- comma7.2 reads a numeric variable with commas and two decimal places for Salary.
- mmddyy6. interprets a date in MMDDYY format for Date.

The output dataset will be:

```
ID       Name    Salary   Date
123456   John    65000.50 01JAN2021
789012   Jane    55000.25 12SEP2021
```

List Input Technique

The list input technique reads free-format data, where fields are separated by one or more delimiters (typically spaces). This technique is simpler and useful when the raw data is well-structured with consistent delimiters.

Given another raw data file freedata.txt with this content:

123456 John 65000.50 01JAN2021
789012 Jane 55000.25 12SEP2021

Reading this data using list input can be done with the following code:

```
data employees;
   infile 'freedata.txt';
   input ID $ Name $ Salary Date mmddyy10.;
run;
```

In this example, the list input technique uses the following:

- $ indicates character variables ID and Name.
- Other variables, Salary and Date, are read as numeric; Date uses the mmddyy10. informat for correct date interpretation.

With list input, SAS assumes that each data entry is separated by spaces, and it automatically advances from one field to the next.

The resulting output will have the same structure as the formatted input example.

Combining Formatted and List Input Techniques

Occasionally, raw data may require a combination of both formatted and list input techniques to handle varying field structures adequately. For complex data scenarios:

```
data employees;
   infile 'complexdata.txt';
   input ID $6. @7 Name $8. @16 Salary comma7.2 Date mmddyy10.;
run;
```

This time, the @ symbol is used to position the pointer at specific columns, allowing for precise reading:

- @7 positions the pointer to column 7 for reading Name.
- @16 positions it to column 16 for reading Salary.

Using a combination enables handling more sophisticated data layouts while maintaining data integrity during input processes, thus ensuring accurate dataset creation.

2.5 Creating Variables in the Data Step

To create new variables within a DATA step, one must employ assignment statements, which assign values to variables. Assignment statements follow the form:

```
variable = expression;
```

Here, variable represents the new or existing variable being defined or modified, and expression can be a constant, another variable, a function, or an arithmetic expression.

Consider the following scenario where we have a dataset containing the heights and weights of individuals, and we wish to compute the Body Mass Index (BMI) for each individual. The formula for BMI is:

$$\text{BMI} = \frac{\text{weight (kg)}}{\text{height (m)}^2}$$

In SAS, this can be achieved as follows:

```
DATA health_data;
    SET raw_data;
    Weight_kg = Weight_lbs * 0.453592;
    Height_m = Height_in * 0.0254;
    BMI = Weight_kg / (Height_m**2);
RUN;
```

In this example, three new variables are created: Weight_kg, Height_m, and BMI. The variables Weight_lbs and Height_in are assumed to be present in the existing dataset raw_data.

Using Functions to Create Variables

SAS offers a comprehensive suite of functions to facilitate variable creation. Commonly used function categories include character functions, numeric functions, and date functions.

Character Functions

Character functions manipulate character variables. For example:

```
DATA string_handling;
    SET text_data;
    Initials = CAT(SUBSTR(First_Name, 1, 1), SUBSTR(Last_Name, 1, 1));
RUN;
```

This example concatenates the first letters of the First_Name and Last_Name variables to create the Initials variable.

Numeric Functions

Numeric functions perform operations on numeric data. For instance:

```
DATA transformations;
    SET numerical_data;
    LogIncome = LOG(Income);
    SquareRootIncome = SQRT(Income);
RUN;
```

This script calculates the log and square root of the Income variable, assigning these values to the new variables LogIncome and SquareRootIncome, respectively.

Date Functions

Date functions enable manipulation and arithmetic with date values:

```
DATA date_manip;
    SET employee_data;
    CurrentDate = TODAY();
    Days_Employed = CurrentDate - Hire_Date;
RUN;
```

In this example, CurrentDate is assigned the current date, and Days_Employed calculates the difference between CurrentDate and Hire_Date.

Conditional Variable Creation

Variables can also be created or modified conditionally using IF-THEN statements. This is particularly useful for deriving new variables based on specific conditions or subsets of data.

```
DATA conditional_vars;
    SET input_data;
    IF Age < 18 THEN Status = ’Minor’;
    ELSE Status = ’Adult’;
RUN;
```

In this case, the Status variable is assigned based on the value of Age.

Retaining Variables

The RETAIN statement retains a variable’s value across iterations of the DATA step. Without RETAIN, SAS reinitializes variables to missing at the start of each iteration.

```
DATA cumulative_sum;
    SET input_data;
    RETAIN Total 0;
    Total = Total + Value;
RUN;
```

Here, Total accumulates the sum of Value across all records in input_data.

The precise and deliberate use of assignment statements, functions, conditional logic, and RETAIN will considerably enhance one's ability to manage and analyze data efficiently within the SAS environment.

2.6 Data Step Programming Statements

Within the SAS data step, programming statements serve as the core building blocks for manipulating, transforming, and analyzing data. These statements enable users to harness the full potential of the SAS programming environment, providing the ability to perform a wide range of operations. Essential programming statements in the data step include conditional processing statements such as IF-THEN-ELSE, loop constructs like DO loops, and other control statements such as STOP. These allow for precise data manipulation and control over the data flow.

IF-THEN-ELSE Statements

The IF-THEN-ELSE statement is a cornerstone of conditional processing within the SAS data step. It enables conditional execution of code based on the evaluation of boolean expressions. The general syntax for an IF-THEN-ELSE statement is:

```
IF condition THEN action;
ELSE alternative-action;
```

IF evaluates the condition; if true, it executes the action. If the condition is false and the ELSE keyword is used, alternative-action is executed. Consider the following example where we classify students based on their scores:

```
DATA students;
    INPUT StudentID $ Score;
    IF Score >= 90 THEN Grade = 'A';
    ELSE IF Score >= 80 THEN Grade = 'B';
    ELSE IF Score >= 70 THEN Grade = 'C';
    ELSE Grade = 'D';
```

```
DATALINES;
101 92
102 85
103 73
104 68
;
RUN;
```

This code assigns a grade based on each student's score. The IF-THEN ladder allows the assignment of different grades corresponding to different score ranges.

DO Loops

DO loops facilitate repetitive processing, enabling the execution of a block of statements multiple times. There are various forms of DO loops in SAS: simple iterative DO loops, DO WHILE loops, and DO UNTIL loops.

The general syntax for a simple DO loop is:

```
DO index-variable = start TO stop BY increment;
    statements;
END;
```

Here, index-variable iterates from start to stop by increments defined by increment. Below is an example that calculates the factorial of a number using a DO loop:

```
DATA factorial;
    Factorial = 1;
    Number = 5;
    DO i = 1 TO Number;
        Factorial = Factorial * i;
    END;
RUN;
```

The DO loop iterates five times, calculating the factorial by multiplying the current value of Factorial by i in each iteration.

DO WHILE and DO UNTIL loops are more suitable when the number of iterations is not known beforehand, but instead determined by a condition.

```
DATA increment;
    Value = 0;
    DO WHILE(Value < 10);
        Value + 1;
    END;
RUN;
```

In this example, the loop continues executing as long as Value is less than 10. The loop increments Value by 1 in each iteration.

SELECT and WHEN Statements

The SELECT statement is an alternative to the IF-THEN-ELSE ladder, providing a more readable structure for multiple conditional branches. The syntax is:

```
SELECT (expression);
    WHEN (value) action;
    WHEN (value) action;
    OTHERWISE alternative-action;
END;
```

Consider the following example where we assign a label based on a numeric variable:

```
DATA categories;
    INPUT Number;
    SELECT (Number);
        WHEN (1) Label = 'One';
        WHEN (2) Label = 'Two';
        WHEN (3) Label = 'Three';
        OTHERWISE Label = 'Other';
    END;
DATALINES;
1
2
3
4
;
RUN;
```

Here, the value of Number determines which block of code is executed, and Label is assigned accordingly. The OTHERWISE keyword handles all cases not explicitly covered by WHEN statements.

STOP and ABORT Statements

STOP terminates the execution of the data step immediately upon execution. Its primary usage is within iterative processing or conditional clauses to prevent further execution once a condition is met. Here is an example demonstrating its usage:

```
DATA check;
    SET source;
    IF count > 10 THEN STOP;
    * Other processing statements;
RUN;
```

ABORT provides a more robust mechanism to halt processing and generate error messages or return codes. It allows for different options such as ABORT ABEND, which forces an abnormal termination of the SAS job. It is typically used in more advanced error handling scenarios.

These programming statements, combined with fundamental data step constructs, empower SAS programmers to execute sophisticated data manipulations, ensuring precise, efficient data handling and analysis.

2.7 Using Functions in the Data Step

In the data step, SAS functions are pivotal tools for performing computations, manipulating data, and generating statistical summaries. Functions streamline the process of transforming and analyzing raw data, ensuring efficiency and accuracy in your SAS programs. This section will explore various SAS functions, their usage, and how they integrate seamlessly within the data step.

Mathematical Functions

SAS provides a wide array of mathematical functions that can be used to perform arithmetic operations, logarithmic transformations, and more. Some common mathematical functions include:

- ABS: Calculates the absolute value of a number.
- SUM: Sums up its arguments.
- LOG: Computes the natural logarithm of a number.
- EXP: Returns the exponential value of a number.

To use these functions within a data step, you can directly incorporate them into assignment statements. For example:

```
data transformed_data;
    set raw_data;
    log_value = log(original_value);
    abs_difference = abs(value1 - value2);
    total = sum(var1, var2, var3);
run;
```

In this example, log_value holds the natural logarithm of original_value, abs_difference computes the absolute difference between value1 and value2, and total is the sum of var1, var2, and var3.

Character Functions

Character functions are essential for manipulating string data. SAS offers numerous functions for substrings, concatenation, trimming, and searching within strings:

- SUBSTR: Extracts a substring from a character variable.

- CAT: Concatenates two or more strings.
- TRIM: Removes trailing spaces from a string.
- INDEX: Returns the position of a substring within a string.

Examples of these functions in use:

```
data string_operations;
    set raw_data;
    first_part = substr(name, 1, 5);
    full_name = cat(first_name, ' ', last_name);
    trimmed_value = trim(extra_spaces);
    position = index(sentence, 'findme');
run;
```

Date and Time Functions

SAS provides robust date and time processing capabilities. Date and time functions facilitate the manipulation of dates and times, ensuring accurate temporal analyses:

- TODAY: Returns the current date.
- DATEPART: Extracts the date part from a datetime value.
- TIMEPART: Extracts the time part from a datetime value.
- INTCK: Computes the interval between two dates.

Example usage in a data step:

```
data date_time_operations;
    set raw_data;
    current_date = today();
    date_only = datepart(datetime_value);
    time_only = timepart(datetime_value);
    days_between = intck('day', start_date, end_date);
run;
```

Statistical Functions

Statistical functions are instrumental in performing preliminary statistical analysis within the data step. Functions such as mean, standard deviation, and minimum/maximum are frequently utilized:

- MEAN: Computes the mean of arguments.
- STD: Calculates the standard deviation of arguments.
- MIN: Returns the minimum value among arguments.

- MAX: Returns the maximum value among arguments.

Example usage:

```
data stats_operations;
    set raw_data;
    average = mean(var1, var2, var3);
    variability = std(var1, var2, var3);
    minimum = min(var1, var2, var3);
    maximum = max(var1, var2, var3);
run;
```

Conditional Functions

Conditional functions such as IFN and IFC are valuable for creating conditional assignments within the data step. IFN handles numeric conditions while IFC is used for character conditions:

- IFN: Selects a value based on a numeric condition.
- IFC: Selects a value based on a character condition.

Example:

```
data conditional_operations;
    set raw_data;
    numeric_result = ifn(test > 100, 1, 0);
    character_result = ifc(control eq 'Y', 'Yes', 'No');
run;
```

This code shows how numeric_result is assigned 1 if test is greater than 100, otherwise 0. character_result is assigned 'Yes' if control equals 'Y', otherwise 'No'.

By incorporating these functions into your data step, you can efficiently process and transform your data, leading to more robust and insightful analysis. Understanding the full breadth of SAS functions and their applications is crucial for mastering data manipulation and achieving expert proficiency in SAS programming.

2.8 Manipulating Data with If-Then Statements

The if-then statement is a control flow construct crucial for conditional processing within a Data Step. It allows specific actions to be taken based on conditions evaluated during program execution. The syntax for an if-then statement is straightforward: IF condition THEN action;.

Every if-then statement starts with the keyword IF, followed by a condition. If the condition evaluates to true, the statement following THEN is executed. Otherwise, the subsequent statement is skipped.

Consider the following example:

```
data new_dataset;
    set original_dataset;
    if age > 18 then adult = 1;
    else adult = 0;
run;
```

In this example, the dataset original_dataset is read observation by observation. If the variable age is greater than 18, the variable adult is assigned the value 1. If age is not greater than 18 (including missing values), adult is assigned the value 0.

Conditions can be as simple or complex as needed, and they can include logical operators such as AND, OR, and NOT. Here's an example with multiple conditions:

```
data classified_dataset;
    set input_dataset;
    if age >= 13 and age <= 19 then class = 'Teenager';
    else if age >= 20 and age <= 64 then class = 'Adult';
    else if age >= 65 then class = 'Senior';
    else class = 'Child';
run;
```

Here we use a series of if-then-else statements to classify observations into one of four categories based on the value of age. Note the use of the ELSE IF construct for additional conditions and the last ELSE clause as a catch-all for any remaining observations.

When working with datasets, it's important to manage complexity carefully. Consider the utility of compound conditions and remember that conditions are evaluated in the order they appear. This order can affect the logical flow and the resulting dataset.

```
data health_status;
    set patient_data;
    if sex = 'F' and age < 50 and status = 'Healthy' then eligible = 1;
    else if sex = 'M' and age < 45 and status = 'Healthy' then eligible = 1;
    else eligible = 0;
run;
```

The segmentation above makes use of logical AND (sex = 'F' and age < 50 and status = 'Healthy') to ensure multiple criteria must be met for the variable eligible to be assigned a value of 1. If none of these compound conditions are true, eligible is set to 0.

For measures of performance and readability, nesting conditional statements can be avoided in favor of clear, linear logic. Consider the following nested example alongside its linear counterpart:

Nested example:

```
data student_grades;
    set class_data;
    if exam_score >= 60 then do;
        if exam_score >= 90 then grade = 'A';
        else if exam_score >= 80 then grade = 'B';
        else if exam_score >= 70 then grade = 'C';
        else grade = 'D';
    end;
    else grade = 'F';
run;
```

Linear example:

```
data student_grades;
    set class_data;
    if exam_score >= 90 then grade = 'A';
    else if exam_score >= 80 then grade = 'B';
    else if exam_score >= 70 then grade = 'C';
    else if exam_score >= 60 then grade = 'D';
    else grade = 'F';
run;
```

While both examples produce the same results, the linear approach eliminates unnecessary nesting, enhancing readability and maintainability.

The else- clause linked to if-then can also be omitted if no alternative action is required. For instance:

```
data credit_risk;
    set applicant_data;
    if income < 20000 then risk = 'High';
run;
```

In this case, only applicants with income less than 20000 are assigned risk = 'High'. The else- clause is left out because no other actions or assignments are necessary.

Another consideration is handling missing values which SAS treats as the smallest possible number for numeric comparisons. This means:

```
data check_missing;
    set survey_results;
    if age = . then age_missing_indicator = 1;
    else age_missing_indicator = 0;
run;
```

In this example, age = . checks for missing values, and assigns age_-

missing_indicator accordingly.

Applying the if-then statement precisely and efficiently within the Data Step is fundamental for effective data manipulation and analysis in SAS. Understanding and leveraging logical conditions enables the creation of clear, purposeful datasets, essential for subsequent analytic tasks.

2.9 Concatenating and Merging Datasets

Concatenating and merging datasets are essential techniques in SAS programming, allowing you to combine and manipulate data from multiple sources effectively. This section covers the fundamental approaches and considerations for concatenating and merging datasets using the DATA step and the MERGE statement.

Concatenating Datasets

Concatenation refers to the process of combining two or more datasets by appending the observations of one dataset to another. This is achieved using the SET statement within the DATA step. To concatenate datasets:

```
data concatenated_data;
   set dataset1 dataset2;
run;
```

In this example, dataset1 and dataset2 are combined into a new dataset called concatenated_data. The resulting dataset will contain all the observations from dataset1 followed by all the observations from dataset2. Note that both datasets must have similar variable names and types; otherwise, SAS will generate warnings or errors.

Merging Datasets

Merging is the process of combining datasets based on the values of common key variables. This is accomplished using the MERGE statement in conjunction with a BY statement. To merge datasets:

```
data merged_data;
   merge dataset1 dataset2;
   by key_variable;
run;
```

In this example, dataset1 and dataset2 are merged into a new dataset called merged_data based on the common variable key_variable. The resulting dataset will contain all variables from both datasets. It's crucial to ensure both datasets are sorted by the key variable prior to merging.

To demonstrate this with an example, let's consider two datasets containing student information:

```
data student_scores;
    input ID \$ Score1 Score2;
    datalines;
    A001 85 90
    A002 88 82
    A003 91 87
    ;
run;

data student_details;
    input ID \$ Name \$ Age;
    datalines;
    A001 John 15
    A002 Emma 16
    A003 Liam 14
    ;
run;
```

To merge these datasets based on the ID:

```
proc sort data=student_scores;
    by ID;
run;

proc sort data=student_details;
    by ID;
run;

data students_merged;
    merge student_scores student_details;
    by ID;
run;
```

After executing this code, the dataset students_merged will have the following structure:

ID	Score1	Score2	Name	Age
A001	85	90	John	15
A002	88	82	Emma	16
A003	91	87	Liam	14

Using Conditional Logic in Merging

Sometimes, it may be necessary to include conditional logic while merging datasets to handle missing values or to update records. This can be done using the IF-THEN statement within the DATA step:

```
data students_updated;
    merge student_scores (in=a) student_details (in=b);
    by ID;
    if a and b then output students_merged;
    else if a then output students_scores_only;
    else if b then output students_details_only;
run;
```

In this example, the datasets student_scores and student_details are merged, but the merged observations are output to students_merged only if they exist in both datasets. Observations unique to student_scores and student_details are output to students_scores_only and students_details_only, respectively.

One-to-Many and Many-to-Many Merging

Merging can also be conducted in one-to-many and many-to-many relationships. In a one-to-many merge, one key value in the primary dataset corresponds to multiple observations in the secondary dataset. In a many-to-many merge, multiple observations in both datasets share key values.

Consider the following example datasets for one-to-many merging:

```
data teachers;
    input TeacherID \$ TeacherName \$;
    datalines;
    T001 MrSmith
    T002 MsJohnson
    ;
run;

data students_teachers;
    input TeacherID \$ StudentID \$;
    datalines;
    T001 S001
    T001 S002
    T002 S003
    ;
run;
```

Merging these datasets on TeacherID:

```
proc sort data=teachers;
    by TeacherID;
run;

proc sort data=students_teachers;
    by TeacherID;
run;

data teacher_student_merge;
    merge teachers students_teachers;
    by TeacherID;
```

```
run;
```

The resulting dataset teacher_student_merge will show each student with their assigned teacher.

These methods and techniques are instrumental in enabling complex data manipulations and facilitating accurate analysis. Understanding and applying these merging and concatenating techniques ensures that data is combined efficiently and correctly, preserving the integrity and utility of the datasets involved.

2.10 Using the RETAIN Statement

The RETAIN statement is fundamental in controlling the value of variables across iterations of the data step in SAS. Without a RETAIN statement or an equivalent mechanism, SAS initializes variables to missing at the beginning of each iteration of the data step and assigns values based on the current observation. The use of RETAIN allows for the preservation of the values of variables from one iteration to the next. This is especially useful in cumulative calculations, comparisons across observations, and flagging specific conditions based on sequences of data.

The syntax of the RETAIN statement is straightforward:

```
RETAIN variable-list <initial-values>;
```

Here, variable-list refers to one or more variables whose values you wish to retain across iterations, and <initial-values> are optional initial values assigned to those variables. If initial values are not provided, SAS retains the variables' existing values.

Consider the following example where we calculate a running total of sales:

```
DATA sales_summary;
    SET sales_data;
    RETAIN running_total 0; /* Initialize running total to 0 */
    running_total + sales; /* Accumulate sales to running total */
RUN;
```

In this example, the RETAIN statement ensures that running_total is initialized only once (with 0) and retains its value across the entire dataset. The line running_total + sales; adds the value of the sales variable to running_total for each iteration, resulting in a cumulative total.

RETAIN is often used in conjunction with the IF-THEN statements to flag specific conditions across data observations. Consider the following example where the dataset contains transactions, and we want to flag the first occurrence of each customer using the RETAIN statement:

```
DATA customer_flag;
    SET transactions;
    BY customer_id; /* Ensure data is sorted by customer_id */
    RETAIN first_transaction;

    IF FIRST.customer_id THEN first_transaction = 1;
    ELSE first_transaction = 0;
RUN;
```

In this example:

- The BY statement ensures that the dataset is processed by customer_id.
- The RETAIN statement is used on first_transaction.
- FIRST.variable is a SAS automatic variable that indicates the first observation in each BY-group. The IF FIRST.customer_id condition sets first_transaction to 1 for the first record of each customer, and 0 otherwise.

Another common scenario is using the RETAIN statement for lag calculations. Suppose we have a dataset of daily stock prices and we want to calculate the difference between the current day's closing price and the previous day's closing price:

```
DATA stock_diff;
    SET stock_prices;
    RETAIN prev_close;
    diff = close - prev_close;
    prev_close = close;
RUN;
```

Here, prev_close retains its value between iterations:

- On each data step iteration, diff computes the difference between close (current day's closing price) and prev_close (previous day's closing price).
- prev_close is then updated to the current day's close for the next iteration.

It's important to note that the RETAIN statement does not affect the ordering or reading of data. Its sole purpose is to maintain the values of specified variables across iterations of the data step. Additionally, unless a variable is explicitly set to missing within the data step or initialized in the RETAIN statement, it holds the value from the previous iteration.

Edge cases to consider include large datasets where memory management and computational efficiency become critical. Properly using the RETAIN statement alongside data step programming can significantly enhance performance. However, misuse can lead to erroneous results and inefficiencies, so understanding the exact implications of variable retention across iterations is crucial.

The RETAIN statement is thus a powerful tool in SAS programming, enabling effective data manipulation techniques that require historical context within a dataset. By carefully integrating RETAIN with other SAS capabilities, programmers can develop sophisticated data analysis and reporting processes.

2.11 Understanding PDV (Program Data Vector)

The Program Data Vector (PDV) is a crucial concept within the SAS Data Step, integral to understanding how data is read and processed. The PDV is a logical area of memory where SAS builds data sets one observation at a time. Comprehending its structure and operation is essential for efficient and effective data manipulation.

When a DATA step executes, SAS processes data line by line through the PDV. The PDV consists of all the variables in the data set and temporary variables created during the processing of the DATA step, including those explicitly declared, such as with the retain statement, and implicit system variables like _N_ and _ERROR_.

- _N_: This system variable counts the number of times the DATA step has iterated.
- _ERROR_: This system variable flags errors during data step execution. It is initialized to 0 and is set to 1 if an error occurs.

When the DATA step begins, the PDV is initialized. The variables take on their initial values, typically missing for numeric variables and blank for character variables. As each record is read from the input data source, the PDV is populated with the values from the record. SAS then sequentially processes each statement in the DATA step, updating the values in the PDV accordingly. After processing all statements for a single record, the PDV values are written to the output data set, creating one observation, then the process repeats for the next record.

An illustrative example can clarify this process. Consider the following data step code:

```
data work.example;
    infile datalines;
    input ID $ Name $ Age;
    AgeGroup = ifn(Age >= 18, 'Adult', 'Minor');
datalines;
001 John 25
002 Alice 17
003 Bob 24
;
run;
```

Let's perform a step-by-step walkthrough of how PDV handles this code.

- data work.example; initializes the PDV with variables: ID, Name, Age, and AgeGroup (though AgeGroup is added later when it's computed).
- The infile datalines; and input statements read data line-by-line and populate the PDV with values for ID, Name, and Age.
- The ifn function computes AgeGroup based on the value of Age, updating the PDV.
- The processed PDV is output as an observation in work.example.

Again, emphasizing system variables, the _N_ variable on first iteration equals 1, indicating the first record processing, and it continues to increment with each subsequent record. Any error during assignment or input output operations sets _ERROR_ to 1, however in this case, assuming no error, it remains 0.

Consequently, each record undergoes evaluation and transformation in the PDV before being written to the dataset, exemplifying the significance of understanding the PDV for debugging and optimizing DATA steps. Practitioners can manipulate the content of the PDV to engineer new variables, manage data transformations, and ensure the accuracy of the output dataset.

The interplay between the input buffer, the PDV, and the output data set underlies the core mechanics of the DATA step – mastery of which augments one's ability to harness the full power of SAS for data manipulation tasks. Enhancing one's adeptness at predicting the state of the PDV grants a deeper debugging insight, allowing for more sophisticated data step manipulations.

2.12 Data Step Efficiency and Optimization

Optimizing the efficiency of a Data Step is crucial for improving the performance of SAS programs, especially when handling large datasets. This section will cover various strategies and best practices for enhancing the execution speed and resource utilization of Data Steps. The focus will be on efficient reading and writing of data, minimizing the use of computationally intensive operations, and leveraging SAS-specific features to optimize performance.

To begin, one of the primary considerations in optimizing a Data Step is the method of reading and writing data. Leveraging the appropriate input method based on the dataset structure can significantly impact the execution time. For instance, when dealing with well-structured data files where each column aligns perfectly, column input or formatted input can be more efficient than list input, which is generally more flexible but might introduce additional overhead with large datasets.

Example of Column Input:

```
DATA work.optimized_data;
    INFILE 'datafile.txt';
    INPUT @1 ID 4. @5 Name $10. @15 Age 2.;
RUN;
```

In this example, the column input method is used to read a dataset with fixed-width fields. This approach ensures that the Data Step reads the exact position of each variable, thereby enhancing performance.

Another crucial aspect of optimization is the use of appropriate data types and lengths for variables. By specifying the minimum necessary lengths for character variables and using numeric variables judiciously, one can reduce the memory footprint and improve processing speed.

```
DATA work.efficient_varusage;
```

```
    LENGTH Name $10.;
    SET work.raw_data;
    Age = Input(AgeString, 2.);
RUN;
```

Here, the LENGTH statement optimizes memory usage by limiting the Name variable to 10 characters. Converting string representations of numeric values using the Input function also ensures efficient type handling.

Leveraging the RETAIN statement can also be instrumental in improving efficiency by eliminating unnecessary reinitialization of variables. The RETAIN statement allows variables to hold their values across iterations of the Data Step, reducing redundant computations.

```
DATA work.aggregated_data;
    SET work.transactions;
    RETAIN TotalSales 0;
    TotalSales + SaleAmount;
RUN;
```

In this example, the TotalSales variable accumulates the SaleAmount values across iterations, avoiding repeated reinitialization.

Efficiencies can also be realized through the strategic use of WHERE statements and INDEX options. Applying a WHERE clause early in the Data Step can filter records at the input stage, thereby reducing the amount of data processed. Similarly, creating indices on frequently queried variables can expedite data retrieval.

```
DATA work.filtered_data;
    SET work.large_data (WHERE=(Age > 30));
RUN;
```

```
DATA work.large_data;
    SET work.raw_large_data;
    INDEX Name / unique;
RUN;
```

The WHERE clause ensures that only records where Age is greater than 30 are processed. Creating an index on the Name variable speeds up queries involving this variable.

Moreover, minimizing the use of computationally intensive operations within the Data Step is essential. For example, combining multiple IF-THEN statements into a SELECT statement can improve readability and performance.

```
DATA work.classified_data;
    SET work.input_data;
    SELECT (Score);
```

```
        WHEN (>=90) Grade = 'A';
        WHEN (>=80) Grade = 'B';
        WHEN (>=70) Grade = 'C';
        WHEN (>=60) Grade = 'D';
        OTHERWISE Grade = 'F';
    END;
RUN;
```

Utilizing the SELECT statement instead of multiple IF-THEN statements streamlines the decision-making process, leading to more efficient code execution.

Efficient use of temporary arrays can also optimize performance, particularly when dealing with repetitive calculations or transformations. By loading data into temporary arrays, one can reduce I/O operations and improve processing speed.

```
DATA work.temp_array_usage;
    ARRAY scores[5] Score1-Score5;
    DO i = 1 TO 5;
        scores[i] = scores[i] * 1.1;
    END;
RUN;
```

The use of the array in this example allows for efficient manipulation of multiple variables in a loop, reducing the need for repetitive code and potentially improving execution speed.

Efficient data management through the proper use of the KEEP and DROP statements can also play a significant role in optimization. By specifying only the necessary variables to be retained, redundant data processing is minimized.

```
DATA work.minimal_vars;
    SET work.raw_data (KEEP=ID Name Age);
RUN;
```

The KEEP statement ensures that only the ID, Name, and Age variables are retained, thus reducing memory consumption and improving Data Step performance.

Employing efficient I/O operations is another key aspect of Data Step optimization. Strategically placing IF-THEN statements to minimize unnecessary I/O operations and reduce the condition checks can improve efficiency.

```
DATA work.optimized_io;
    SET work.raw_data;
    IF Age > 18 THEN OUTPUT work.adult_data;
    ELSE IF Age <= 18 THEN OUTPUT work.minor_data;
RUN;
```

The placement of the IF-THEN statements strategically reduces the number of logical checks, improving efficiency by minimizing unnecessary evaluations.

Understanding and utilizing the Program Data Vector (PDV) effectively is vital. Recognizing how the PDV works, ensuring that variables are initialized and used appropriately within it, and minimizing the overhead introduced by implicit and explicit function calls within the PDV can contribute to Data Step efficiency.

By combining these methods and strategies, SAS programmers can achieve significant improvements in the performance and efficiency of their Data Steps, leading to faster execution times and more efficient resource utilization.

Chapter 3

Creating and Applying Formats

This chapter focuses on the use of formats in SAS to control and customize the appearance of data values. It begins with an introduction to predefined SAS formats and guides readers through creating custom formats using PROC FORMAT. Key topics include defining value ranges and labels, applying formats to variables, and utilizing formats in various procedures. The chapter also covers specialized formats for date, time, numeric, and character data, along with managing format catalogs and troubleshooting common format-related issues.

3.1 Introduction to Formats in SAS

In SAS, a format is an instruction that determines how data values are displayed in output. Formats do not alter the actual data but control the representation of data, enhancing readability and facilitating interpretation. They are especially useful when dealing with date, time, and numeric data, as well as categorical variables. In SAS, formats can be predefined or user-defined, allowing for a high degree of customization.

Predefined formats in SAS cover a wide range of data types and display preferences. For instance, numeric data can be displayed in various formats, such as currency, percentage, or with a specified number of decimal places. Date and time data can be exhibited in numerous configurations, illustrating the flexibility and robustness of SAS formats.

To apply a format in SAS, the FORMAT statement is typically employed within procedures or data steps. The syntax for the FORMAT statement is straightforward:

```
FORMAT variable-name format-name.;
```

Here, variable-name refers to the name of the variable to which the format is applied, and format-name denotes the name of the format. For example:

```
DATA example;
    INPUT date_var date9.;
    FORMAT date_var mmddyy10.;
    DATALINES;
    01JAN2020
    15FEB2021
    ;
RUN;

PROC PRINT DATA=example;
RUN;
```

The data step above reads in dates in the date9. format and then applies the mmddyy10. format to the date_var variable. The output will display the dates in mm/dd/yyyy format, improving interpretability for users familiar with this date representation.

The utility of formats extends beyond simple display preferences. Formats can categorize continuous data into discrete groups, a practice known as binning. This is particularly useful in statistical analysis where continuous variables need to be segmented into categories. For instance, income data can be grouped into ranges such as "Low", "Medium", and "High".

For complex scenarios, user-defined formats can be created using the PROC FORMAT procedure. This process involves defining value ranges and associating them with specific labels. The basics of creating a custom format using PROC FORMAT are illustrated below:

```
PROC FORMAT;
    VALUE income_fmt
        Low = '0-20000'
        Medium= '20001-50000'
        High = '50001-100000'
        VeryHigh='>100000';
RUN;
```

In this example, an income format named income_fmt categorizes values into four groups: Low, Medium, High, and VeryHigh. This format can then be applied to an income variable to facilitate analysis and reporting:

```
DATA income_data;
    INPUT income;
    FORMAT income income_fmt.;
    DATALINES;
    18000
    25000
    60000
    120000
    ;
RUN;

PROC PRINT DATA=income_data;
RUN;
```

The resulting output will display the categorized income levels based on the defined ranges.

In summary, SAS formats provide an efficient way to control data presentation. They improve data readability and facilitate categorical analysis. Whether using predefined formats for common data types or creating custom formats with PROC FORMAT, SAS offers immense flexibility to meet diverse data representation needs. Understanding how to leverage formats is crucial for achieving expert proficiency in SAS programming.

3.2 Predefined SAS Formats

Predefined SAS formats provide a way to uniformly present and analyze data within the SAS environment. SAS offers a robust set of built-in formats that cater to a wide array of data types, including numeric, date/-time, and character data. Understanding and effectively utilizing these formats is crucial for accurate data representation and interpretation.

Numeric Formats:

SAS includes predefined numeric formats to control the appearance of numeric values in various outputs. These formats allow the specification of decimal places, comma inclusion, and the presentation of numbers as percentages, among other options. Here are some commonly used numeric formats:

- w.d: This is the basic number format where w represents the total width of the number including the decimal point, and d represents the number of decimal places. For example, 8.2 will display a number with a total width of 8 characters, including 2 decimal places.

- COMMAw.d: This format includes commas in the number at every thousand. For instance, COMMA10.2 will display a number such as 1,234.56.

- DOLLARw.d: This format is similar to COMMAw.d but also includes a dollar sign. For example, DOLLAR10.2 will display $1,234.56.

- PERCENTw.d: This format multiplies the number by 100 and then displays it with a percent sign. For instance, PERCENT8.2 will convert 0.123 to 12.30

Date and Time Formats:

SAS supports various formats for presenting date and time values, which are critical in data analysis involving temporal data. These formats facilitate the representation of dates and times in a human-readable form and support a range of temporal resolutions from days to seconds.

- DATEw.: This format displays dates in the form DDMMYYYY or MMDDYYYY based on the operating environment. DATE9. will display the date as 03FEB2023.

- MMDDYYw.: This format strictly displays dates in the form MM/DD/YY. For example, MMDDYY10. will display 02/03/2023.

- TIMEw.d: This format presents the time portion of datetime values. TIME8. will display the time as 12:34:56.

- DATETIMEw.d: This format combines both date and time, displaying the complete timestamp. DATETIME19. will display 03FEB2023:12:34:56.

Character Formats:

Character formats in SAS manage the presentation of string data. While most character data are user-defined, SAS provides some formats to control string display, including:

- $w.: This is the basic character format where w indicates the width. For example, $20. ensures the output string will have a width of 20 characters.

- $UPCASEw.: This format converts all character data to uppercase. For instance, $UPCASE10. applied to "hello" will produce "HELLO".

- $QUOTEw.: This format adds quotation marks around the character string. $QUOTE15. applied to "Yale" will produce "Yale".

Applying Predefined Formats:

Predefined formats are applied to variables using the FORMAT statement. The syntax is:

```
FORMAT variable-name format-name;
run;
```

For example:

```
DATA example;
    input Sales $10. Date mmddyy10.;
    FORMAT Date mmddyy10. Sales dollar10.2;
    DATALINES;
    2000 01/31/2021
    1500 02/28/2021
    ;
RUN;
```

In the above example, the Sales variable is formatted with the DOLLAR10.2 format and the Date variable is formatted with the MMDDYY10. format to ensure correct presentation.

```
Sales        Date
$2,000.00    01/31/2021
$1,500.00    02/28/2021
```

Understanding these predefined formats allows users to efficiently control the presentation of data in reports and analyses. The ability to customize outputs ensures clarity and precision, which is fundamental to effective data analysis in SAS.

3.3 Custom Formats with PROC FORMAT

Creating custom formats in SAS is performed using the PROC FORMAT procedure. This functionality enables users to create formats tailored to specific data interpretation needs, enhancing readability and usability. Custom formats can categorize data values and assign meaningful labels, thus improving data presentation in reports and analyses.

Basic Syntax

The basic syntax of the PROC FORMAT statement involves the VALUE statement for defining value formats. The general syntax is as follows:

```
PROC FORMAT;
    VALUE format-name
        value-range = 'formatted-value'
        ...;
RUN;
```

Here, format-name is the name of the user-defined format, value-range specifies the data values to be formatted, and 'formatted-value' is the label or description assigned to the value range.

Example: Creating a Custom Format

Consider a scenario where you have a dataset containing numerical codes representing different departments. To enhance readability, you can define a custom format to assign descriptive labels to these codes:

```
PROC FORMAT;
    VALUE deptfmt
        1 = 'Human Resources'
        2 = 'Finance'
        3 = 'IT'
        4 = 'Marketing'
        OTHER = 'Unknown';
RUN;
```

In this example, deptfmt is the name of the format, and specific numeric values are associated with department names. The keyword OTHER is used to handle any values not explicitly listed.

Applying Custom Formats

Once a custom format is created, it can be applied to variables using the FORMAT statement in a DATA step or within various SAS procedures. To apply the deptfmt format to a variable named dept_code, use the following syntax:

```
DATA formatted_data;
    SET original_data;
    FORMAT dept_code deptfmt.;
RUN;
```

Alternatively, formats can be applied in procedures such as PROC PRINT:

```
PROC PRINT DATA=original_data;
   FORMAT dept_code deptfmt.;
RUN;
```

Defining Range Formats

Value ranges can be defined using various operators:

- Hyphen (-) for an inclusive range
- Less than (<)
- Greater than (>)
- Combining these for complex ranges

For example, to create a custom format for scoring intervals:

```
PROC FORMAT;
   VALUE scorefmt
      90 - HIGH = 'Excellent'
      70 - <90 = 'Good'
      50 - <70 = 'Average'
      LOW - <50 = 'Poor';
RUN;
```

Here, LOW and HIGH are predefined keywords representing the lowest and highest possible values.

Character Formats

Custom formats can also be defined for character values. Consider an example to format product categories:

```
PROC FORMAT;
   VALUE $catfmt
      'A' = 'Apparel'
      'E' = 'Electronics'
      'H' = 'Home Goods'
      'T' = 'Toys'
      OTHER = 'Miscellaneous';
RUN;
```

In this case, the $ prefix indicates a character format, and the $catfmt format is applicable to character variables.

Multilabel Formats

Multilabel formats allow a single value to have multiple labels. They are useful for categorizing data under multiple criteria. To enable multilabel formats, the MULTILABEL option is used:

```
PROC FORMAT;
    VALUE $multilab (MULTILABEL)
        'A' = 'Category A'
        'A' = 'High Priority'
        'B' = 'Category B'
        'B' = 'Low Priority';
RUN;
```

To utilize multilabel formats in procedures, the MISSING and MULTILABEL options must be specified.

```
PROC MEANS DATA=example_data MISSING MULTILABEL;
    CLASS category / MLF;
    VAR some_variable;
    FORMAT category $multilab.;
RUN;
```

Storing Formats Permanently

When you require formats to be reused across different sessions or datasets, store them in a permanent format library. This involves specifying the FMTLIB option and using the LIBRARY statement:

```
LIBNAME mylib '/path/to/format/library';

PROC FORMAT LIBRARY=mylib;
    VALUE custfmt
        1 = 'Customer A'
        2 = 'Customer B';
RUN;
```

The formats can then be accessed in future SAS programs by referencing the library:

```
LIBNAME mylib '/path/to/format/library';

OPTIONS FMTSEARCH=(mylib);

DATA formatted_data;
    SET original_data;
    FORMAT customer_id custfmt.;
RUN;
```

The FMTSEARCH option determines the search order for format catalogs. Ensure the library is specified correctly to avoid format retrieval issues.

By leveraging PROC FORMAT, you can create sophisticated and versatile custom formats that significantly enhance the clarity and interpretability of your datasets.

3.4 Creating Value Ranges and Labels

To create custom formats based on specific value ranges and assign them descriptive labels, you can employ the PROC FORMAT procedure in SAS. This section elaborates on the syntactic elements and logical structuring for constructing meaningful formats, which can significantly enhance the interpretability of your dataset.

PROC FORMAT allows for the creation of various formats using the VALUE statement. The basic structure is as follows:

```
PROC FORMAT;
    VALUE format-name
        range1 = 'label1'
        range2 = 'label2'
        ...
        rangen = 'labeln';
RUN;
```

Here, format-name must adhere to SAS naming conventions: it should start with a letter or underscore and can contain letters, numbers, and underscores. The name must also be unique to avoid conflicts with pre-existing formats or variables.

Ranges can be specified in various ways:

- **Single Values**: Define a label for an exact value.
- **Value Lists**: Assign a label to a comma-separated list of values.
- **Range Intervals**: Use inclusive and exclusive range delimiters such as -, <, and combinations thereof.
- **Keywords**: Handle missing (.), low (LOW), and high (HIGH) values.

The inclusive range delimiter - indicates that both the lower and upper bounds are part of the range. For instance, 1-10 corresponds to values from 1 to 10, inclusive. The exclusive range is denoted by either < or combinations like -<. For example, 1-<10 encompasses values from 1 to just less than 10.

Consider the following practical example:

```
PROC FORMAT;
    VALUE AgeGroup
        0-12 = 'Child'
        13-19 = 'Teenager'
        20-<65 = 'Adult'
```

```
        65-HIGH = 'Senior';
RUN;
```

In this example, the AgeGroup format categorizes age into four groups: 'Child', 'Teenager', 'Adult', and 'Senior'.

When specifying ranges, you should be cognizant of the overlap and order. SAS processes ranges in the sequence they appear; hence, overlapping ranges could lead to unexpected categorization if not ordered and defined correctly. For instance, consider if we had overlapping ranges, such as:

```
PROC FORMAT;
    VALUE OverlapExample
        0-18 = 'Minor'
        18-65 = 'Adult'; /* Incorrect */
RUN;
```

This code results in the value 18 being labeled ambiguously. To correctly manage this, you should decide which category the overlapping edge belongs to and adjust the ranges accordingly:

```
PROC FORMAT;
    VALUE CorrectedExample
        0-<18 = 'Minor'
        18-65 = 'Adult';
RUN;
```

This clearly demarcates 18 as an 'Adult'.

The VALUE statement can also be enriched with special keywords:

- LOW-> *−value*: This range includes all values from the lowest possible value up to, but not including, a specified value.
- value-HIGH: This designates a range from a particular value to the highest possible value.
- OTHER: This keyword can label any value not explicitly covered by other defined ranges.
- MISSING: To specifically format missing values.

Utilizing these keywords ensures comprehensive coverage of all potential data values. For example:

```
PROC FORMAT;
    VALUE ExtendedAgeGroup
        LOW-<0 = 'Invalid Age'
        0-12 = 'Child'
```

```
        13-19 = 'Teenager'
        20-<65 = 'Adult'
        65-HIGH = 'Senior'
        . = 'Missing';
RUN;
```

In this example, negative ages are flagged as 'Invalid Age', while missing values are explicitly labeled 'Missing'.

To apply your custom format to a variable, use the FORMAT statement within a DATA step or procedure. For instance:

```
DATA Persons;
    INPUT Name $ Age;
    DATALINES;
    John 25
    Mary 70
    Mike .
    Susan -5
    Tom 15
    ;
    FORMAT Age ExtendedAgeGroup.;
RUN;
```

Name	Age
John	Adult
Mary	Senior
Mike	Missing
Susan	Invalid Age
Tom	Teenager

This applies the ExtendedAgeGroup format to the Age variable, modifying the appearance of these data points for improved clarity.

The ability to create coherent value ranges and labels is a crucial skill in SAS, allowing for better data presentation and interpretation. Properly crafted value labels enhance the readability and analytic potential of your datasets, leading to more accurate and insightful analyses.

3.5 Applying Formats to Variables

In SAS programming, applying formats to variables is a fundamental step that greatly enhances the readability and presentation of data. To apply a format to a variable, one typically uses the FORMAT statement within a DATA step or a PROC step. This section elaborates on various methods to apply formats, covering both temporary and permanent formats, and emphasizes using formats within dataset manipulations and procedure outputs.

To apply a format temporarily, you can include the FORMAT statement directly within a PROC step. The temporary format only affects the output of the specific procedure where it is applied. Here is an example illustrating this approach:

```
proc print data=sashelp.class;
    format age 3.;
run;
```

In the example above, the age variable is displayed with a format of 3 digits, controlling its appearance in the output of the PROC PRINT step. This does not permanently alter the format of the age variable in the dataset; it solely applies to the printed output.

On the other hand, formats can be applied permanently within a DATA step, ensuring that the variable consistently appears with the specified format in all subsequent procedures unless explicitly overridden. This is accomplished by including the FORMAT statement inside the DATA step, as shown below:

```
data class_formatted;
    set sashelp.class;
    format age 3.;
run;
```

In this scenario, the class_formatted dataset is created with the age variable permanently formatted to display with three digits. Any procedure executed on class_formatted henceforth will adhere to this format by default.

Additionally, one can simultaneously apply multiple formats to different variables within a single DATA or PROC step. This is particularly useful when dealing with datasets that contain various types of data requiring distinct formatting:

```
data sales_formatted;
    set sales_data;
    format date yymmdd10. amount dollar10.2;
run;
```

Here, the date variable is formatted to display in YYYY-MM-DD format, while the amount variable is formatted as a dollar amount with two decimal places.

Applying formats to variables can significantly improve the clarity and interpretability of data. For example, when dealing with date and time data, special formats ensure these are presented meaningfully. Consider a dataset where transaction dates need to be in a particular format for reporting purposes:

```
data transactions_formatted;
    set transactions;
    format transaction_date date9.;
run;
```

In this example, the date9. format is applied to the transaction_date variable, ensuring dates are consistently presented as ddMMMyyyy, where MMM represents the three-letter abbreviation of the month.

When working with numeric data, applying formats to variables can help manage the representation of large numbers, decimals, and currency. For instance, to display sales figures in a human-readable format with commas for thousands separators, one can apply the comma format:

```
data revenue_formatted;
    set financials;
    format revenue comma12.;
run;
```

In this illustrative case, the revenue variable is displayed with up to twelve digits with commas separating thousands, improving readability in financial reports.

Formats can also be dynamically applied within procedures. An example using the PROC MEANS procedure to summarize dataset statistics while controlling the formatting of output is given below:

```
proc means data=sales_data mean median maxdec=2;
    var amount;
    format amount dollar10.2;
run;
```

By integrating the FORMAT statement within the PROC MEANS step, the amount variable is summarized and displayed in a dollar format with two decimal places, while the maxdec=2 option rounds the median and mean to two decimal places.

For datasets with character variables, custom formats defined using PROC FORMAT can be applied to categorize or reformat textual data. Here is an example demonstrating this:

```
proc format;
    value $genderfmt
        'M' = 'Male'
        'F' = 'Female';
run;

data demographics_formatted;
    set demographics;
    format gender $genderfmt.;
run;
```

In this case, a custom format $genderfmt maps the values 'M' and 'F' to 'Male' and 'Female' respectively. Applying this format to the gender variable in the demographics dataset facilitates more intuitive understanding of gender data in subsequent analyses.

Overall, applying formats to variables allows for the customization of data presentation, making the output more comprehensible and user-friendly. Whether applied temporarily within procedures or permanently within DATA steps, formats are essential in ensuring the clarity and interpretability of SAS data outputs.

3.6 Using Formats in Procedures

In the previous sections, we have explored the creation and application of both predefined and custom formats. This section delves into employing these formats within various SAS procedures. Utilizing formats in procedures enriches the dataset display and analysis by controlling the appearance of data values consistently. The knowledge and application of formats in procedures consolidate understanding of how formats enhance report generation and data presentation.

PROC PRINT

The PROC PRINT procedure lists the contents of a SAS dataset, displaying the formatted values of variables. By applying formats within PROC PRINT, you illuminate the dataset with meaningful value displays.

```
proc print data=sample;
  format salary dollar8.2 hiredate date9.;
run;
```

In this example, the format statement within PROC PRINT applies the dollar8.2 format to the salary variable and the date9. format to the hiredate variable. The formatted output provides a user-friendly display:

```
Obs   salary    hiredate
 1   $50,000   01JAN2000
 2   $60,000   15FEB2010
```

PROC MEANS

The PROC MEANS procedure computes descriptive statistics such as mean, median, and standard deviation. When using formats in PROC MEANS, it impacts how grouping variables are displayed.

```
proc means data=sample;
```

```
  class gender;
  format gender $genderfmt.;
  var salary;
run;
```

Here, the class statement identifies the gender variable for calculating statistics by groups. The format statement uses the $genderfmt. format, which could look as follows in the dataset:

```
Female:
  N: 10
  Mean: $55,000
Male:
  N: 12
  Mean: $57,500
```

PROC FREQ

PROC FREQ produces frequency tables. By incorporating formats, you can deliver more insightful and readable frequency tables.

```
proc freq data=sample;
  tables department;
  format department $deptfmt.;
run;
```

Assuming $deptfmt. formats department codes as readable department names, the output elucidates:

Department name	Frequency	Percent
HR	8	28.57%
Finance	7	25.00%
IT	13	46.43%

PROC REPORT

PROC REPORT offers advanced data presentation with extensive formatting capabilities. By using custom formats in PROC REPORT, you control both the report layout and the data display precision.

```
proc report data=sample nowd;
  column department salary;
  define department / group format=$deptfmt.;
  define salary / analysis sum format=dollar10.2;
run;
```

In this example, $deptfmt. formats the department variable, and dollar10.2 provides a formatted sum for the salary variable within the report:

Department	Total Salary
HR	$400,000.00
Finance	$300,000.00
IT	$650,000.00

PROC TABULATE

Another powerful procedure, PROC TABULATE, allows multi-dimensional table creation with a high degree of customization, where formats play a crucial role.

```
proc tabulate data=sample;
  class department;
  var salary;
  table department, salary*(mean*format=dollar10.2);
  format department $deptfmt.;
run;
```

This script creates a table displaying the mean salary per department, using $deptfmt. for department formatting. It results in:

```
Department    Mean Salary
HR            $50,000.00
Finance       $42,857.14
IT            $50,000.00
```

Employing formats within procedures like PROC PRINT, PROC MEANS, PROC FREQ, PROC REPORT, and PROC TABULATE ensures data presentation is not only accurate but tailored to the end user's understanding and requirements. Each application underscores the transformative role formats play, enhancing the analytical clarity and interpretability of the data outputs. This section, marrying the conceptual premises and practical applications of formats, empowers users with the skills needed to leverage SAS capabilities fully.

3.7 Date and Time Formats

In SAS, handling date and time data effectively significantly enhances dataset manipulations. Understanding the appropriate formats to apply to such fields is crucial in ensuring data consistency and readability. SAS provides several predefined formats to cater to diverse date and time representation needs.

The most commonly used predefined date formats encompass instructions to display dates in a variety of national and international conventions. For example, one may use formats ranging from MMDDYY to DATE9. for American-style dates or DDMMYY for European-style dates. The following example illustrates the application of these predefined formats:

```
data date_formats_example;
    input date1 mmddyy10. date2 ddmmyy10.;
    format date1 mmddyy10. date2 ddmmyy10.;
    datalines;
    12/25/2022 25/12/2022
```

```
    07/04/2023 04/07/2023
    ;
run;

proc print data=date_formats_example;
run;
```

```
Obs   date1        date2
1     12/25/2022   25/12/2022
2     07/04/2023   04/07/2023
```

Date formats such as DATE9. facilitate the rendering of dates in a more universally understood format:

```
format date1 date9. date2 date9.;
```

Next, consider SAS time formats which also offer varied styles for displaying time values. The common formats include TIME8., showing time in HH:MM:SS, and TOD11., which displays time as HH:MM:SS.ss. Here is an illustration:

```
data time_formats_example;
    input time1 time8. time2 tod11.;
    format time1 time8. time2 tod11.;
    datalines;
    13:30:45 13:30:45.67
    08:15:00 08:15:00.00
    ;
run;

proc print data=time_formats_example;
run;
```

```
Obs     time1        time2
1       13:30:45     13:30:45.67
2       08:15:00     08:15:00.00
```

For situations where both date and time need representation, SAS provides formats like DATETIME18. and DTG12.. These formats encapsulate date and time in one field. Consider the following example:

```
data datetime_formats_example;
   input datetime datetime21.;
   format datetime datetime18.;
   datalines;
   25DEC2022 13:30:45
   04JUL2023 08:15:00
   ;
run;

proc print data=datetime_formats_example;
run;
```

```
Obs        datetime
1     25DEC22:13:30:45
2     04JUL23:08:15:00
```

Creating custom date and time formats using PROC FORMAT further allows users to refine how date and time data is displayed. The following example shows how to define a custom date format:

```
proc format;
    picture custdate
        low-high = '%0d-%0b-%Y' (datatype=date);
run;

data custom_date_format_example;
    input date date9.;
    format date custdate.;
    datalines;
    25DEC2022
    04JUL2023
    ;
run;

proc print data=custom_date_format_example;
run;
```

```
Obs        date
1       25-Dec-2022
2       04-Jul-2023
```

Here, PROC FORMAT defines a new format custdate which presents dates in %d-%b-%Y format. The low-high term ensures that the format is applied universally to all date values within a valid range.

Timezone adjustments and fractional seconds precision can also be handled seamlessly using specific SAS formats, aiding in applications requiring precise time tracking and transformation across different time zones.

Correctly applying SAS date and time formats is paramount in achieving clarity and accuracy in the representation of temporal data. By leveraging both predefined and custom formats, users can tailor their data display to specific needs, facilitating improved data analysis and reporting.

3.8 Numeric and Character Formats

Numeric and character formats in SAS are essential tools for controlling the display of data values. These formats enable the presentation of numbers and text in a readable, informative manner, aligning with both standard conventions and custom specifications. Understanding and effectively utilizing these formats is crucial for data reporting and analysis.

Numeric formats in SAS primarily deal with the representation of numbers, including decimals, integers, and dates. The predefined numeric formats cover a broad spectrum of requirements. Key numeric formats include BEST, COMMA, DOLLAR, E, F, and PERCENT formats, among others.

The BEST format is the default format for numeric variables. It dynamically adjusts the width of the number to display it in the most compact form without loss of precision. For example, compare the use of BEST and F formats:

```
data _null_;
    num = 12345.6789;
    put num= best12.;
    put num= f12.2;
run;
```

```
num=12345.6789
num=12345.68
```

The COMMA format adds commas as thousand separators which is useful when dealing with large numbers. The DOLLAR format further enhances readability by adding a currency symbol.

```
data _null_;
    num = 12345.6789;
    put num= comma12.2;
    put num= dollar12.2;
run;
```

```
num=12,345.68
num=$12,345.68
```

The E format is used for scientific notation. It is particularly useful for representing very large or very small numbers.

```
data _null_;
    num = 12345.6789;
    put num= e12.4;
run;
```

```
num=1.2346E4
```

Character formats, on the other hand, deal with the representation of text data. Predefined character formats such as $UPCASE, $DOWNCASE, $CHAR, and $QUOTE are widely used. The $UPCASE format converts all lowercase letters to uppercase, whereas $DOWNCASE converts all uppercase letters to lowercase.

```
data _null_;
    text = "Hello World!";
    put text= $upcase14.;
    put text= $downcase14.;
```

```
run;
```

text=HELLO WORLD!
text=hello world!

The $CHAR format ensures that trailing blanks in character strings are preserved, which can be critical for aligning text in reports.

To create custom numeric and character formats, the PROC FORMAT procedure is utilized. Custom formats allow detailed control over data presentation and can accommodate specialized use cases. For example, creating a custom numeric format that categorizes values into specified ranges:

```
proc format;
    value income
        low-<20000 = 'Low'
        20000-<50000 = 'Medium'
        50000-high = 'High';
run;

data income_data;
    input income;
    datalines;
15000
30000
65000
;
run;

proc print data=income_data;
    format income income.;
run;
```

income
Low
Medium
High

Custom character formats can be created similarly. For example, converting coded values to meaningful labels:

```
proc format;
    value $gender
        'M' = 'Male'
        'F' = 'Female'
        'U' = 'Unknown';
run;

data gender_data;
    input gender $;
    datalines;
M
F
U
;
run;
```

```
proc print data=gender_data;
    format gender $gender.;
run;
```

gender
Male
Female
Unknown

Both numeric and character formats can be used within the DATA and PROC steps to customize the display and analysis of datasets. For instance, in the DATA step, formats are applied while reading or modifying data:

```
data sales_data;
    input sales date mmddyy10.;
    format date mmddyy10. sales dollar12.2;
    datalines;
12345.67 01/15/2021
54321.89 02/15/2021
;
run;
```

Formats provide a powerful mechanism to enhance the clarity and relevance of data presentations. The appropriate use of numeric and character formats can significantly improve the interpretability of reports and facilitate better data-driven decisions. Continuous practice and exploration of these formats further solidify one's command over SAS programming and data presentation.

3.9 Using Formats in the Data Step

In SAS, formats add a significant degree of flexibility and control over data presentation and manipulation. When working within the Data Step, it is often necessary to apply these formats to ensure the data is interpreted and displayed correctly according to the specific requirements of the analysis. Utilizing formats in the Data Step involves applying pre-defined or custom formats to variables and ensuring these formats persist across different SAS procedures and data manipulations.

Applying a format within the Data Step typically involves the FORMAT statement. The FORMAT statement allows you to associate one or more variables with specific formats, ensuring the data adheres to the required representation. The syntax for using the FORMAT statement is straightforward:

```
FORMAT variable-name1 format-name1. variable-name2 format-name2.;
```

For example, consider a dataset containing employee information, including salaries and hire dates. To apply a currency format to salaries and a date format to hire dates, one would use the following code:

```
DATA employees;
   SET original_employees;
   FORMAT salary dollar12.2 hire_date mmddyy10.;
RUN;
```

In this example, salary is formatted using the dollar12.2 format, which displays the value as currency with two decimal places and appropriate commas. The hire_date is formatted using the mmddyy10. format, which displays the date in the MM/DD/YYYY format.

To further illustrate the utility of formats within the Data Step, consider another example where a custom format is applied. Custom formats are defined using the PROC FORMAT procedure, and then applied within the Data Step:

```
PROC FORMAT;
   VALUE $deptfmt
       'A' = 'Accounting'
       'B' = 'Human Resources'
       'C' = 'Operations';
RUN;

DATA employees;
   SET original_employees;
   FORMAT department $deptfmt.;
RUN;
```

The $deptfmt format associates the department codes (A, B, C) with their respective department names (Accounting, Human Resources, Operations). Applying this custom format within the Data Step ensures that when the department variable is printed or displayed, it appears with the appropriate departmental names.

Another vital aspect of using formats in the Data Step involves conditional logic based on formatted values. By employing the PUT function, formatted values can be retrieved and used in conditional statements. This is especially useful when making decisions based on user-friendly representations of data rather than the raw values.

Consider the following code snippet that conditionsally assigns bonus eligibility based on a formatted salary:

```
DATA employee_bonus;
   SET employees;
   IF PUT(salary, dollar12.2) > 100000 THEN bonus = 1000;
```

```
   ELSE bonus = 500;
RUN;
```

In this example, the PUT function converts the salary variable to its formatted string, and the conditional logic determines the bonus amount. This method leverages the human-readable format to make decisions within the Data Step.

In addition to straightforward formatting, it's possible to transform data based on applied formats. This transformation can be essential when input data must be modified before further analysis or when generating reports. For instance, transforming date values into a different format for further processing might involve the DATE9. to MMDDYY10. formats, ensuring compatibility with external systems or particular reporting requirements.

```
DATA transformed_dates;
   SET original_dates;
   FORMAT new_date mmddyy10.;
   new_date = INPUT(PUT(old_date, date9.), mmddyy10.);
RUN;
```

In this transformation example, old_date initially formatted as DATE9., is converted to a character string using the PUT function, then subsequently re-interpreted and transformed into MMDDYY10. format using the INPUT function.

Overall, using formats within the Data Step enhances data readability, aligns data representation with business requirements, and supports more intuitive conditional logic and transformations. Proper use of formats ensures data is consistently displayed and interpreted correctly across all procedural steps, facilitating accurate analysis and reporting.

3.10 Managing and Storing Formats

In SAS, managing and storing formats efficiently is crucial for maintaining data integrity and ensuring that custom formats are available for use across different sessions and programs. This section delves into methods for saving formats in permanent catalogs, referencing formats stored in different libraries, and leveraging these capabilities to enhance your data management practices.

Creating custom formats is typically carried out using the PROC FORMAT statement. For formats to be reusable across different SAS sessions, they need to be stored in a permanent format catalog. By default, formats created using PROC FORMAT are stored in the work.formats catalog, which is temporary and gets deleted at the end of the SAS session. To create a permanent format catalog, specify the lib option in the PROC FORMAT statement.

```
libname mylib 'C:\sas\formats';

proc format library=mylib.formats;
    value agefmt
        0 - 12 = 'Child'
        13 - 19 = 'Teenager'
        20 - 64 = 'Adult'
        65 - high = 'Senior';
run;
```

In the example above, the agefmt format is stored in a permanent format catalog located in the mylib library. This ensures that the format is available for future use even after the current SAS session ends.

To apply a stored format in another SAS session or program, reference the appropriate library where the format is saved. This can be done using the OPTIONS FMTSEARCH=() statement, which tells SAS where to look for the format catalogs.

```
libname mylib 'C:\sas\formats';
options fmtsearch=(mylib.formats);

data sample;
    input age;
    format age agefmt.;
    datalines;
5
16
45
72
;
run;

proc print data=sample;
run;
```

When executing the PROC PRINT statement, SAS will search the mylib.formats catalog for the agefmt format. This streamlined access ensures consistency in data presentation across various datasets and analyses.

Another important aspect of managing formats is catalog compatibility and migration between different systems or versions of SAS. SAS provides tools for copying formats between catalogs and verifying their integrity. The PROC CATALOG statement aids in the management of format catalogs by providing options for tasks like copying, deleting, and renaming entries.

```
proc catalog catalog=mylib.formats entrytype=format;
    copy out=backlib.formats;
    select agefmt;
run;
```

In this example, the agefmt format is copied from mylib.formats to a backup catalog backlib.formats. Catalog management operations like this ensure that formats can be effectively backed up and migrated, safeguarding against data loss and facilitating collaborative workflows.

Formats can also be exported and imported using the PROC FORMAT CNTLOUT= and CNTLIN= options for interoperability across different environments. This feature becomes extremely useful for complex environments where formats need to be shared or moved between different SAS installations.

```
proc format cntlout=fmtout;
    select agefmt;
run;

proc format cntlin=fmtout;
run;
```

The CNTLOUT= option exports the details of agefmt to the dataset fmtout, while the CNTLIN= option imports it back to a new catalog, thereby recreating the format from the dataset.

Effective format management also entails periodic cleanup of obsolete or redundant formats. The CATALOG DELETE and CATALOG CLEAN options can be used to delete specific entries or cleanup unused formats from a catalog, keeping the catalog organized and efficient.

```
proc catalog catalog=mylib.formats;
    delete agefmt / entrytype=format;
run;

proc catalog catalog=mylib.formats;
    clean;
run;
```

The delete operation removes the agefmt entry, whereas the clean operation ensures that any corrupted or incomplete entries are tidied up, ensuring the integrity of the format catalog.

Ensuring that formats are managed and stored correctly enhances reproducibility and consistency in SAS programs. By utilizing permanent format catalogs, referencing formats correctly across sessions, and maintaining catalog hygiene, users can effectively manage custom formats and apply them seamlessly to their datasets.

3.11 Format Catalogs

The efficient organization and management of formats within SAS are facilitated by format catalogs. A format catalog is a collection of user-defined formats stored in a single location, making format management and reusability more manageable. Format catalogs allow users to separate format definitions from the program code that uses them, promoting modularity and reducing the risk of format-related errors.

To begin working with format catalogs, it is crucial to understand how to create and store these catalogs. Format catalogs are stored in SAS libraries, with each library having its catalog. By default, formats created during a SAS session are stored in the WORK library, which is temporary. For permanent storage, formats must be saved in a permanent library.

To create a permanent format catalog, you need to specify a library in the LIBNAME statement. For example, assume you want to create a library named mylib. The LIBNAME statement for this can be:

```
LIBNAME mylib 'path-to-your-library';
```

Once the library is defined, use the LIBRARY= option in PROC FORMAT to specify the library where the formats should be stored. For example:

```
PROC FORMAT LIBRARY=mylib;
  VALUE $gender
    'M' = 'Male'
    'F' = 'Female';
RUN;
```

This code stores the $gender format in the mylib library. When you run the PROC FORMAT step, SAS creates a format catalog named formats.sas7bcat within the specified library. The created catalog includes the formats defined in the PROC FORMAT step.

To use a format stored in a permanent catalog, you must specify the library reference in a FORMAT statement or when applying formats in procedures. For example:

```
LIBNAME mylib 'path-to-your-library';
```

```
DATA sample_data;
  INPUT gender $;
  DATALINES;
  M
  F
  ;
RUN;

PROC PRINT DATA=sample_data;
  FORMAT gender $gender.;
  LIBNAME'=path-to-your-'libraryFORMAT gender $gender.; /* Applying the format
        */
RUN;
```

This code demonstrates how to assign the gender format to the gender variable in the PROC PRINT step. The LIBNAME statement ensures that SAS has access to the library containing the format catalog.

Additionally, you can manage and list the contents of format catalogs using the PROC DATASETS procedure. For example, to list all formats in a catalog:

```
PROC DATASETS LIBRARY=mylib MEMTYPE=catalog;
  CONTENTS;
RUN;
QUIT;
```

The PROC DATASETS step with the CONTENTS statement provides detailed information about the formats stored in the mylib library's catalog. The MEMTYPE=catalog option restricts the listing to catalogs only.

Another critical aspect of format catalogs is the ability to copy, move, or delete formats between catalogs. The PROC CATALOG procedure in SAS is used to perform these operations. To copy a format from one catalog to another, for instance:

```
PROC CATALOG CATALOG=mylib.formats;
  COPY OUT=anotherlib.formats;
  SELECT gender;
RUN;
QUIT;
```

This example copies the gender format from the catalog in mylib to the catalog in anotherlib. The SELECT statement specifies the format to be copied. Similarly, formats can be deleted using the PROC CATALOG procedure:

```
PROC CATALOG CATALOG=mylib.formats;
  DELETE gender;
RUN;
QUIT;
```

This command deletes the gender format from the mylib catalog, helping maintain an organized set of formats by removing outdated or unused entries.

In the case of creating multiple formats, SAS provides the ability to utilize format search options. By default, SAS searches the WORK library for formats. To enable SAS to search multiple format catalogs, use the FMTSEARCH= system option. For instance:

```
OPTIONS FMTSEARCH=(mylib, anotherlib);
```

The FMTSEARCH= option tells SAS to search both mylib and anotherlib libraries for formats in the specified order, increasing the flexibility and efficiency of format application.

Finally, when documenting and sharing SAS programs, it is important to ensure that the necessary format catalogs accompany the program. Packaging format catalogs with SAS datasets and code files helps maintain consistency across different environments and user sessions, preventing format-not-found errors and ensuring that data presentation remains consistent.

3.12 Troubleshooting Format Issues

A comprehensive understanding of formats in SAS can significantly enhance data manipulation and presentation. However, issues with formats can arise, necessitating effective troubleshooting strategies. This section addresses common problems and their resolutions, ensuring seamless use of formats in your SAS programs.

One of the primary issues encountered with formats is the ERROR: Format not found or couldn't be loaded message. This error implies that SAS cannot locate the specified format. This issue typically occurs due to one of the following reasons:

- The format library is not specified or incorrectly referenced.
- The format does not exist in the specified catalog.
- There is a typographical error in the format name.

To resolve this, ensure the format library is correctly referenced using the LIBNAME statement. For instance:

```
LIBNAME myfmts '/path/to/format/library';
OPTIONS FMTSEARCH=(myfmts);
```

If the format still cannot be found, verify its existence using the PROC DATASETS procedure:

```
PROC DATASETS LIBRARY=myfmts;
   CONTENTS;
RUN;
```

Another frequent problem is the mismatch between the format type (character vs. numeric) and the variable type. SAS requires the variable type to match the format type. For example, a numeric variable cannot be associated with a character format and vice versa. Ensure compatibility as follows:

```
data example;
    format age 8.; /* Correct: 'age' is a numeric variable */
    format gender $char1.; /* Correct: 'gender' is a character variable */
run;
```

Using formats across different datasets can introduce scope-related issues. If formats are defined within a specific data step and not stored in a permanent catalog, they will not be available in other data steps or procedures. Store formats permanently by creating a format catalog:

```
LIBNAME myfmts '/path/to/format/library'; /* Specify the format library */
proc format library=myfmts;
    value agegrp
        0-12 = 'Child'
        13-19 = 'Teen'
        20-high = 'Adult';
run;
```

To ensure the formats are applied correctly across sessions, include the FMTSEARCH option in your autoexec file:

```
OPTIONS FMTSEARCH=(myfmts);
```

Custom formats with overlapping ranges or conflicting values can cause unexpected results. Ensure ranges do not overlap and values do not conflict when defining custom formats:

```
proc format;
    value grade
        0-59 = 'F'
        60-69 = 'D'
        70-79 = 'C'
        80-89 = 'B'
        90-100 = 'A';
run;
```

Date and time formats can sometimes display unintended outputs if the underlying variable is not appropriately handled. SAS stores dates as the number of days since January 1, 1960, and times as the number of seconds since midnight. Ensure dates and times are read and formatted correctly:

```
data date_example;
    format birthdate date9.;
    input birthdate date9.;
    datalines;
    01JAN2000
    23FEB2012
    ;
run;
```

Lastly, managing format catalogs is crucial for preventing bloated libraries and ensuring efficiency. Use the PROC CATALOG procedure to manage and clean up format catalogs:

```
proc catalog catalog=myfmts.sas7bcat;
   contents;
   delete agegrp / description='Obsolete format';
run;
```

By addressing these common issues, you can maintain efficient and error-free use of formats in your SAS programs. Proper troubleshooting ensures that formats enhance data presentation and functionality without introducing complications.

Chapter 4

Using Functions in SAS

This chapter provides an in-depth look at the wide array of functions available in SAS for data manipulation and analysis. It covers character, numeric, date and time, and descriptive statistical functions, as well as data conversion functions. Readers will learn how to effectively use these functions within the data step and apply conditional functions and array functions. The chapter also introduces specialized functions and the creation of custom functions using PROC FCMP, with a focus on function efficiency and performance optimization.

4.1 Introduction to SAS Functions

In SAS, functions are essential tools that perform specific operations or calculations on data. These functions take one or more arguments as input and return a value. SAS provides a wide array of functions to handle various types of data manipulation, including character, numeric, date and time, descriptive statistical, and data conversion functions. Understanding and effectively using these functions can significantly enhance the power and efficiency of your SAS programs.

SAS functions are categorized into the following main types:

- **Character Functions**
- **Numeric Functions**

- **Date and Time Functions**
- **Descriptive Statistical Functions**
- **Data Conversion Functions**

Each category of functions serves a specific purpose. For instance, character functions are used to manipulate text data, numeric functions perform mathematical calculations, date and time functions handle date-time values, descriptive statistical functions compute statistical measures, and data conversion functions transform data from one type to another.

To illustrate the usage of SAS functions, consider the following example. Suppose you have a dataset named sales that contains the following variables: product_name, sales_amount, and sale_date. You might want to calculate the total sales amount, extract the year from the sale_date, or convert the sales_amount to a different format. SAS functions facilitate these operations through simple and efficient syntax.

```
data sales;
  input product_name $ sales_amount sale_date : date9.;
  format sale_date date9.;
  datalines;
  WidgetA 100.50 10JAN2020
  WidgetB 200.75 12FEB2020
  WidgetC 150.30 23MAR2020
  ;
run;

data sales_analysis;
  set sales;
  total_sales_amount = sum(total_sales_amount, sales_amount);
  sale_year = year(sale_date);
  formatted_sales_amount = put(sales_amount, dollar8.2);
run;
```

In this example, the sum function calculates the cumulative total of sales_amount for each observation. The year function extracts the year from sale_date, and the put function converts sales_amount to a formatted dollar amount.

The output of the sales_analysis dataset will be:

product_name	sales_amount	sale_date	total_sales_amount	sale_year	formatted_sales_amount
WidgetA	100.50	10JAN2020	100.50	2020	$100.50
WidgetB	200.75	12FEB2020	301.25	2020	$200.75
WidgetC	150.30	23MAR2020	451.55	2020	$150.30

Character functions include operations like extracting substrings, concatenating strings, and trimming spaces. Examples of these functions are substr, cat, and trim.

Numeric functions include arithmetic calculations, rounding numbers, and finding absolute values. Examples are sqrt, round, and abs.

Date and time functions involve extracting components from a date, calculating the difference between dates, and formatting date and time values. Some commonly used functions are datepart, intck, and timeofday.

Descriptive statistical functions are used to obtain summary statistics such as mean, standard deviation, and median. Examples of these functions are mean, std, and median.

Data conversion functions include converting data from one type to another, such as from numeric to character and vice versa. Examples are input and put.

By familiarizing yourself with these functions, you can perform complex data manipulations with greater ease and precision. Integrating these functions into your SAS programs will result in more efficient and readable code.

4.2 Character Functions

Character functions in SAS are instrumental for manipulating and transforming character strings. These functions allow you to perform a broad spectrum of tasks such as searching, modifying, extracting, and formatting character data. This section elaborates on various essential character functions, providing precise examples and explanations to consolidate understanding.

1. LENGTH Function

The LENGTH function returns the number of characters in a character string, excluding trailing blanks. Its syntax is as follows:

LENGTH(character-variable)

For example, given a character variable name containing the value 'John Doe ' (note the trailing spaces), the LENGTH function returns 8, not counting the trailing blanks.

```
data _null_;
    name = 'John Doe ';
    len = length(name);
    put len;
run;
```

Output:

8

2. SUBSTR Function

The SUBSTR function extracts a substring from a character variable. Its syntax is:

SUBSTR(character-variable, start, length)

Here, start specifies the position of the first character of the substring, and length specifies the number of characters to extract.

```
data _null_;
    name = 'John Doe';
    subset = substr(name, 6, 3);
    put subset;
run;
```

Output:

Doe

3. UPCASE and LOWCASE Functions

The UPCASE function converts a character string to uppercase, whereas the LOWCASE function converts it to lowercase. Their syntax is similar:

UPCASE(character-variable)
LOWCASE(character-variable)

Example for UPCASE:

```
data _null_;
    text = 'Hello World';
    upper_text = upcase(text);
    put upper_text;
run;
```

Output:

HELLO WORLD

Example for LOWCASE:

```
data _null_;
    text = 'Hello World';
    lower_text = lowcase(text);
    put lower_text;
run;
```

Output:

hello world

4. COMPBL and COMPRESS Functions

The COMPBL function compresses multiple blanks in a character string to a single blank. The COMPRESS function removes blanks or specified characters from a character string. Their syntax is as follows:

COMPBL(character-variable)
COMPRESS(character-variable <, characters-to-remove>)

Example for COMPBL:

```
data _null_;
    text = ' Too many spaces ';
    compressed_text = compbl(text);
    put compressed_text;
run;
```

Output:

Too many spaces

Example for COMPRESS:

```
data _null_;
    text = 'Hello, World!';
    text_without_commas = compress(text, ',');
    put text_without_commas;
run;
```

Output:

Hello World!

5. CAT, CATT, CATS, and CATX Functions

These functions are used for concatenating character variables. Their differences lie in how they handle leading and trailing blanks.

- CAT: Concatenates character variables. - CATT: Concatenates character variables after trimming trailing blanks. - CATS: Concatenates character variables after trimming both leading and trailing blanks. - CATX: Concatenates character variables with a specified delimiter after trimming leading and trailing blanks.

```
data _null_;
    var1 = 'Hello';
    var2 = ' ';
    var3 = 'World';
    concatenated = cat(var1, var2, var3);
    put concatenated;
    concatenated_trailing = catt(var1, var2, var3);
    put concatenated_trailing;
    concatenated_all = cats(var1, var2, var3);
    put concatenated_all;
    concatenated_delim = catx(',', var1, var3);
    put concatenated_delim;
run;
```

Output:

Hello World
HelloWorld
HelloWorld
Hello,World

6. FIND and FINDC Functions

The FIND function searches for a substring within a string and returns the position of the substring's first character. The FINDC function searches for a set of characters and returns the position of the first occurrence of any character in the set.

FIND(character-variable, substring <, modifiers> <, startposition>)
FINDC(character-variable, char-set <, modifiers> <, startposition>)

Example for FIND:

```
data _null_;
    text = 'Hello World';
    position = find(text, 'World');
    put position;
run;
```

Output:

7

Example for FINDC:

```
data _null_;
    text = 'Hello World';
    position = findc(text, 'oe');
    put position;
run;
```

Output:

2

7. TRANWRD and TRANSLATE Functions

The TRANWRD function replaces all occurrences of a substring with another substring within a string. The TRANSLATE function translates characters in a string.

TRANWRD(character-variable, old-substring, new-substring)
TRANSLATE(character-variable, to-characters, from-characters)

Example for TRANWRD:

```
data _null_;
    text = 'Good morning';
    new_text = tranwrd(text, 'morning', 'night');
```

```
    put new_text;
run;
```

Output:

Good night

Example for TRANSLATE:

```
data _null_;
    text = 'abcabc';
    new_text = translate(text, '123', 'abc');
    put new_text;
run;
```

Output:

123123

Proficiency in these character functions allows for efficient data manipulation, ensuring that character data suits various analytical and reporting requirements, thereby enhancing the flexibility and power of your SAS programs.

4.3 Numeric Functions

Numeric functions in SAS provide the capability to perform various arithmetic operations, comparisons, and transformations on numeric data. These functions are essential for data analysis, allowing users to manipulate, restructure, and derive insights from numerical datasets. This section explores several commonly used numeric functions and their applications.

Basic Arithmetic Functions

SAS incorporates a variety of functions to handle basic arithmetic computations. These functions often take one or more numeric arguments and return a numeric result.

- SUM - Calculates the sum of its arguments.
- MEAN - Determines the arithmetic mean of its arguments.
- MEDIAN - Yields the median value from its arguments.
- MIN - Finds the smallest value among its arguments.
- MAX - Identifies the largest value from its arguments.

```
data sample_data;
    input var1 var2 var3;
    datalines;
    10 20 30
    40 50 60
    70 80 90
    ;
run;

data calc_data;
    set sample_data;
    sum_var = sum(of var1-var3);
    mean_var = mean(of var1-var3);
    median_var = median(of var1-var3);
    min_var = min(of var1-var3);
    max_var = max(of var1-var3);
run;

proc print data=calc_data;
run;
```

Obs	var1	var2	var3	sum_var	mean_var	median_var	min_var	max_var
1	10	20	30	60	20	20	10	30
2	40	50	60	150	50	50	40	60
3	70	80	90	240	80	80	70	90

Mathematical Functions

Several mathematical functions allow users to perform complex numerical transformations. These functions include:

- ABS - Computes the absolute value of a given number.
- SQRT - Returns the square root of a number.
- LOG - Provides the natural logarithm (base e) of a number.
- LOG10 - Returns the logarithm of a number to base 10.
- EXP - Calculates the exponential value of a number.
- CEIL - Rounds up to the nearest integer.
- FLOOR - Rounds down to the nearest integer.
- ROUND - Rounds a number to the nearest specified unit.

```
data math_functions;
    input num;
    abs_value = abs(num);
    sqrt_value = sqrt(num);
    log_value = log(num);
    log10_value = log10(num);
    exp_value = exp(num);
    ceil_value = ceil(num);
```

```
    floor_value = floor(num);
    round_value = round(num, 0.1);
    datalines;
    -25
    0.5
    10
    25.35
    ;
run;

proc print data=math_functions;
run;
```

Obs	num	abs_value	sqrt_value	log_value	log10_value	exp_value	ceil_value
1	25	25	.	.	0	-25	
2	0.5	0.5	0.7071	-0.6931	-0.3010	1.6487	1
3	10	10	3.1623	2.3026	1	22026.4658	10
4	25.35	25.35	5.0349	3.2319	1.4031	1052015.0635	26

Trigonometric Functions

Trigonometric functions are used for calculations in fields requiring geometry and physics, among others. SAS supports several standard trigonometric functions:

- SIN - Computes the sine of a specified angle in radians.
- COS - Calculates the cosine of an angle in radians.
- TAN - Returns the tangent of an angle in radians.
- ARSIN - Provides the arcsine (inverse sine) of a value.
- ARCOS - Yields the arccosine (inverse cosine) of a value.
- ATAN - Computes the arctangent (inverse tangent) of a given value.

```
data trig_functions;
    input angle_rad;
    sine_value = sin(angle_rad);
    cosine_value = cos(angle_rad);
    tangent_value = tan(angle_rad);
    arcsine_value = arsin(sine_value);
    arccosine_value = arcos(cosine_value);
    arctangent_value = atan(tangent_value);
    datalines;
    0
    1.5708 /* pi/2 */
    3.1416 /* pi */
    4.7124 /* 3pi/2 */
    6.2832 /* 2pi */
    ;
run;

proc print data=trig_functions;
run;
```

Obs	angle_rad	sine_value	cosine_value	tangent_value	arcsine_value	arccosine_value	arctangent_value
1	0	0	1	0	0	0	0
2	1.5708	1	6.1232E-17	1.6331E16	1.5708	1.5708	1.5708
3	3.1416	-9.2792E-16	-1	9.2792E-16	-9.2792E-16	-9.2792E-16	3.1416
4	4.7124	-1	-1.8369E-16	5444566620	4.7124	4.7124	4.7124
5	6.2832	1.2246E-16	1	1.2246E-16	1.2246E-16	1.2246E-16	6.2832

Specialized Numeric Functions

Apart from basic arithmetic and trigonometric functions, SAS provides a range of specialized numeric functions tailored for specific use cases in data analysis.

- RANUNI - Generates random numbers uniformly distributed between 0 and 1.
- RANNOR - Produces random numbers from a standard normal distribution.
- PROBIT - Computes the quantile function (inverse cumulative distribution function) for the standard normal distribution.
- CUMUL - Provides cumulative frequency or percentage for a series of numbers.

```
data special_num_functions;
    do i = 1 to 10;
        random_uni = ranuni(123);
        random_nor = rannor(123);
        probit_value = probit(random_uni);
        output;
    end;
run;

proc print data=special_num_functions;
run;
```

Obs	i	random_uni	random_nor	probit_value
1	1	0.726369	0.820691	0.59857
2	2	0.579738	-0.847193	0.44631
3	3	0.787662	0.820695	0.79345
4	4	0.729227	-0.112353	0.60734
5	5	0.966766	-0.502373	1.82139
6	6	0.303079	0.848192	-0.52251
7	7	0.849938	-0.188678	1.03664
8	8	0.895283	0.865044	1.24987
9	9	0.362001	0.182029	-0.35643
10	10	0.684211	-1.529026	0.48180

Understanding numeric functions in SAS enhances the ability to perform a wide array of analytical tasks, from simple calculations to complex data modeling. By leveraging these functions, users can efficiently process and interpret numerical data within their datasets.

4.4 Date and Time Functions

In SAS, date and time functions are essential for handling and manipulating date and time values within datasets. These functions facilitate operations such as extracting specific components of a date or time, computing differences between dates, formatting dates, and converting between date and time formats. Understanding and effectively utilizing these functions is crucial for accurate time-based data analysis.

Extracting Components of Date and Time

SAS provides a set of functions specifically designed to extract components from date and time values. These functions help retrieve parts such as the year, month, day, hour, minute, and second. Here are some common extraction functions:

- YEAR() - Extracts the year from a SAS date value.
- MONTH() - Extracts the month from a SAS date value.
- DAY() - Extracts the day of the month from a SAS date value.
- HOUR() - Extracts the hour from a SAS time or datetime value.
- MINUTE() - Extracts the minute from a SAS time or datetime value.
- SECOND() - Extracts the second from a SAS time or datetime value.

Illustrating an example, consider the extraction of year, month, and day from a given date value:

```
data extract_example;
    input date_value date9.;
    year_value = year(date_value);
    month_value = month(date_value);
    day_value = day(date_value);
    format date_value date9.;
    datalines;
    01JAN2021
    15JUL2022
    31DEC2020
    ;
run;
```

The year_value, month_value, and day_value will contain the extracted components of the given date_value.

Computing Differences Between Dates

Computing the difference between dates is an essential operation for time-based analysis. SAS provides several functions to calculate the number of days, months, or years between two dates:

- INTCK() - Counts the number of interval boundaries between two dates.
- DATDIF() - Computes the difference between two dates in days.
- YRDIF() - Computes the difference between two dates in years.

Example of using INTCK() to compute the number of months between two dates:

```
data diff_example;
    start_date = '01JAN2021'd;
    end_date = '15JUL2022'd;
    months_diff = intck('month', start_date, end_date);
    days_diff = datdif(start_date, end_date, 'actual');
    years_diff = yrdif(start_date, end_date, 'actual');
run;
```

In this example, months_diff will contain the number of months, days_-diff the number of days, and years_diff the number of years between start_date and end_date.

Formatting Dates and Times

SAS provides a wide array of formats for displaying date and time values. Formatting allows for the customization of the output appearance of these values. Some common formats include:

- DATE9. - Displays a date value in day-month-year format with a 3-letter abbreviation for the month.
- MMDDYY10. - Displays a date value in month/day/year format with 2-digit day, month, and 4-digit year.
- YYMMDD10. - Displays a date value in year/month/day format with 2-digit day, month, and 4-digit year.
- TIME8. - Displays a time value in hour:minute:second format.
- DATETIME20. - Displays a datetime value in day-month-year hour:minute:second format.

Example of formatting a date and datetime value:

```
data format_example;
    date_value = '15JUL2022'd;
    datetime_value = '15JUL2022:12:34:56'dt;
    format date_value date9. datetime_value datetime20.;
run;
```

Here, date_value will be displayed as 15JUL2022 and datetime_value as 15JUL2022:12:34:56.

Conversions Between Date and Time Formats

Converting between different date and time formats is often required for consistency and compatibility within datasets and reports. SAS provides functions for such conversions:

- MDY() - Combines month, day, and year into a SAS date value.
- DHMS() - Combines date, hour, minute, and second into a SAS datetime value.
- DATEPART() - Extracts the date part from a SAS datetime value.
- TIMEPART() - Extracts the time part from a SAS datetime value.

Example of converting components into a SAS datetime value:

```
data convert_example;
    month = 7;
    day = 15;
    year = 2022;
    hour = 12;
    minute = 34;
    second = 56;
    datetime_value = dhms(mdy(month, day, year), hour, minute, second);
    format datetime_value datetime20.;
run;
```

The datetime_value will represent the datetime as 15JUL2022:12:34:56.

Understanding and efficiently using date and time functions in SAS enhances the ability to manipulate and analyze time-based data accurately. This knowledge is pivotal in domains where temporal data plays a critical role, such as finance, healthcare, and operations research.

4.5 Descriptive Statistical Functions

Descriptive statistical functions in SAS are instrumental for summarizing and understanding the properties of datasets. These functions help in calculating key summary statistics such as mean, median, standard deviation, variance, and percentiles. Using these functions effectively can provide valuable insights into data distributions, central tendencies, and the variability within a dataset.

Mean Function:

The MEAN function computes the arithmetic mean of non-missing values. For instance, let us compute the mean of several numeric variables in a dataset.

```
data summary;
    set original_data;
    mean_value = mean(var1, var2, var3, var4);
run;
```

In this example, mean_value will be assigned the mean of the non-missing values of var1, var2, var3, and var4 for each observation in the dataset original_data.

Median Function:

The MEDIAN function calculates the middle value of the non-missing values when sorted in ascending order. Here's how it can be applied:

```
data summary;
    set original_data;
    median_value = median(var1, var2, var3, var4);
run;
```

This code assigns the median of the non-missing values of the listed variables to median_value.

Standard Deviation and Variance:

The STD function returns the sample standard deviation, while the VAR function provides the sample variance. They can be used as follows:

```
data summary;
    set original_data;
    std_value = std(var1, var2, var3, var4);
    var_value = var(var1, var2, var3, var4);
run;
```

Here, std_value is the sample standard deviation and var_value is the sample variance of the non-missing values of the specified variables.

Percentile Calculation:

To compute specific percentiles, the PCTL functions such as PCTL75 can be utilized. The example below demonstrates how to obtain the 75th percentile:

```
proc univariate data=original_data noprint;
    var var1 var2 var3 var4;
    output out=percentiles pctlpts=75 pctlpre=PCT;
run;
```

The PROC UNIVARIATE procedure computes the 75th percentile (or any specified percentile) for each variable (var1, var2, var3, and var4) and outputs the results to a new dataset named percentiles, with the percentile variable names prefixed by PCT.

Other Descriptive Statistics:

Additional descriptive statistics can be derived using various built-in SAS functions. For instance, the RANGE function computes the difference between the maximum and minimum values, whereas the CV function calculates the coefficient of variation.

```
data summary;
    set original_data;
    range_value = range(var1, var2, var3, var4);
    cv_value = cv(var1, var2, var3, var4);
run;
```

range_value denotes the range, and cv_value represents the coefficient of variation for the non-missing values of the variables specified.

Through combining these descriptive statistical functions, comprehensive datasets can be summarized to provide an overview of the underlying data characteristics. It is crucial to ensure these functions are applied considering the presence of non-missing values to avoid skewed results.

4.6 Functions for Data Conversion

Functions for data conversion are essential in SAS programming when it is necessary to convert data from one type or format to another. This section discusses various SAS functions available for converting character data to numeric data, numeric data to character data, and handling date and time formats. Understanding these functions is crucial for data preprocessing and ensuring compatibility across different types of data analyses.

Character to Numeric Conversion

When working with data, it is often required to convert character values to numeric values for computation purposes. The INPUT function performs this conversion efficiently. The INPUT function requires the source character variable and an appropriate informat as arguments.

```
data char_to_num;
    char_var = '12345';
    num_var = input(char_var, 5.);
run;
```

In this example, the char_var is a character variable containing the string '12345', and the input function converts it into a numeric value num_var with an informat of 5..

Numeric to Character Conversion

Conversely, there are situations where numeric values need to be converted to character strings. This is achieved using the PUT function, which requires the numeric variable and a suitable format.

```
data num_to_char;
    num_var = 67890;
    char_var = put(num_var, 5.);
run;
```

Here, the put function converts the numeric variable num_var to a character variable char_var using a format of 5..

Handling Missing Values

Handling missing values during conversion is another critical aspect. For character-to-numeric conversion, SAS returns a missing value if the character string cannot be successfully converted. The following example demonstrates this:

```
data handle_missing;
    char_var = 'abc';
    num_var = input(char_var, 5.);
run;
```

In the resulting dataset, num_var will have a missing value since 'abc' cannot be converted to a numeric format.

Similarly, when converting numeric to character with missing values, the put function handles it gracefully:

```
data handle_missing_num_to_char;
    num_var = .;
    char_var = put(num_var, 5.);
run;
```

In this case, char_var will contain a missing value (represented often as a blank string) corresponding to the missing numeric value.

Date and Time Conversion

Date and time data are frequently encountered in data sets, and SAS provides robust functions to manipulate these values. Conversion between date formats, numeric timestamps, and character representations can be performed using specific functions.

DATEPART and TIMEPART functions extract the date and time parts from a datetime value respectively.

```
data date_time_conversion;
    datetime_var = '01JAN2023:10:30:00'dt;
    date_var = datepart(datetime_var);
    time_var = timepart(datetime_var);
    format date_var date9.;
    format time_var time8.;
run;
```

In this dataset, date_var contains the date part of datetime_var while time_var retains the time part. Proper formats (date9. and time8.) ensure the output is human-readable.

For converting character dates to SAS date values, the INPUT function with a date informat is used.

```
data char_to_date;
    char_date = '15MAR2022';
    sas_date = input(char_date, date9.);
    format sas_date date9.;
run;
```

Here, the input function converts the character string char_date to a SAS date value sas_date with the date9. informat.

Format Manipulation and Conversion Functions

The PUTN and PUTC functions enable conversion based on variable formats. They can be particularly useful for dynamic formatting needs.

```
data dynamic_format;
    num_var = 1234.56;
    formatted_value = putn(num_var, 'dollar12.2');
run;
```

In this example, putn converts the numeric variable num_var to a character string with a dollar format (dollar12.2).

These data conversion functions enhance the flexibility and dynamism of SAS programming, enabling seamless transitions between data types and formats, essential for comprehensive data analysis and preprocessing tasks.

4.7 Using Functions in the Data Step

In SAS, the Data Step is a fundamental construct used for data manipulation and analysis. Within the Data Step, functions are vital tools that allow for a wide range of transformations and analyses on the dataset. This section elaborates on the integration of functions within the Data Step, providing detailed examples and explanations to enhance understanding.

The basic syntax of a Data Step in SAS is as follows:

```
DATA output_dataset;
    SET input_dataset;
    /* Function usage and data transformations */
RUN;
```

In this framework, functions perform specific operations on the dataset's variables. Multiple categories of functions—such as character, numeric, date and time, and others—can be employed to achieve the desired data manipulations.

Character Functions:

Consider a dataset where we have a variable Name, and we want to compute the length and first name from it.

```
DATA transformed_data;
    SET raw_data;
    name_length = LENGTH(Name);
    first_name = SCAN(Name, 1, ' ');
RUN;
```

In this example, LENGTH calculates the number of characters in the variable Name, and SCAN returns the first word, assuming names are separated by spaces.

Numeric Functions:

Numeric functions are used for arithmetic calculations and statistical transformations within the Data Step. For instance, to compute the absolute value and the square root of a variable Score:

```
DATA numeric_transforms;
    SET scores_data;
    absolute_score = ABS(Score);
    sqrt_score = SQRT(Score);
RUN;
```

Here, ABS computes the absolute value, and SQRT evaluates the square root of the variable Score.

Date and Time Functions:

Date and time functions in the Data Step allow for manipulation and transformation of temporal data. For example, to find the difference between two dates, Date1 and Date2, and to extract the year from Date1:

```
DATA date_transforms;
    SET date_data;
    days_diff = DATE1 - DATE2;
    year_date1 = YEAR(DATE1);
RUN;
```

The subtraction operator calculates the difference in days, and the YEAR function extracts the year part of the date.

Conditional Functions:

Conditional functions like IF-THEN statements can be used to apply conditions to the data.

```
DATA conditional_transforms;
    SET data;
    IF score >= 50 THEN grade = 'Pass';
    ELSE grade = 'Fail';
RUN;
```

This logic conditionally assigns values to grade based on the value of score.

Array Functions:

Array functions are used within loops to process group variables efficiently.

```
DATA array_example;
   SET raw_data;
   ARRAY scores[3] score1-score3;
   do i = 1 to 3;
      scores[i] = scores[i] * 1.1; /* Apply some transformation */
   end;
RUN;
```

This code defines an array called scores, loops through the array elements, and applies a transformation.

Algorithm 1: Using Functions in Data Step

Data: Dataset containing numerical and character variables
Result: Transformed dataset using various functions

```
for each record in dataset do
    Apply character functions;
    Apply numeric functions;
    Apply date and time functions;
    Apply conditional functions;
    Apply array functions;
```

Functions significantly enhance the versatility and power of the Data Step by enabling detailed manipulations and calculations. Proficient use of these functions helps streamline data preprocessing and analysis workflows in SAS, contributing to more efficient and effective data analysis.

4.8 Conditional Functions

Conditional functions are a powerful resource in SAS programming for enabling logic-based decisions within code. These functions facilitate the execution of operations depending on specified conditions, which is essential in data analysis and manipulation tasks. They commonly contribute to making code more concise and readable while enhancing functionality.

The primary conditional functions in SAS include IF-THEN/ELSE, IFN, IFC, WHICHN, and WHICHC. Each has specific use cases and advantages, aiding in streamlined decision-making processes directly within the data step.

- IF-THEN/ELSE: A fundamental construct in SAS that allows

branching based on condition evaluation.

- IFN: Returns one of the numeric values depending on the evaluation of a condition.
- IFC: Returns a character value based on the evaluation of a condition.
- WHICHN/WHICHC: Determines the position of a specific value within a list of numeric or character values.

IF-THEN/ELSE Construct

IF-THEN/ELSE is the most basic and versatile conditional function, suitable for a variety of scenarios.

```
data example;
    set input_data;
    if age > 18 then adult = 1;
    else adult = 0;
run;
```

The above example demonstrates a simple condition where an individual is classified as an adult if their age is greater than 18.

IFN **Function**

The IFN function serves a similar purpose but is used for more succinctly writing numeric conditional operations. It can be particularly useful when simplifying code to avoid more verbose IF-THEN/ELSE blocks.

```
data example;
    set input_data;
    adult = ifn(age > 18, 1, 0);
run;
```

Here, IFN evaluates the condition $age > 18$ and returns 1 if true and 0 if false.

IFC **Function**

The IFC function is the character equivalent of IFN. It evaluates a condition and returns a character string based on the outcome.

```
data example;
    set input_data;
    status = ifc(age > 18, 'Adult', 'Minor');
run;
```

In this instance, IFC returns 'Adult' if $age > 18$ evaluates to true, and 'Minor' otherwise.

WHICHN and WHICHC Functions

WHICHN and WHICHC are utilized for identifying the position of a value within a list of numeric or character values respectively. This is particularly useful for mapping or lookup operations within a dataset.

```
data example;
    set input_data;
    position = whichn(target_var, var1, var2, var3, var4);
run;
```

In this command, WHICHN returns the position of target_var within the list of variables var1, var2, var3, var4. If target_var matches var3, position will be assigned the value 3.

For character values, use WHICHC:

```
data example;
    set input_data;
    position = whichc(target_var, 'A', 'B', 'C', 'D');
run;
```

Here, WHICHC searches the list of character values and assigns the position of the target character string.

Combining Conditional Functions with Arrays

Combining conditional functions with arrays can offer significant flexibility and efficiency in data processing. For instance, transforming a set of variables based on a condition can be efficiently accomplished using arrays in conjunction with IFN or IFC.

```
data example;
    set input_data;
    array scores {*} score1-score5;
    array passed {*} pass1-pass5;

    do i = 1 to dim(scores);
        passed{i} = ifn(scores{i} >= 60, 1, 0);
    end;
run;
```

In this example, an array of scores is evaluated, and a corresponding array of pass/fail indicators is generated using IFN. Each element in the scores array is checked; if the score is greater than or equal to 60, the respective element in passed is set to 1, otherwise, it is set to 0.

These applications exemplify the utility of conditional functions, highlighting their ability to introduce efficient, readable, and logic-driven decision making into SAS programs. Proper implementation can significantly optimize data workflows and processing efficiency.

4.9 Array Functions

Array functions in SAS offer robust capabilities for handling multidimensional data structures. They allow for streamlined operations on datasets by treating individual variables as elements of an array, thereby reducing repetitive code and enhancing readability.

Definition and Declaration of Arrays in SAS: An array in SAS is a set of variables that can be iterated through using a do-loop. The syntax for defining an array is straightforward:

```
array array_name{dimension} <$> variable_list;
```

Here, array_name is the name given to the array, dimension denotes the size of the array, the dollar sign $ indicates if the array elements are character variables, and variable_list specifies the variables that constitute the array.

Example:

```
data scores;
    input Subject $ Score1-Score5;
    array scores_array{5} Score1-Score5;
    datalines;
    Math 85 92 78 88 90
    Science 90 94 88 96 85
    ;
run;
```

In this example, scores_array consists of five elements corresponding to the variables Score1 through Score5.

Using Array Functions: Array functions enable a range of operations on array elements. Some common array functions include: - DIM(): Returns the number of elements in the array. - LBOUND(): Returns the lower bound of the array dimension. - HBOUND(): Returns the upper bound of the array dimension.

Example:

```
data scores_with_average;
    set scores;
    array scores_array{*} Score1-Score5;
    total=0;

    * Calculating the total score using a do loop;
    do i = 1 to dim(scores_array);
        total + scores_array{i};
    end;
    average = total / dim(scores_array);
run;
```

In this example, the DIM() function is used to determine the number of elements in scores_array, which enables dynamic array processing within the do-loop. The average variable is then computed by dividing the total by the number of elements in the array.

Multidimensional Arrays: SAS also supports multidimensional arrays, which are useful for more complex data operations. The syntax for declaring a two-dimensional array is as follows:

```
array array_name{rows, columns} <$> variable_list;
```

Example:

```
data matrix_operations;
    array matrix{2,3} m1-m6;
    array result{2} sum_row1 sum_row2;

    * Initializing the array with data;
    m1=1; m2=2; m3=3;
    m4=4; m5=5; m6=6;

    * Summing rows of the matrix;
    do i = 1 to 2;
        result{i} = 0;
        do j = 1 to 3;
            result{i} + matrix{i,j};
        end;
    end;
run;
```

Here, matrix is a 2x3 array containing six elements. The inner do-loop processes each column, while the outer do-loop iterates through the rows, performing row-wise summation.

Temporary Arrays: In some situations, it is beneficial to use temporary arrays, which are not associated with variables in the data set but are used for intermediate computations. Temporary arrays are declared by omitting the variable list:

```
array temp_array{5};
```

Example:

```
data calculate_moving_average;
    set scores;
    array scores_array{5} Score1-Score5;
    array temp_array{5} _temporary_;

    * Calculating moving average;
    do i = 1 to dim(scores_array);
        if i = 1 then temp_array{i} = scores_array{i};
        else temp_array{i} = (temp_array{i-1} + scores_array{i}) / 2;
    end;
run;
```

Handling Missing Values: Arrays can efficiently handle datasets with missing values using conditional statements within an array loop. This ensures that operations do not propagate missing values unnecessarily.

Example:

```
data handle_missing_values;
    set scores;
    array scores_array{5} Score1-Score5;

    * Summing scores excluding missing values;
    total=0;
    num_non_missing=0;

    do i = 1 to dim(scores_array);
        if not missing(scores_array{i}) then do;
            total + scores_array{i};
            num_non_missing + 1;
        end;
    end;
    average = total / num_non_missing;
run;
```

In this scenario, the code checks each element for missing values using the missing() function, ensuring that only non-missing scores contribute to the total and average calculations.

The implementation and utilization of array functions significantly enhance the efficiency and readability of SAS programs, particularly when dealing with repetitively structured data. This capability reduces code redundancy and improves both processing time and maintainability of SAS scripts.

4.10 Specialized Functions

SAS provides a variety of specialized functions that are particularly useful for specific tasks in data manipulation, analysis, and reporting. These functions extend beyond the basic character, numeric, and date and time functions, addressing more complex requirements in statistical analysis, financial computations, random number generation, and other specialized tasks. This section delves into several key specialized functions, their syntax, and how to use them effectively.

One notable group of specialized functions in SAS includes the financial functions. These functions allow for the calculation of various financial metrics such as interest rates, future value, present value, and loan payment amounts. For example, the FINANCE function suite includes:

- PV(rate, nper, pmt, fv, type): Computes the present value of an investment.
- FV(rate, nper, pmt, pv, type): Calculates the future value of an investment.
- PMT(rate, nper, pv, fv, type): Determines the payment required for a loan or investment based on constant payments and interest rates.

These functions are highly useful for financial analysts and accountants who need to incorporate financial computations directly within SAS.

Another essential set of specialized functions revolves around probability and random number generation. The RANXXX functions generate random numbers from various distributions:

- RANNOR(seed): Generates a random number from the standard normal distribution.
- RANUNI(seed): Produces a random number from a uniform distribution on the interval (0,1).
- RANBIN(seed, n, p): Generates a random number from a binomial distribution with parameters n and p.

These functions are essential in statistical simulations and Monte Carlo studies. For example, to generate 10000 random normal variates with a mean of 0 and standard deviation of 1, you can use the following code:

```
data random_normals;
   do i = 1 to 10000;
      rand_num = rannor(0);
      output;
   end;
run;
```

The RANBIN function is particularly useful for generating binomial variates. Suppose you need to simulate the number of successes in a series of trials with a probability of success equal to 0.3. The following code illustrates this:

```
data binomial_samples;
   do i = 1 to 10000;
      successes = ranbin(0, 10, 0.3);
      output;
   end;
run;
```

In more complex statistical applications, SAS provides a suite of specialized statistical functions. For instance, the CDF function computes the cumulative distribution function for various distributions. The syntax is CDF(’distribution’, x, <parameters>). Some examples include:

- CDF(’NORMAL’, x, mu, sigma): Returns the cumulative probability up to x for a normal distribution.
- CDF(’T’, x, df): Computes the cumulative probability up to x for a Student’s t-distribution.
- CDF(’BINOMIAL’, x, n, p): Calculates the cumulative probability up to x for a binomial distribution.

To compute the cumulative probability of getting a value less than 1.5 from a normal distribution with mean 0 and standard deviation 1, you can use:

```
data cdf_example;
    prob = cdf('NORMAL', 1.5, 0, 1);
run;
```

For distributions requiring inverse CDF calculations, SAS provides the QUANTILE function. Its syntax is QUANTILE(’distribution’, p, <parameters>). Examples include:

- QUANTILE(’NORMAL’, p, mu, sigma): Returns the quantile for a given probability p from a normal distribution.
- QUANTILE(’T’, p, df): Finds the quantile for a given probability p from a Student’s t-distribution.
- QUANTILE(’BINOMIAL’, p, n, p): Determines the quantile for a given probability p from a binomial distribution.

To determine the value corresponding to the 95th percentile of a standard normal distribution:

```
data quantile_example;
    value = quantile('NORMAL', 0.95, 0, 1);
run;
```

Beyond statistical and random number functions, SAS also offers specialized functions for data aggregation. The LAG and DIFF functions are extremely useful in time series analysis:

- LAGn(variable): Returns the value of variable from n observations prior.
- DIFFn(variable): Computes the difference between the current value of variable and its value n observations prior.

An example of using the LAG function to compute a 3-observation lag:

```
data time_series;
    set original_data;
    lag3_variable = lag3(variable);
run;
```

The LAG function is fundamental in creating autoregressive models or dealing with time-dependent data. Combining both LAG and DIFF functions can be invaluable for detecting trends over time.

Another important set of functions revolves around handling missing values. The NMISS and CMISS functions are efficient tools for identifying and counting missing values within datasets:

- NMISS(of variable-list): Counts the number of missing numeric values.
- CMISS(of variable-list): Counts the number of missing character or numeric values.

For example, to count the number of missing values in a dataset:

```
data missing_counts;
    set original_data;
    nmiss_count = nmiss(of num1-num5);
    cmiss_count = cmiss(of char1-char5 num1-num5);
run;
```

This section has covered a range of specialized functions available in SAS, each integral for handling specific types of data analysis tasks efficiently. Selecting the appropriate specialized function can significantly optimize both the computational performance and the clarity of SAS programs, allowing for more effective data analysis and reporting.

4.11 Creating Custom Functions with PROC FCMP

The ability to create custom functions in SAS can significantly extend the power and flexibility of your SAS programs. Customized functions allow you to encapsulate frequently-used code into reusable units, thus promoting code modularity and ease of maintenance. The PROC FCMP procedure is the main mechanism in SAS for defining such user-defined functions (UDFs) and subroutines.

The PROC FCMP (Function Compiler) offers a structured syntax to define, compile, and store custom functions and subroutines. These can be later invoked just like any built-in SAS function or procedure within your data steps or other SAS procedures.

The general syntax for defining a custom function with PROC FCMP is as follows:

```
proc fcmp outlib=libref.dataset.package;
    function function-name(argument-1 <length_1> ..., argument-n <length_n>);
        /* Function logic and operations */
        return (result);
    endsub;
quit;
```

In this syntax: - libref is the library reference where the compiled function will be stored. - dataset specifies the dataset name. - package is a grouping construct for the functions. - The function-name indicates the name of the function. - argument-1, argument-2, ..., argument-n are the parameters passed to the function.

Let's illustrate the process of creating a custom function using a specific example. Assume we need a custom function to calculate the Body Mass Index (BMI) given weight and height.

```
proc fcmp outlib=work.functions.health;
    function BMI(weight, height);
        bmi = weight / (height * height);
        return (bmi);
    endsub;
quit;
```

In this example: - work.functions.health specifies that the function will be stored in the WORK library, tucked inside the FUNCTIONS dataset, categorized under the HEALTH package. - The function BMI accepts two arguments: weight and height. - The body of the function performs the calculation bmi = weight / (height * height); and returns the result using return (bmi);

After defining the function, it can be used in a DATA step similarly to any built-in SAS function.

```
options cmplib=work.functions;
data test_bmi;
    set sample_data;
    BMI_Value = BMI(weight, height);
```

```
run;
```

In this code: - options cmplib=work.functions; specifies the location of the compiled functions so SAS knows where to find them. - A DATA step processes the sample_data dataset. The new variable BMI_-Value is computed using our custom BMI function.

Advanced Usage with Arrays:

Custom functions can also handle arrays. Suppose we want a function that calculates the mean of an array of numbers. First, we would gather the sum of the array elements and then divide by the number of elements.

```
proc fcmp outlib=work.functions.stats;
    function ArrayMean(x[*]);
        sum = 0;
        do i = 1 to dim(x);
            sum + x[i];
        end;
        mean = sum / dim(x);
        return (mean);
    endsub;
quit;
```

Here: - The function ArrayMean accepts an array x[*] as its parameter. - The index i iterates over the dimensions of the array, summed up in sum, and the mean is calculated as mean = sum / dim(x);

This function can also be invoked within a DATA step where datasets consist of array structures.

```
options cmplib=work.functions;
data test_mean;
    set sample_data;
    array scores[5] score1-score5;
    Avg_Score = ArrayMean(scores);
run;
```

Error Handling:

It is prudent to include error handling in your custom functions. Let's modify the BMI function to ensure positive values for weight and height.

```
proc fcmp outlib=work.functions.health;
    function BMI(weight, height);
        if weight <= 0 or height <= 0 then
            return (.);
        bmi = weight / (height * height);
        return (bmi);
    endsub;
quit;
```

This enhanced version checks if weight and height are positive. If not, it returns a missing value.

Creating Subroutines:

In addition to functions, PROC FCMP also supports the creation of subroutines. Subroutines differ from functions as they do not return a value but can modify their input parameters.

```
proc fcmp outlib=work.functions.geography;
    subroutine SwapCoordinates(x, y);
        outargs x, y;
        temp = x;
        x = y;
        y = temp;
    endsub;
quit;
```

In this example, the subroutine SwapCoordinates swaps the values of x and y. The keyword outargs specifies parameters that the subroutine modifies.

Using this subroutine in a DATA step requires calling it with the call statement:

```
options cmplib=work.functions;
data test_swap;
    x = 10;
    y = 20;
    call SwapCoordinates(x, y);
run;
```

Here, x and y are swapped through the subroutine SwapCoordinates.

As demonstrated, PROC FCMP not only allows for the creation of custom functions but also enables the incorporation of complex logic and parameter handling, thus enhancing the modularity and flexibility of SAS programming. Using these customized tools can greatly boost productivity by reducing repetitive code and fostering reusable logic.

4.12 Function Efficiency and Performance

Efficient use of functions in SAS programming is crucial for optimizing performance, especially when dealing with large datasets and complex analyses. This section explores various strategies to enhance function efficiency, including selecting appropriate functions, minimizing computational overhead, and leveraging SAS architecture optimally.

Selecting Appropriate Functions

Choosing the right function for the task is fundamental to achieving efficiency. SAS offers multiple functions to perform similar tasks; however, their performance characteristics can vary significantly. For instance, to concatenate strings, using CAT functions can be more efficient compared to the traditional || operator. Here's a comparison:

```
data example;
    length str1 str2 str3 $200;
    set old_data;
    str_combined = catx(' ', str1, str2, str3); /* More efficient */
    str_combined_op = str1 || ' ' || str2 || ' ' || str3; /* Less efficient */
run;
```

When handling numerical data transformations, functions like SUM and MEAN are optimized for performance, especially in scenarios involving missing values. For instance:

```
data example;
    set old_data;
    total = sum(of var1-var5); /* Handles missing values efficiently */
    avg = mean(of var1-var5); /* Efficient calculation of mean */
run;
```

Minimizing Computational Overhead

Computational overhead can be minimized by avoiding redundant function calls within data steps. Functions should be called as few times as necessary to produce the required result. Consider the following code example, which minimizes overhead by storing intermediate results:

```
data example;
    set old_data;
    length_full_name = length(trim(first_name) || ' ' || trim(last_name));
    /* More efficient */
    trimmed_first = trim(first_name);
    trimmed_last = trim(last_name);
    length_full_name_opt = length(trimmed_first || ' ' || trimmed_last);
run;
```

In this example, trimming the first_name and last_name fields only once and reusing the result reduces the total number of function calls, thereby enhancing efficiency.

Leveraging SAS Architecture

Understanding and leveraging the underlying SAS architecture is key to optimizing function performance. SAS processes data in a sequential manner within the data step, making it crucial to structure code that aligns with this flow. Efficient use of BY processing and FIRST. and LAST. variables can greatly improve the performance of functions applied to groups of data.

For instance, when calculating group-level statistics, using BY groups efficiently can significantly reduce processing time:

```
proc sort data=old_data;
    by group_var;
run;

data group_stats;
    set old_data;
    by group_var;
    if first.group_var then group_sum = 0;
    group_sum + value_var;
    if last.group_var then output;
run;
```

Here, the SUM accumulator (group_sum) is reset only at the start of each group, and the sum is calculated incrementally, which enhances performance.

Parallel Processing

Utilizing parallel processing can further optimize the performance of function execution in SAS. By dividing tasks into smaller, independent units that can be executed concurrently, overall processing time can be reduced. This approach is particularly useful when dealing with large datasets in a multiprocessor environment.

Parallel processing can be achieved using the MP Connect feature in SAS, which allows for splitting and distributing data processing tasks among multiple processors. Here is an example of how this can be implemented:

```
options sascmd="!sascmd" autosignon;
signon task1;
signon task2;

rsubmit task1 wait=no sysrputsync=yes;
    data part1;
        set old_data(where=(mod(_N_,2)=1));
        /* Function-intensive operations */
    run;
endrsubmit;

rsubmit task2 wait=no sysrputsync=yes;
    data part2;
        set old_data(where=(mod(_N_,2)=0));
        /* Function-intensive operations */
    run;
endrsubmit;

waitfor _all_ task1 task2;

data final;
    set part1 part2;
run;
```

```
signoff task1;
signoff task2;
```

This example demonstrates splitting a dataset into two parts and processing them concurrently, thus reducing overall computation time.

Avoiding Resource-Intensive Functions

Certain functions in SAS are more resource-intensive than others. Whenever possible, these functions should be avoided or used sparingly. For instance, the CALL SYMPUT routine and similar functions that interact with the macro facility can introduce significant overhead. Instead, utilizing data step variables and retaining data within the data step can be more efficient.

Additionally, functions that perform complex mathematical operations or involve extensive string manipulations may also be resource-intensive. Profiling and benchmarking different functions on sample datasets can help identify and avoid those that are less performant for specific tasks.

Efficient function usage not only improves the performance of individual data steps but also contributes to the overall optimization of SAS programs. By selecting appropriate functions, minimizing redundant computations, leveraging SAS architecture, utilizing parallel processing techniques, and avoiding resource-intensive functions, programmers can achieve significant gains in performance.

Chapter 5

Data Manipulation Techniques

This chapter explores various data manipulation techniques in SAS, including sorting data with PROC SORT, filtering data using WHERE and IF statements, and merging and joining datasets. It covers aggregating data with PROC MEANS and PROC SUMMARY, reshaping data with PROC TRANSPOSE, and concatenating datasets. Additionally, readers will learn how to create and modify variables, use arrays for data manipulation, handle missing values, and apply advanced data transformation techniques, culminating in data manipulation using PROC SQL.

5.1 Introduction to Data Manipulation

Data manipulation is a crucial aspect of working with datasets in SAS, enabling researchers and programmers to transform, manage, and prepare data for analysis. This section introduces fundamental data manipulation techniques that lay the groundwork for more complex operations detailed later in the chapter. Data manipulation in SAS involves modifying datasets by sorting, filtering, merging, reshaping, and performing various transformations on the data.

Data manipulation begins with understanding the structure of SAS datasets, which consist of rows (observations) and columns (variables).

Each variable is assigned a specific data type, such as numeric or character, determining how the data is handled during manipulation.

Sorting Data: Sorting data is one of the primary steps in data manipulation. In SAS, the PROC SORT procedure sorts the dataset by one or more variables. Sorting facilitates data analysis, merging operations, and preparation for reporting.

```
proc sort data=work.mydata;
  by variable1 variable2;
run;
```

In this example, mydata is sorted by variable1 and variable2. The by statement specifies the variables used for sorting. When sorting, SAS orders the data based on the variable values, allowing for ascending or descending order specifications if necessary using the descending keyword.

Filtering Data: Filtering data involves selecting subsets of data based on specified criteria. This can be accomplished using WHERE and IF statements. The WHERE statement is typically used within procedures, while the IF statement is used within data steps.

```
data filtered_data;
  set work.mydata;
  if variable1 > 100;
run;
```

Here, filtered_data contains only the observations from mydata where variable1 has values greater than 100. The IF statement within the data step filters the data efficiently during processing.

Merging and Joining Datasets: Combining datasets is another essential aspect of data manipulation. Datasets can be merged or joined based on common variables. This is often necessary when data resides in multiple datasets and needs to be analyzed together. SAS offers several methods for merging data, with the MERGE statement being the simplest.

```
data merged_data;
  merge work.dataset1 work.dataset2;
  by common_variable;
run;
```

dataset1 and dataset2 are merged based on the common_variable. The by statement indicates the variable shared between the datasets, aligning the rows accordingly.

Aggregating Data: Aggregating data means summarizing it, often using statistical measures such as sum, mean, or count. The PROC MEANS and PROC SUMMARY procedures in SAS are powerful tools for data aggregation.

```
proc means data=work.mydata;
  var numeric_variable;
  output out=summary_data mean=mean_value;
run;
```

This example calculates the mean of numeric_variable and outputs the result into summary_data. PROC MEANS offers numerous summary statistics which can be tailored to specific analytical needs.

Reshaping Data: Reshaping data includes transforming the structure of a dataset to suit particular analytical or reporting requirements. One commonly used approach in SAS is the PROC TRANSPOSE procedure, converting datasets from wide format to long format or vice versa.

```
proc transpose data=work.mydata out=transposed_data;
  by id_variable;
  var variable1 variable2;
run;
```

In this example, mydata is transposed, transforming variable1 and variable2 while retaining the id_variable. The result, transposed_data, restructures the original dataset making it suitable for specific types of analysis.

Adhering to these foundational data manipulation techniques enables efficient and accurate dataset preparation, ensuring that the subsequent analytical processes produce meaningful insights. Each of these operations builds upon the previous one, creating a continuum of data transformation steps that can accommodate increasingly complex analytical tasks.

5.2 Sorting Data with PROC SORT

Sorting data is a fundamental technique in data analysis, helping to organize datasets for further manipulation and visualization. In SAS, the PROC SORT procedure is used to sort observations in a dataset by one or more variables efficiently.

The syntax for PROC SORT is straightforward. Here is its basic form:

```
PROC SORT DATA=input_dataset OUT=output_dataset;
    BY variable1 variable2 ... variableN;
RUN;
```

input_dataset refers to the original dataset you want to sort, and output_dataset is the name of the dataset that will contain the sorted observations. If the OUT statement is omitted, the original dataset will be overwritten with the Sorted data. The BY statement lists the variables by which the dataset should be sorted, from the primary sorting variable (variable1) to secondary sorting variables (variable2, ... variableN).

To demonstrate the use of PROC SORT, consider the following example dataset:

```
DATA employees;
    INPUT EmployeeID $ Name $ Department $ Salary;
    DATALINES;
    E001 John HR 55000
    E002 Jane IT 65000
    E003 Mark HR 48000
    E004 Linda IT 54000
    E005 Gary Sales 60000
    E006 Helen Sales 62000
;
RUN;
```

The example dataset, employees, contains employee ID, name, department, and salary. To sort this dataset by the Department and then by Salary within each department in ascending order, use the following code:

```
PROC SORT DATA=employees OUT=sorted_employees;
    BY Department Salary;
RUN;
```

The PROC SORT step sorts the employees data first by the Department and then by Salary within each department. The sorted output is stored in a new dataset named sorted_employees. When executed, the resulting dataset will be:

EmployeeID	Name	Department	Salary
E001	John	HR	55000
E003	Mark	HR	48000
E002	Jane	IT	65000
E004	Linda	IT	54000
E005	Gary	Sales	60000
E006	Helen	Sales	62000

To sort data in descending order, the DESCENDING keyword is used before the variable name in the BY statement. To sort the employees by Salary in descending order within each department, modify the code as follows:

```
PROC SORT DATA=employees;
    BY Department DESCENDING Salary;
RUN;
```

The DESCENDING keyword instructs SAS to sort the Salary variable in descending order. The result is as follows:

EmployeeID	Name	Department	Salary
E001	John	HR	55000
E003	Mark	HR	48000
E002	Jane	IT	65000
E004	Linda	IT	54000
E006	Helen	Sales	62000
E005	Gary	Sales	60000

In SAS, sorting by multiple variables can refine the dataset organization substantially. When sorting by multiple variables, ensure their order in the BY statement reflects the desired hierarchy. For instance, when organizing large datasets or preparing for merges, precise sorting criteria are crucial.

Additionally, to sort data while preserving the original dataset, the OUT keyword creates a new sorted dataset without modifying the original. This is beneficial for maintaining data integrity and enabling comparison between different sorting methods. Sorting is a crucial step in many data processing pipelines and preparing datasets for subsequent analyses, such as merging or summarization.

Advanced PROC SORT options include handling duplicates with the NODUPKEY and NODUPREC options. The NODUPKEY option removes duplicate observations based on the BY variable(s), while NODUPREC removes duplicate records entirely. For example:

```
PROC SORT DATA=employees OUT=unique_employees NODUPKEY;
   BY EmployeeID;
RUN;
```

EmployeeID	Name	Department	Salary
E001	John	HR	55000
E002	Jane	IT	65000
E003	Mark	HR	48000
E004	Linda	IT	54000
E005	Gary	Sales	60000
E006	Helen	Sales	62000

Conformance with these practices ensures well-organized, clean datasets, facilitating subsequent analysis steps and leading to more accurate and insightful data interpretations.

5.3 Filtering Data with WHERE and IF Statements

Filtering data is an essential task in data manipulation, allowing analysts to subset datasets and focus on relevant observations. In SAS, two primary methods for filtering data are the WHERE statement and the IF statement. Both serve the purpose of subsetting datasets, but they differ in their application and performance implications.

The WHERE statement is used in procedures and the DATA step to filter observations before they are processed. It applies conditions to decide which rows to include based on the specified criteria. The WHERE statement can significantly enhance performance because it reduces the number of observations read into the memory.

The IF statement, on the other hand, is used solely within the DATA step and processes observations after they are read into the program data vector (PDV). The IF statement conditionally processes or excludes observations based on the specified criteria.

Examples illustrate the practical application of both statements:

```
/* Using WHERE statement in PROC PRINT */
proc print data=sashelp.class;
    where age >= 14;
run;
```

The above code uses the WHERE statement within the PROC PRINT procedure to filter and display only those students from the sashelp.class dataset who are 14 years old or older.

```
/* Using IF statement in DATA step */
data teenagers;
    set sashelp.class;
    if age >= 14;
run;
```

Here, the IF statement within a DATA step creates a new dataset teenagers containing only the students aged 14 or older.

Both WHERE and IF statements can handle more complex conditions using logical operators such as AND, OR, and NOT, as shown below:

```
/* WHERE statement with multiple conditions */
proc print data=sashelp.class;
    where age >= 14 and sex = 'F';
run;
```

```
/* IF statement with multiple conditions */
```

```
data female_teenagers;
    set sashelp.class;
    if age >= 14 and sex = 'F';
run;
```

In the examples, both the WHERE and IF statements filter data to include only female students who are at least 14 years old.

It is important to understand when to use the WHERE statement over the IF statement. The WHERE statement should be used outside the DATA step, particularly in procedures like PROC PRINT, PROC SORT, etc., for improved performance. The IF statement should be used within the DATA step to create new datasets.

The following example demonstrates using the WHERE statement for improved performance:

```
/* Efficient use of WHERE statement */
data filtered_class;
    set sashelp.class (where=(age >= 14));
run;
```

This specifies the WHERE condition directly in the SET statement, thereby filtering the data immediately as it is read into the memory. Another method is using the WHERE statement in combination with procedures:

```
/* Using WHERE with PROC SORT */
proc sort data=sashelp.class out=sorted_class;
    where age >= 14;
    by name;
run;
```

This approach filters the dataset before sorting it, reducing the number of observations processed during sort operation.

When dealing with dates or formats in filtering data, the WHERE statement proves beneficial. Dates should be formatted appropriately to ensure accurate filtering.

```
/* Using WHERE with date filtering */
data recent_births;
    set births_records;
    where birth_date >= '01JAN2020'd;
run;
```

This filters observations in the births_records dataset to include only births on or after January 1, 2020.

In addition, the WHERE statement supports the use of IN operators to filter based on a list of values.

```
/* Using WHERE with IN operator */
proc print data=sashelp.class;
    where sex in ('F', 'M') and age in (13, 15, 16);
run;
```

This code filters records where sex is either 'F' or 'M', and age is 13, 15, or 16.

Using the WHERE ALSO and WHERE ALSO IF constructs allows adding multiple WHERE conditions incrementally:

```
/* Using WHERE ALSO */
data filtered_data;
    set large_dataset;
    where condition1;
    where also condition2;
run;
```

The WHERE ALSO statement adds another layer of filtering without overwriting the previous condition.

Proficiency in leveraging both WHERE and IF statements for filtering enriches data manipulation skills and enhances operational efficiency within SAS programming.

5.4 Merging and Joining Datasets

Merging and joining datasets are fundamental operations in data manipulation, allowing for the synthesis of information from multiple sources. In SAS, these operations are primarily conducted using the DATA step with MERGE statement, and PROC SQL.

The DATA Step with MERGE Statement

The MERGE statement within a DATA step is used to combine datasets by columns. This operation requires datasets to be sorted by the merging key variables. Consider two datasets: data1 and data2, both sorted by a common key variable ID.

```
data combined;
    merge data1 data2;
    by ID;
run;
```

In this example, data1 and data2 are merged by ID, resulting in a combined dataset.

Controlling MERGE with IN= Option

To distinguish between observations coming from different datasets during the merge, the IN= option can be employed. This assists in identifying the source of each observation, which is particularly useful for inner and outer joins.

```
data combined;
    merge data1 (in=in1) data2 (in=in2);
    by ID;
    if in1 and in2 then output; /* Inner Join */
    /* if in1 or in2 then output; /* Full Outer Join */ */
run;
```

Here, in1 and in2 are temporary variables that indicate the inclusion of ID in data1 and data2 respectively. The condition if in1 and in2 executes an inner join, while if in1 or in2 performs a full outer join.

One-to-Many and Many-to-Many Merges

DATA step merges assume one-to-one or one-to-many relationships. However, many-to-many merges can lead to incorrect results as SAS performs a Cartesian product on the matching keys.

```
data many_to_many;
    merge data1 data2;
    by ID;
run;
```

In many-to-many merges, use caution and verify the relationship between datasets.

Using PROC SQL for Joins

PROC SQL provides a flexible alternative for merging and joining datasets, supporting a variety of join types, including inner, outer, left, and right joins.

Inner Join:

```
proc sql;
    create table combined as
    select a.*, b.*
    from data1 a
    inner join data2 b
    on a.ID = b.ID;
quit;
```

Left Join:

```
proc sql;
    create table left_join as
    select a.*, b.*
    from data1 a
    left join data2 b
    on a.ID = b.ID;
```

```
quit;
```

Right Join:

```
proc sql;
    create table right_join as
    select a.*, b.*
    from data1 a
    right join data2 b
    on a.ID = b.ID;
quit;
```

Full Outer Join:

```
proc sql;
    create table full_outer_join as
    select a.*, b.*
    from data1 a
    full join data2 b
    on a.ID = b.ID;
quit;
```

With PROC SQL, users can join multiple datasets in a single query, making it a powerful tool for complex data manipulations.

Considerations for Merging Datasets

Ensure datasets are sorted by key variables before using the MERGE statement. Address any inconsistencies in variable names or types to avoid conflicts. When merging large datasets, assess memory requirements and optimize performance by minimizing unnecessary operations, employing indexing, and leveraging efficient coding practices.

Understanding the specific requirements of your analysis is crucial in selecting the appropriate method for merging or joining datasets. Whether using DATA step merges or the more versatile PROC SQL joins, each approach offers unique advantages tailored to different data manipulation scenarios.

5.5 Aggregating Data with PROC MEANS and PROC SUMMARY

Aggregating data is a crucial step in data analysis and involves summarizing datasets to understand their central tendency, variability, and overall distribution. SAS provides powerful procedures for this purpose: PROC MEANS and PROC SUMMARY. Both procedures perform similar functionalities but have distinct differences in default behaviors and options.

PROC MEANS calculates descriptive statistics for numeric variables across the entire dataset or within groups. Common statistics generated include mean, median, standard deviation, minimum, and maximum values. PROC SUMMARY, while highly similar, is more flexible for producing output datasets without default output displays.

```
/* Example usage of PROC MEANS */
proc means data=sashelp.class;
    var age height weight;
run;
```

This example calculates the statistics for the variables age, height, and weight from the dataset sashelp.class. The output includes the mean, standard deviation, minimum, and maximum values for each variable.

```
The MEANS Procedure

Variable    N     Mean     Std Dev   Minimum   Maximum
-------------------------------------------------------
Age        19    13.32     1.492     11.00     16.00
Height     19    62.336    5.127     51.30     72.00
Weight     19    100.03    22.773    50.50     150.00
```

To calculate grouped statistics, use the CLASS statement:

```
/* Example of grouped statistics using PROC MEANS */
proc means data=sashelp.class;
    class sex;
    var age height weight;
run;
```

The results are then provided separately for each group defined by the sex variable.

```
The MEANS Procedure

Gender=F
Variable    N     Mean     Std Dev   Minimum   Maximum
-------------------------------------------------------
Age         9    13.00     1.323     11.00     15.00
Height      9    60.422    5.210     51.30     66.50
Weight      9    92.67     19.758    50.50     112.50

Gender=M
Variable    N     Mean     Std Dev   Minimum   Maximum
-------------------------------------------------------
Age        10    13.60     1.577     11.00     16.00
Height     10    64.640    4.585     57.30     72.00
Weight     10    106.33    23.263    83.00     150.00
```

For more customization, PROC MEANS can output results to a new dataset using the OUTPUT statement:

```
/* Outputting results to a new dataset */
proc means data=sashelp.class noprint;
```

```
    var age height weight;
    output out=summary_stats mean=mean_age mean_height mean_weight;
run;
```

The NPRINT option suppresses the display of results, and the OUTPUT statement directs results to the dataset summary_stats with specified variable names.

PROC SUMMARY syntax is similar but provides flexibility to suppress output by default:

```
/* Example usage of PROC SUMMARY */
proc summary data=sashelp.class;
    var age height weight;
    output out=summary_stats mean=mean_age mean_height mean_weight;
run;
```

The above code generates the same output dataset as with PROC MEANS. When detailed control over grouping and output is required, PROC SUMMARY offers additional options, such as TYPES statement to specify multiple groupings.

Another critical aspect is the BY statement for both procedures. It involves sorting the dataset by specified variables beforehand:

```
/* Using the BY statement */
proc sort data=sashelp.class out=sorted_class;
    by sex;
run;

proc means data=sorted_class;
    by sex;
    var age height weight;
run;
```

This segment first sorts the sashelp.class dataset by the sex variable and then performs the PROC MEANS analysis within each group defined by sex.

Utilizing formats in PROC MEANS and PROC SUMMARY enhances grouped analysis further. The FORMAT statement applies a predefined format to analysis variables facilitating precise groupings:

```
/* Applying formats in PROC MEANS */
proc format;
    value agefmt low-<13='Preteen' 13-high='Teen';
run;

proc means data=sashelp.class;
    class age;
    var height weight;
    format age agefmt.;
run;
```

In this example, the format agefmt categorizes age into Preteen and Teen, and PROC MEANS applies these groups during analysis.

Advanced usage includes ways statement in PROC SUMMARY for specifying multiple combinations of class variables:

```
/* Advanced grouping with WAYS statement */
proc summary data=sashelp.class;
    class sex age;
    ways 1 2;
    var height weight;
    output out=summary_stats mean=mean_height mean_weight;
run;
```

The WAYS statement dictates that PROC SUMMARY calculates statistics for single-level and two-level combinations of sex and age.

Choosing between PROC MEANS and PROC SUMMARY depends on the application's specific needs. While PROC MEANS is straightforward for quick summary statistics, PROC SUMMARY offers more control and is apt for large-scale data summarization suitable for further processing. Proper usage of these procedures enhances data analysis capabilities, providing meaningful insights and facilitating decision-making based on summarized data.

5.6 Reshaping Data with PROC TRANSPOSE

Reshaping data is a crucial aspect of data manipulation tasks, allowing analysts to pivot datasets for various analytical needs. The PROC TRANSPOSE procedure in SAS is a powerful tool designed to transpose data, enabling the transformation of data from wide format to long format and vice versa.

Basic Usage of PROC TRANSPOSE

The fundamental syntax of PROC TRANSPOSE is straightforward. Consider the following simple dataset:

```
data sample;
    input Year Q1 Q2 Q3 Q4;
    datalines;
    2020 10 15 20 25
    2021 12 18 24 30
    ;
run;
```

This dataset comprises quarterly data for the years 2020 and 2021. To pivot this data from wide format (horizontal) to long format (vertical), the PROC TRANSPOSE procedure can be used as follows:

```
proc transpose data=sample out=transposed_sample;
    by Year;
run;
```

The BY statement signifies that the transposition should group the data by the specified variable, Year. The resulting dataset transposed_sample will appear as follows:

```
Year _NAME_ _COL1_
2020 Q1 10
2020 Q2 15
2020 Q3 20
2020 Q4 25
2021 Q1 12
2021 Q2 18
2021 Q3 24
2021 Q4 30
```

Specifying Variables with VAR and ID Statements

The VAR and ID statements refine the PROC TRANSPOSE process by specifying which variables to transpose and which to use as identifiers.

```
proc transpose data=sample out=transposed_sample;
    by Year;
    var Q1 Q2 Q3 Q4;
    id Year;
run;
```

In this example, the var statement explicitly lists the variables to transpose. Although not necessary in this case (since the default behavior is to transpose all variables not in the BY statement), it can be useful for more complex datasets. The id statement assigns unique identifiers for each value in the transposed dataset.

Handling Multiple BY Variables

When dealing with more complex datasets, it's often necessary to use multiple BY variables. Here is an example dataset that includes an additional Product variable:

```
data sample_multi;
    input Year Product $ Q1 Q2 Q3 Q4;
    datalines;
```

```
    2020 A 10 15 20 25
    2020 B 11 16 21 26
    2021 A 12 18 24 30
    2021 B 13 19 25 31
    ;
run;
```

Using multiple BY variables in the PROC TRANSPOSE statement:

```
proc transpose data=sample_multi out=transposed_sample_multi;
    by Year Product;
    var Q1 Q2 Q3 Q4;
run;
```

The resulting dataset groups the transposed data by both Year and Product:

Year Product _NAME_ _COL1_
2020 A Q1 10
2020 A Q2 15
2020 A Q3 20
2020 A Q4 25
2020 B Q1 11
2020 B Q2 16
2020 B Q3 21
2020 B Q4 26
2021 A Q1 12
2021 A Q2 18
2021 A Q3 24
2021 A Q4 30
2021 B Q1 13
2021 B Q2 19
2021 B Q3 25
2021 B Q4 31

Customizing Output Variable Names

The PROC TRANSPOSE procedure allows customization of output variable names using the prefix option. For instance:

```
proc transpose data=sample out=transposed_sample prefix=Quarter_;
    by Year;
run;
```

This command will produce a dataset with renamed variables:

Year _NAME_ Quarter_1
2020 Q1 10
2020 Q2 15
2020 Q3 20
2020 Q4 25
2021 Q1 12
2021 Q2 18
2021 Q3 24
2021 Q4 30

Utilizing the prefix option provides clarity and context to the transposed variables, which can be particularly useful when merging or joining datasets later in the workflow.

Example of Real-World Application

Consider a healthcare dataset where patient data is recorded over multiple visits. Each record is initially wide format:

```
data patient;
    input PatientID $ Visit1 Weight1 Height1 BP1 Visit2 Weight2 Height2 BP2;
    datalines;
    001 2021Q1 70 175 120/80 2021Q2 72 175 118/79
    002 2021Q1 68 165 122/82 2021Q2 69 165 121/80
    ;
run;
```

Applying PROC TRANSPOSE to reshape this data for easier longitudinal analysis:

```
proc transpose data=patient out=transposed_patient;
    by PatientID;
    var Visit1-Visit2 Weight1-Weight2 Height1-Height2 BP1-BP2;
run;
```

The transformed data facilitates analysis per visit over time:

PatientID _NAME_ Col1 Col2
001 Visit1 2021Q1 2021Q2
001 Weight1 70 72
001 Height1 175 175
001 BP1 120/80 118/79
002 Visit1 2021Q1 2021Q2
002 Weight1 68 69
002 Height1 165 165
002 BP1 122/82 121/80

The PROC TRANSPOSE procedure is indispensable for transforming datasets into the suitable structure for further analytical processes, offering flexibility and control over data reshaping tasks.

5.7 Concatenating Datasets

Concatenating datasets is a crucial aspect of data manipulation in SAS, allowing the integration of multiple datasets into a single dataset. This task is frequently required when working with data distributed across multiple tables or files. SAS provides several methods to concatenate datasets, from the simple SET statement in a Data Step to more advanced procedures like PROC APPEND. Below, we will delve into these methods in detail, ensuring a comprehensive understanding of their application and nuances.

Using the SET Statement in a Data Step

The most straightforward method to concatenate datasets in SAS is by using the SET statement within a Data Step. This approach is particularly useful when the datasets to be concatenated share a similar structure, i.e., the same columns.

```
data combined_data;
    set dataset1 dataset2 dataset3;
run;
```

In the above example, dataset1, dataset2, and dataset3 are concatenated into a single dataset named combined_data. The SET statement reads observations from all the specified datasets in the order listed and writes them to the combined_data dataset.

Important Considerations

1. Variable Mismatches: If the input datasets have variables with different attributes (e.g., different lengths or types), SAS will align the variables by name. However, if there are type mismatches (numerical vs. character), an error will occur. 2. Missing Values: When concatenating datasets with missing variables, SAS will fill these variables with missing values (. for numeric and blank for character variables).

```
data combined_data;
    set dataset1 dataset2;
    by common_variable;
run;
```

Here, BY statement is used to ensure the concatenated data is sorted by common_variable. This necessitates that the individual datasets are pre-sorted by the common_variable.

Using PROC APPEND

PROC APPEND offers an alternative to concatenate datasets when the primary concern is efficiency. This procedure appends the contents of a source dataset to a base dataset without the need to read and write the base dataset during the process. This efficiency saves processing time, especially for large datasets.

```
proc append base=dataset1 data=dataset2;
run;
```

In this example, dataset2 is appended to dataset1. Note the absence of a DATA statement; only the BASE (existing dataset) and DATA (dataset to append) are required. PROC APPEND is efficient but comes with constraints:

1. Variable Structures: The BASE and DATA datasets must have identical variable structures. If they differ, use the FORCE option to force concatenation, potentially dropping misaligned variables in the DATA dataset.

```
proc append base=dataset1 data=dataset2 force;
run;
```

2. Index Handling: If the BASE dataset has an index, PROC APPEND will maintain the index but at the cost of performance due to index update necessity.

Advanced Concatenation with PROC SQL

For more complex concatenation tasks, PROC SQL offers a highly flexible and powerful alternative. PROC SQL can handle a wide array of operations beyond simple concatenation, providing functionalities akin to those found in standard SQL environments.

```
proc sql;
    create table combined_data as
    select * from dataset1
    outer union corr
    select * from dataset2;
quit;
```

Here, the OUTER UNION CORR clause ensures a comprehensive union of dataset1 and dataset2, aligning variables with the same name and introducing missing values where necessary. This method is robust for datasets with differing structures.

Column Aliases and Order

When concatenating datasets via PROC SQL, it is often essential to manage column names and orders explicitly.

```
proc sql;
    create table combined_data as
    select col1 as new_col1, col2 from dataset1
    outer union corr
    select col_a, col_b from dataset2;
quit;
```

In this example, columns from dataset1 and dataset2 are renamed and aligned explicitly, enhancing clarity and ensuring the desired structure in the combined_data.

Concatenating datasets is fundamental for SAS programmers, enabling the effective integration of diverse data sources into cohesive analytical datasets. By mastering methods such as the SET statement in a Data Step, PROC APPEND, and PROC SQL, programmers can handle a variety of data concatenation scenarios efficiently and accurately.

5.8 Creating and Modifying Variables

Creating and modifying variables in SAS is foundational for effective data manipulation. This section delves into techniques for generating new variables and altering existing ones using Data Steps, functions, and conditional constructs.

Creating Variables in a Data Step

Variables can be created within a Data Step using assignment statements. The syntax follows the form variable_name = expression;, where expression can include constants, other variable values, or functions.

```
data new_dataset;
    set original_dataset;
    new_variable = existing_variable * 2;
    formatted_date = input(date_string, mmddyy10.);
run;
```

In this example, new_variable is twice the value of existing_variable. Additionally, formatted_date converts a character string date_string to a SAS date value using the input function and the mmddyy10. informat.

Modifying Variables

To modify an existing variable, assign a new value to it within a Data Step. The new value can result from applying a computation or function to its current value.

```
data modified_dataset;
    set original_dataset;
    existing_variable = existing_variable + 5;
run;
```

Here, the value of existing_variable is increased by 5. This in-place modification updates the variable directly.

Using Conditional Statements for Variable Creation and Modification

Conditional statements, such as IF-THEN/ELSE, allow for the creation or modification of variables based on specific conditions.

```
data conditional_dataset;
    set original_dataset;
    if condition_variable > 100 then new_variable = 1;
    else new_variable = 0;
run;
```

The Data Step checks the value of condition_variable. If it's greater than 100, new_variable is set to 1; otherwise, it is set to 0.

Using Functions for Advanced Variable Creation and Modification

SAS provides numerous functions for comprehensive data manipulation. Below are common functions used to create and modify variables:

- SUM() for summing values. - MEAN() for calculating the average. - SUBSTR() for extracting substrings. - TRIM() for trimming spaces. - CATX() for concatenating strings.

```
data function_dataset;
    set original_dataset;
    sum_value = sum(of var1-var3);
    average_value = mean(of var1-var3);
    first_three_chars = substr(text_variable, 1, 3);
    trimmed_text = trim(text_variable);
    combined_text = catx("-", text_variable1, text_variable2);
run;
```

These functions offer an efficient way to derive new variables based on existing data.

Array Usage for Bulk Variable Creation and Modification

Arrays in SAS can simplify the process of creating and modifying multiple variables simultaneously.

```
data array_dataset;
    set original_dataset;
    array temps {3} temp1-temp3;
    array newtemps {3} newtemp1-newtemp3;
    do i = 1 to 3;
        newtemps{i} = temps{i} * 1.8 + 32; /* Celsius to Fahrenheit conversion */
    end;
    drop i;
run;
```

Here, temps and newtemps are arrays holding three temperature values each. A DO loop iterates over these arrays, converting temperatures from Celsius to Fahrenheit, and stores the results in the newtemps array.

Retaining Variable Values Across Iterations

The RETAIN statement preserves a variable's value across iterations of the Data Step, enabling cumulative calculations and other advanced manipulations.

```
data cumulative_dataset;
    set original_dataset;
    retain cumulative_sum 0;
    cumulative_sum + increment_variable;
run;
```

In this example, cumulative_sum maintains its value across iterations, cumulatively adding increment_variable.

These techniques collectively empower users to adeptly create and modify variables within SAS, facilitating robust data manipulation workflows essential for any data analysis task.

5.9 Using Arrays for Data Manipulation

In SAS, arrays are utilized as a powerful tool for simplifying repetitive tasks on groups of variables. Arrays can significantly streamline code for complex data manipulation tasks by making operations on multiple variables more concise and manageable. Arrays are not physical data structures but rather a name given to a set of variables that can then be operated upon collectively. The array statement associates the names of a group of variables with an array name.

The general syntax for defining an array in SAS is as follows:

```
ARRAY array-name {n} $ length array-elements;
```

Here, array-name is the name assigned to the array, n is the number of variables in the array, $ indicates character variables (if omitted, numeric variables are assumed), length specifies the length of character variables, and array-elements lists the variables included in the array. Variables defined within arrays can be pre-existing in the dataset or new variables that will be created by the array definition.

Consider a practical example where array manipulation is used to standardize scores stored in five different variables across each observation into a standardized score:

```
DATA standardized_scores;
    SET raw_scores;
    ARRAY scores{5} score1-score5;
    ARRAY std_scores{5} std_score1-std_score5;
    DO i = 1 TO 5;
```

```
        std_scores{i} = (scores{i} - MEAN(of score1-score5)) / STD(of score1-score5);
    END;
    DROP i;
RUN;
```

In the example above, the ARRAY scores{5} statement defines an array named scores containing the variables score1 through score5. The ARRAY std_scores{5} statement defines a corresponding array for the standardized scores. The DO loop iterates over each variable in the arrays, calculating the standardized score by subtracting the mean and dividing by the standard deviation of the scores, and stores the result in the std_scores array. The loop variable i is dropped after the loop to ensure it does not appear in the final dataset.

Arrays are particularly useful in scenarios requiring conditional updates. For instance, to set negative values in a set of variables to zero, one could use:

```
DATA clean_data;
    SET raw_data;
    ARRAY vars{8} var1-var8;
    DO i = 1 TO 8;
        IF vars{i} < 0 THEN vars{i} = 0;
    END;
    DROP i;
RUN;
```

In this code, an array vars{8} is created to include variables from var1 to var8. The DO loop checks each variable value and sets it to zero if it is less than zero.

Multidimensional arrays can be defined for more complex data structures. For example, a 2-dimensional array is useful for handling data in a matrix or table format:

```
DATA matrix;
    ARRAY matrix_vals{3, 4} val1-val12;
    DO i = 1 TO 3;
        DO j = 1 TO 4;
            matrix_vals{i, j} = val1 + (i-1)*4 + j-1;
        END;
    END;
    DROP i j;
RUN;
```

In this example, matrix_vals is a 3x4 array filled with values computed based on the indices i and j. The nested DO loops iterate over the rows and columns of the matrix.

To effectively handle missing values in arrays, SAS provides functions such as NMISS and CMISS to count the number of missing numeric and character values, respectively. Consider the following scenario where they are used to check for missing values:

```
DATA check_missing;
    SET data_with_missing;
    ARRAY num_vars{*} _NUMERIC_;
    ARRAY char_vars{*} _CHARACTER_;
    missing_numeric = NMISS(of num_vars{*});
    missing_character = CMISS(of char_vars{*});
RUN;
```

The _NUMERIC_ and _CHARACTER_ array definitions automatically include all numeric and character variables in the dataset, respectively. The NMISS and CMISS functions then compute the number of missing values in these arrays.

Arrays can also facilitate the renaming of variables, transforming wide datasets into long datasets, or applying the same transformation to similar variables across a dataset. Mastery in using arrays entails efficiency in SAS programming, ensuring the code is not only correct but also succinct and maintainable. Arrays thus play an instrumental role in sophisticated data manipulation techniques within the SAS environment.

5.10 Handling Missing Values

Handling missing values is critical in data analysis and manipulation, as they can significantly impact the integrity and accuracy of statistical analyses. SAS provides various methods and techniques for identifying, handling, and imputing missing values. This section delves into these methods, focusing on efficient strategies to manage missing data within datasets.

Identifying Missing Values

In SAS, missing values for numeric variables are represented by a period (.) and for character variables by a blank space (' '). Identifying missing values is the first step in handling them, and SAS provides several functions and procedures to detect missing data.

To identify missing values in a dataset, the NMISS and CMISS functions are particularly useful. NMISS counts the number of missing numeric variables, while CMISS can handle both numeric and character variables.

```
data example;
    input x y $ z;
    datalines;
    1 A .
    . B 3
    2 . 4
    ;
run;

proc print data=example;
run;

data example_check;
    set example;
    nmiss = nmiss(x, z);
    cmiss = cmiss(x, y, z);
run;

proc print data=example_check;
run;
```

The output of the example_check dataset will illustrate the columns nmiss and cmiss, indicating the number of missing values in the specified variables.

Obs	x	y	z	nmiss	cmiss
1	1	A	.	1	1
2	.	B	3	1	1
3	2	.	4	0	1

Handling Missing Values in Data Steps

To handle missing values during data manipulation, it is often necessary to use conditional logic to replace or omit these values. The IF-THEN/ELSE statement is commonly used.

```
data handle_missing;
    set example;
    if x = . then x = 0;
    if y = ' ' then y = 'Unknown';
run;

proc print data=handle_missing;
run;
```

This code replaces missing numeric values in x with 0 and missing character values in y with 'Unknown'.

Obs	x	y	z
1	1	A	.
2	0	B	3
3	2	Unknown	4

IFN and IFC functions provide another approach. They are particularly useful for inline conditional replacements.

```
data handle_missing_inline;
    set example;
    x_replaced = ifn(x = ., 0, x);
    y_replaced = ifc(y = ' ', 'Unknown', y);
run;

proc print data=handle_missing_inline;
run;
```

Obs	x	y	z	x_replaced	y_replaced
1	1	A	.	1	A
2	.	B	3	0	B
3	2	.	4	2	Unknown

Replacing Missing Values Using PROC SQL

PROC SQL offers a flexible approach to handle missing values, particularly useful when integrating multiple conditional replacements.

```
proc sql;
    create table sql_missing as
    select x,
           y,
           z,
           case when x is missing then 0 else x end as x_replaced,
           case when y is missing then 'Unknown' else y end as y_replaced
    from example;
quit;

proc print data=sql_missing;
run;
```

Obs	x	y	z	x_replaced	y_replaced
1	1	A	.	1	A
2	.	B	3	0	B
3	2	.	4	2	Unknown

Imputing Missing Values

Imputation involves replacing missing values with substituted values. Simple imputation methods include mean, median, or mode imputation. The following example demonstrates mean imputation using PROC STDIZE.

```
proc stdize data=example reponly method=mean out=imputed;
    var x z;
run;

proc print data=imputed;
run;
```

Obs	x	y	z
1	1	A	3.5
2	1.5	B	3
3	2	.	4

PROC MI offers a more sophisticated approach by employing multiple imputation methods suitable for advanced statistical analysis.

```
proc mi data=example nimpute=5 out=mi_multiple;
    var x z;
run;

proc print data=mi_multiple (obs=10);
run;
```

Multivariate Imputation by Chained Equations.

While handling missing values, it is essential to consider the context and the potential impact on the analysis. Replacing, omitting, or imputing missing data should be done with caution to avoid introducing biases. Techniques discussed here equip the user with the tools necessary for effective data preparation in SAS environments.

5.11 Data Transformation Techniques

Data transformation is a crucial aspect of data manipulation in SAS, enabling the restructuring and alteration of data to improve its usability and interpretability. This section delves into various techniques, including creating new variables, recoding existing variables, using functions for data transformation, and employing date and time functions, among other methods.

PROC SQL in SAS provides a powerful toolset for data transformation. Techniques will extend upon previous concepts, allowing you to perform complex operations efficiently.

```
data sales;
  set old_sales;
  Total_Sales = Sales_Amount * Quantity;
run;
```

The example above demonstrates the creation of a new variable Total_Sales by multiplying Sales_Amount and Quantity. This is a fundamental transformation technique to generate new insights from existing data.

```
data recoded_sales;
  set sales;
  if Sales_Region = 'North' then Region_Code = 1;
```

```
  else if Sales_Region = 'South' then Region_Code = 2;
  else if Sales_Region = 'East' then Region_Code = 3;
  else if Sales_Region = 'West' then Region_Code = 4;
run;
```

Recoding variables can simplify analysis and improve data consistency. Here, Sales_Region is transformed into Region_Code with numerical values, making it easier to perform statistical analyses.

Using Functions for Data Transformation

SAS offers a broad range of functions to manipulate data. Functions such as UPCASE, LOWCASE, SUBSTR, TRIM, COMPRESS, and CATX can be employed to alter the structure and content of character variables.

```
data transformed_sales;
  set sales;
  Product_Name_Upper = upcase(Product_Name);
  Product_Code_Prefix = substr(Product_Code, 1, 3);
  Trimmed_Name = trim(Product_Name);
  Clean_Product_Code = compress(Product_Code, '-');
  Full_Product_Info = catx(' - ', Product_Name, Product_Code);
run;
```

In this example:

- UPCASE(Product_Name) converts the product names to uppercase.
- substr(Product_Code, 1, 3) extracts the first three characters from Product_Code.
- trim(Product_Name) removes any trailing blanks from Product_Name.
- compress(Product_Code, '-') removes hyphens from Product_Code.
- catx(' - ', Product_Name, Product_Code) concatenates Product_Name and Product_Code with a hyphen and space.

Date and Time Functions

Handling and transforming date and time variables are common requirements. SAS provides numerous date and time functions such as DATEPART, TIMEPART, MDY, YRDIF, INTCK, and INTNX.

```
data date_transformed_sales;
  set sales;
```

```
  Sales_Date = mdy(5, 21, 2021); /* Create a date value */
  Sales_Year = year(Sales_Date); /* Extract the year */
  Sales_Month = month(Sales_Date); /* Extract the month */
  Sales_Day = day(Sales_Date); /* Extract the day */
  Days_Since_Sale = intck('day', Sales_Date, today()); /* Calculate the difference in
       days */
run;
```

In this dataset transformation:

- mdy(5, 21, 2021) creates a SAS date value.
- year(Sales_Date), month(Sales_Date), and day(Sales_Date) extract the year, month, and day from the date.
- intck('day', Sales_Date, today()) computes the number of days between the sale date and the current date.

Advanced Transformations

Advanced data transformations often involve more complex operations such as reshaping datasets, transposing data, and using arrays. These are crucial for tasks requiring intricate manipulations.

Reshaping can be done using PROC TRANSPOSE to convert data from wide format to long format or vice versa.

```
proc transpose data=sales out=transposed_sales;
  by Product_Code;
  var Q1_Sales Q2_Sales Q3_Sales Q4_Sales;
  id Quarter;
run;
```

Transposing reorganizes the sales data to have a single column for sales and a column indicating the quarter.

Using arrays can facilitate complex data transformations, especially when dealing with repetitive tasks.

```
data array_transformed_sales;
  set sales;
  array qtr_sales{4} Q1_Sales Q2_Sales Q3_Sales Q4_Sales;
  array qtr_growth{4} Q1_Growth Q2_Growth Q3_Growth Q4_Growth;
  do i = 1 to 4;
    qtr_growth{i} = (qtr_sales{i} - lag(qtr_sales{i})) / lag(qtr_sales{i});
  end;
run;
```

In this example, arrays are used to calculate the growth rate for each quarter dynamically.

By combining these techniques, data in SAS can be transformed to meet a wide range of analytical needs. Understanding and applying these transformations is essential for effective data manipulation and analysis.

5.12 Advanced Data Manipulation with PROC SQL

PROC SQL is a powerful procedure available in SAS for performing advanced data manipulation tasks. The versatility of SQL, combined with the powerful data handling capabilities of SAS, makes PROC SQL an invaluable tool for data analysts and programmers. This section covers advanced topics including subqueries, inline views, complex joins, and data summarization with SQL functions. We will also discuss the creation of macro variables within PROC SQL.

To use PROC SQL, we begin with a PROC SQL statement and conclude with a QUIT statement. Within these boundaries, we define our SQL queries.

```
PROC SQL;
  /* SQL code goes here */
QUIT;
```

Subqueries in PROC SQL

Subqueries are nested queries that provide data to the main query. They are utilized for filtering data subsets and constructing more complex data manipulations. Consider a scenario where we want to select employees whose salaries are above the average salary:

```
PROC SQL;
    SELECT Name, Salary
    FROM Employees
    WHERE Salary > (SELECT AVG(Salary) FROM Employees);
QUIT;
```

In this example, the subquery (SELECT AVG(Salary) FROM Employees) calculates the average salary, which is then used in the WHERE clause to filter employees.

Inline Views

Inline views are subqueries that are treated as temporary tables within the main query. They are useful when performing complex operations that require intermediate results. Here, we compute the total sales per region and then filter regions with sales exceeding 100,000:

```
PROC SQL;
    SELECT region, total_sales
    FROM (SELECT region, SUM(sales) AS total_sales
          FROM sales_data
          GROUP BY region) AS regional_sales
    WHERE total_sales > 100000;
QUIT;
```

In this instance, the inline view (SELECT region, SUM(sales) AS total_sales FROM sales_data GROUP BY region) creates a temporary table of total sales by region. The main query then filters these results.

Complex Joins

PROC SQL supports various types of joins, including inner joins, outer joins, and self-joins. A complex join might involve multiple tables and various join conditions. Suppose we have two tables, Orders and Customers, and we want to list all orders along with corresponding customer information, including customers with no orders (left join):

```
PROC SQL;
    SELECT o.OrderID, o.OrderDate, c.CustomerName, c.ContactName
    FROM Orders o
    LEFT JOIN Customers c
    ON o.CustomerID = c.CustomerID;
QUIT;
```

This query joins tables Orders and Customers on the CustomerID field while including all customers, even those without corresponding orders.

Data Summarization with SQL Functions

SQL provides numerous functions for data summarization, including SUM, AVG, MAX, MIN, and COUNT. These functions facilitate efficient data aggregation and summary. To calculate the total, average, minimum, and maximum salaries from the Employees table, we execute:

```
PROC SQL;
    SELECT SUM(Salary) AS TotalSalary,
           AVG(Salary) AS AvgSalary,
           MIN(Salary) AS MinSalary,
           MAX(Salary) AS MaxSalary
    FROM Employees;
QUIT;
```

GROUP BY clauses can also be integrated with summary functions for grouped data aggregation. For example, to summarize salaries by department:

```
PROC SQL;
    SELECT Department,
           SUM(Salary) AS TotalSalary,
```

```
        AVG(Salary) AS AvgSalary,
        MIN(Salary) AS MinSalary,
        MAX(Salary) AS MaxSalary
    FROM Employees
    GROUP BY Department;
QUIT;
```

Creating Macro Variables

PROC SQL allows the creation of macro variables for use in subsequent SAS code. This is achieved using the INTO clause. For instance, we can store the average salary in a macro variable:

```
PROC SQL;
    SELECT AVG(Salary)
    INTO :AvgSalary
    FROM Employees;
QUIT;

%PUT The average salary is &AvgSalary;
```

This code snippet creates the macro variable AvgSalary, which can be referenced subsequently in the SAS program. The statement %PUT The average salary is &AvgSalary; displays the value of the macro variable.

Familiarity with these advanced techniques in PROC SQL allows for sophisticated data analysis and manipulation, significantly enhancing the capabilities of SAS programming. Practical application of these methods can lead to efficient and effective data management solutions.

Chapter 6

Working with SAS Procedures

This chapter provides a detailed exploration of the various SAS procedures used for data analysis and reporting. Readers will learn the basic syntax of the PROC step and how to use procedures like PROC PRINT, PROC MEANS, and PROC FREQ for data inspection and summarization. The chapter covers statistical analysis with PROC UNIVARIATE, creating reports with PROC TABULATE and PROC REPORT, and data manipulation with PROC SQL. Additionally, it includes procedures for data visualization, import and export operations, and techniques for debugging and optimizing SAS procedures.

6.1 Introduction to SAS Procedures

SAS (Statistical Analysis System) Procedures, commonly referred to as PROCs, are essential tools for performing various data analyses, reporting, and management tasks within the SAS software environment. These procedures allow the execution of complex data manipulations and statistical operations through concise and structured commands. Each SAS procedure is designed to perform specific functions, such as printing data, summarizing statistics, generating frequency distributions, and creating sophisticated data visualizations.

The fundamental structure of a SAS procedure comprises the PROC keyword, followed by the procedure name and relevant options or statements. The basic syntax for invoking a SAS procedure is as follows:

```
PROC procedure-name;
    statements;
RUN;
```

The RUN; statement signifies the end of the procedure step and triggers the execution of the specified commands. It is worth noting that the RUN; statement is not always mandatory but is recommended for clarity and to ensure correct execution order.

An exemplary SAS procedure is PROC PRINT, which is used to display the contents of a dataset. For instance, to print all observations and variables in the dataset sashelp.class, one can use the following code:

```
PROC PRINT DATA = sashelp.class;
RUN;
```

Executing the above code will result in the following output:

```
Obs   Name      Sex   Age   Height   Weight
1     Alfred    M     14    69.0     112.5
2     Alice     F     13    56.5     84.0
...
19    William   M     15    66.5     112.0
```

Each SAS procedure may include various options and statements to customize output, perform specific calculations, or apply particular conditions. For instance, in PROC PRINT, the VAR statement can be used to select specific variables for display:

```
PROC PRINT DATA = sashelp.class;
    VAR Name Age Height;
RUN;
```

This will produce an output with only the Name, Age, and Height variables displayed.

The flexibility and power of SAS procedures are further enhanced by the ability to include multiple statements within a single procedure call. For instance, PROC MEANS is employed to compute descriptive statistics such as mean, median, and standard deviation. By default, it calculates statistics for all numeric variables in a dataset but can be customized with additional statements:

```
PROC MEANS DATA = sashelp.class;
    VAR Height Weight;
RUN;
```

Output from this code would summarise the Height and Weight variables:

	The MEANS Procedure Analysis Variable : Height	Weight
N	19.00000	19.00000
Mean	62.33789	100.02632
...		
Std Deviation	5.12707	22.43923

Another pertinent feature of SAS procedures is the use of BY and CLASS statements, which facilitate analysis based on particular subsets or groupings within the data. For example, to compute means by gender, one may utilize:

```
PROC MEANS DATA = sashelp.class;
   CLASS Sex;
   VAR Height Weight;
RUN;
```

The output of this command would classify the summary statistics according to the Sex variable, allowing comparative analysis between male and female subsets.

Additionally, procedures such as PROC FREQ provide the means to obtain frequency distributions, crucial for categorical data analysis. For example:

```
PROC FREQ DATA = sashelp.class;
   TABLES Sex;
RUN;
```

This will yield the frequency count and percentage distribution of the Sex variable:

Sex	Frequency	Cumulative Percent	Cumulative Frequency	Percent
F	9	47.37	9	47.37
M	10	52.63	19	100.00

Procedures like PROC UNIVARIATE, PROC TABULATE, PROC SQL, and PROC SGPLOT extend the capabilities further into statistical analysis, tabular reporting, SQL-like data manipulation, and data visualization, respectively. Each procedure comes with its specific set of options and statements to tailor the analysis or reporting to the user's needs.

The seamless integration and interoperability of these procedures within the SAS environment enable users to build sophisticated data workflows and analyses efficiently. Careful use of procedure-specific features and options will ensure precise and insightful data handling, meeting a broad range of analytical requirements.

6.2 Basic Syntax of PROC Step

The PROC (Procedure) step in SAS is a powerful structure designed for data analysis and reporting. The essence of a PROC step is to invoke a predefined SAS procedure that operates on a dataset. The basic syntax of a PROC step is as follows:

```
PROC procedure-name options;
    BY variables;
    ID variables;
    VAR variables;
    WHERE (condition);
    OtherStatements;
RUN;
```

The PROC step begins with the keyword PROC followed by the procedure-name, which specifies the procedure to be invoked. The options can be used to modify the behavior of the procedure.

Several key statements that may be included within a PROC step are:

- BY: Specifies variables to create BY groups for conducting separate analyses on each group.
- ID: Identifies variables to include in printed output.
- VAR: Specifies variables to include in the analysis.
- WHERE: Filters observations based on a condition.
- OtherStatements: Additional statements specific to the procedure.

An Example of a PROC Step

Consider the following example where we use the PROC PRINT procedure to display the contents of a dataset named work.dataset:

```
PROC PRINT DATA=work.dataset;
    VAR name age;
    WHERE age > 18;
RUN;
```

In this example:

- DATA=work.dataset specifies the dataset on which the procedure will operate.

- VAR name age instructs SAS to display only the name and age variables.
- WHERE age > 18 filters the data to include only observations where age is greater than 18.

Executing the code will display a table of names and ages for individuals older than 18.

Understanding PROC Step Options

Several options can be specified in the PROC step to control the output and behavior of the procedures:

```
PROC PRINT DATA=work.dataset NOOBS LABEL;
    VAR name age;
    LABEL name = 'Name' age = 'Age in Years';
RUN;
```

Here:

- NOOBS suppresses the printing of observation numbers.
- LABEL allows assigning new labels to variables for more informative output.

Combining Multiple Statements in PROC Step

Multiple statements can be used within a PROC step to achieve complex analyses. Consider the PROC MEANS procedure, which calculates descriptive statistics:

```
PROC MEANS DATA=work.dataset N MEAN STD MIN MAX;
    VAR age income;
    BY gender;
    WHERE age > 18;
RUN;
```

In this example:

- N MEAN STD MIN MAX requests the number of non-missing values, mean, standard deviation, minimum, and maximum for the specified variables.
- VAR age income specifies the variables for which to calculate the statistics.

- BY gender groups the data by gender, performing the analysis separately for each gender.
- WHERE age > 18 restricts the analysis to individuals older than 18.

The output of this procedure will provide a detailed statistical summary for age and income, separated by gender groups.

Error Handling in PROC Step

Errors in PROC steps often arise due to incorrect syntax or incompatible options. SAS provides comprehensive error messages that can guide users to identify and fix issues.

```
PROC MEANS DATA=work.dataset N MEAN STD MIN MAX;
    VAR age income;
    BY gender;
    WHERE ages > 18; /*Purposeful error: 'ages' should be 'age' */
RUN;
```

Executing the above code, which contains a purposeful error (ages instead of age), would generate an error message:

```
ERROR: Variable ages not found in dataset work.dataset.
```

Reading and understanding error messages is crucial for debugging and ensuring the correct execution of PROC steps.

Best Practices for Writing PROC Steps

When writing PROC steps, adhering to best practices enhances readability, maintainability, and performance:

- Always use meaningful names for datasets and variables.
- Leverage the LABEL option for clear and informative output.
- Utilize the WHERE clause to filter data before processing, improving efficiency.
- Group logically related statements for better organization.
- Comment your code to explain complex logic and assumptions.

Applying these principles ensures that PROC steps are not only functional but also easy to understand and modify. This forms a foundational skill for mastering SAS programming and leveraging its full analytical capabilities.

6.3 Using PROC PRINT for Data Inspection

The PROC PRINT procedure is essential for examining the contents of a SAS dataset efficiently. It enables users to display observations and variables directly to the SAS output window, which assists in verifying data accuracy and ensuring that the dataset is correctly processed at various stages of the analysis.

PROC PRINT employs a straightforward syntax. At its core, it requires the specification of the dataset to be printed. By default, the procedure prints all observations and variables within the dataset. Consider the following basic example that prints the work.mydata dataset:

```
proc print data=work.mydata;
run;
```

When executed, the output displays all variables and their corresponding observations from the dataset work.mydata.

Obs	Var1	Var2	Var3
1	...	...	...
2	...	...	...
3	...	...	...

For more refined control over the contents displayed, several options and statements can be incorporated within PROC PRINT. Commonly used options include NOOBS, OBS, VAR, and WHERE statements.

The NOOBS option suppresses the observation numbers. This is especially useful when the focus is solely on the values of the variables without the distraction of observation indices:

```
proc print data=work.mydata noobs;
run;
```

Additionally, the OBS option can be used to print a certain range of observations. This is valuable for displaying a dataset subset, which can be particularly beneficial for large datasets or when validating specific sections of data:

```
proc print data=work.mydata(obs=10);
run;
```

This example will restrict the output to the first 10 observations of the dataset work.mydata.

To print only specific variables, the VAR statement is utilized. By including the desired variable names in the VAR statement, users can generate a more concise and focused output:

```
proc print data=work.mydata;
  var Var1 Var3;
run;
```

Here, only Var1 and Var3 are printed, omitting other variables from the output.

The WHERE statement enables conditional selection of observations based on specified criteria. This enhances data inspection by allowing targeted querying within a dataset:

```
proc print data=work.mydata;
  where Var1 > 10 and Var2 = 'Category1';
run;
```

This command prints observations where the Var1 value exceeds 10 and Var2 equals 'Category1'.

For datasets with large numbers of observations, sorting the data before printing can be advantageous. Integrating PROC SORT ensures that the observations are organized according to specified variable(s). Here is how you can sort and print the work.mydata dataset by Var1 in ascending order:

```
proc sort data=work.mydata;
  by Var1;
run;

proc print data=work.mydata;
run;
```

The power and flexibility of PROC PRINT extend with various formatting options to enhance the clarity of the output. Labels can be assigned to variables to provide more descriptive column headers using the label statement within a data step or directly in the proc print statement:

```
proc print data=work.mydata label;
  label Var1 = 'Variable 1'
        Var2 = 'Variable 2';
run;
```

Column headers will now display 'Variable 1' and 'Variable 2' instead of Var1 and Var2.

Another feature worth exploring is the use of formats to control the appearance of the data outputs. SAS formats can be applied directly in the PROC PRINT step to modify the display without altering the underlying data. For instance, to format numeric outputs to show only two decimal places:

```
proc print data=work.mydata;
   format Var1 8.2;
run;
```

This command formats Var1 to display numeric values with two decimal points, which can improve readability for datasets with extensive numerical precision.

To underscore effectiveness within real-world applications, consider printing a subset of customer data where high-value transactions are highlighted. First, use PROC SORT to sort the dataset by transaction value, and then apply PROC PRINT with desired filters:

```
proc sort data=sales.customers;
   by descending TransactionValue;
run;

proc print data=sales.customers;
   where TransactionValue > 1000;
   var CustomerID TransactionValue Date;
   label CustomerID = 'Customer ID'
         TransactionValue = 'Value'
         Date = 'Transaction Date';
   format TransactionValue dollar8.2;
run;
```

In this application, high-value transactions are displayed, formatted with currency notation ($), and augmented with descriptive labels, thereby providing clear, actionable data insights.

Employing PROC PRINT efficiently facilitates data validation, troubleshooting, and preliminary analysis, playing an integral role in ensuring data integrity throughout the analytical process.

6.4 Summarizing Data with PROC MEANS

The PROC MEANS procedure is a powerful tool for summarizing data in SAS. It allows the calculation of various statistical measures such as mean, standard deviation, minimum and maximum values, and count. This section details the syntax and usage of PROC MEANS, illustrating how to extract meaningful insights from datasets.

The basic syntax of PROC MEANS is as follows:

```
PROC MEANS DATA=data-set <options>;
   VAR variables;
   CLASS classification-variables;
   OUTPUT OUT=output-data-set <statistics>;
RUN;
```

The DATA statement specifies the input data set, while the VAR statement lists the variables on which the statistical metrics are to be computed. The CLASS statement allows grouping data by one or more classification variables. The OUTPUT statement specifies an output data set and the desired statistics.

Basic Example Consider a dataset named sashelp.class, which contains information about students such as name, sex, age, height, and weight. A simple PROC MEANS example to compute the mean, minimum, and maximum values of height and weight is shown below:

```
PROC MEANS DATA=sashelp.class;
   VAR height weight;
RUN;
```

The output will display the mean, minimum, and maximum of height and weight for the entire dataset.

```
                 The MEANS Procedure

Variable      N        Mean      Std Dev     Minimum      Maximum
-----------------------------------------------------------------
height       19     62.3368      5.1270     51.3000      72.0000
weight       19    100.0263     22.7723     50.5000     150.0000
```

Using the CLASS Statement The CLASS statement is employed to segregate summary statistics by a particular classification variable. Suppose we want to compute the same statistics for height and weight but group them by gender:

```
PROC MEANS DATA=sashelp.class;
   CLASS sex;
   VAR height weight;
RUN;
```

The MEANS Procedure
Class Level Information

Variable	Levels	Values
sex	2	F M

N = Number of Observations, IBS = Independent By Statement

Variable	sex	N	Mean	Std Dev	Minimum	Maximum
height	F	10	60.5600	5.6976	51.3000	66.5000
height	M	9	64.1111	3.5378	57.3000	72.0000
weight	F	10	90.2800	19.8055	50.5000	112.5000
weight	M	9	110.3333	20.6733	83.0000	150.0000

Specifying Statistics By default, PROC MEANS computes N (number of non missing values), Mean, Std Dev, Minimum, and Maximum. Additional statistics can be specified using keywords such as MEDIAN, SUM, RANGE, etc., within the PROC MEANS statement:

```
PROC MEANS DATA=sashelp.class NOPRINT;
   VAR height weight;
   OUTPUT OUT=stats_results
      MEAN=mean_height mean_weight
      MIN=min_height min_weight
      MAX=max_height max_weight;
RUN;
```

This generates the requested statistics and saves them into a new dataset stats_results without printing the results. The NOPRINT option suppresses the output to the results window.

Output Dataset The OUTPUT statement creates a new dataset containing the summary statistics. The example from above produces the following output for stats_results:

stats_results

Variable	_TYPE_	_FREQ_	mean_height	mean_weight	min_height	min_weight	max_height	max_weight
1	0	1	62.3368	100.0263	51.3000	50.5000	72.0000	150.0000

Including Additional Options The inclusion of options such as CHARTYPE, Q3, Q1, or QRANGE enables more customized output. For instance, to include the first quartile, third quartile, and interquartile range:

```
PROC MEANS DATA=sashelp.class Q1 Q3 QRANGE;
   CLASS sex;
   VAR height weight;
   OUTPUT OUT=quartile_stats
      Q1=q1_height q1_weight
      Q3=q3_height q3_weight
      QRANGE=qrange_height qrange_weight;
RUN;
```

This command will produce a dataset quartile_stats including the specified statistics.

Understanding and utilizing PROC MEANS efficiently can significantly enhance data analysis and reporting capabilities in SAS. By mastering its various options and configurations, users can tailor summaries to meet specific requirements, facilitating insightful data interpretations.

6.5 Generating Frequencies with PROC FREQ

The PROC FREQ procedure in SAS is designed for calculating and analyzing the frequency distribution of categorical data. This procedure provides insights into how frequent different categories of a variable occur, which is instrumental in data inspection and preliminary analysis. The core of the PROC FREQ syntax is straightforward, and its versatility allows for detailed customization based on the analysis requirements.

The basic syntax of PROC FREQ involves specifying the input dataset and the variables for which the frequency distribution is to be computed. Below is a simple example demonstrating the basic use of PROC FREQ.

```
PROC FREQ DATA=sashelp.class;
   TABLES sex age;
RUN;
```

In this example, the TABLES statement specifies the variables sex and age from the dataset sashelp.class for which the frequency distributions will be calculated. The output lists the frequency counts, percentages, cumulative frequency, and cumulative percentages for each level of the specified variables.

To extend the functionality, PROC FREQ can also compute two-way and multi-way crosstabulations. Crosstabulations are useful for understanding the relationship between categorical variables. The following example illustrates a two-way crosstabulation.

```
PROC FREQ DATA=sashelp.class;
   TABLES sex * age;
RUN;
```

This code produces a contingency table of sex by age, displaying the joint frequency counts for each combination of sex and age categories.

PROC FREQ also allows for the inclusion of several options to modify the output and add statistical measures. Commonly used options include NOCUM (to suppress cumulative statistics), LIST (to display the output in list format), and CHISQ (to perform chi-square tests for independence in crosstabulation tables). Below is an example that demonstrates these options:

```
PROC FREQ DATA=sashelp.class;
   TABLES sex * age / NOCUM LIST CHISQ;
RUN;
```

Here, the / symbol following the TABLES statement specifies the options for the frequency analysis. The NOCUM option will suppress cumulative frequencies and percentages, LIST will present the crosstabulation in a list format, and CHISQ will add chi-square test statistics to the output.

Consider an environmental dataset where we would like to analyze the frequency distribution of pollution levels. This example demonstrates the generation of a frequency table for a variable named PollutionLevel.

```
PROC FREQ DATA=envdata.pollution;
   TABLES PollutionLevel;
RUN;
```

This command will output the frequency distribution of the PollutionLevel variable, providing counts and percentages for each pollution level category. Additionally, if suppression of the cumulative statistics is desired, the following command can be used:

```
PROC FREQ DATA=envdata.pollution;
   TABLES PollutionLevel / NOCUM;
RUN;
```

Sometimes, it's useful to analyze how the frequency distribution of a categorical variable differs across different levels of another categorical variable. This can be done by generating multi-way tables using the list format to present the data succinctly. For instance, analyzing pollution levels across various cities could be illustrated as follows:

```
PROC FREQ DATA=envdata.pollution;
   TABLES City * PollutionLevel / LIST;
RUN;
```

In this example, the output will display a list format table showing the frequency distribution of PollutionLevel within each City.

To enhance the statistical rigor of your analysis, PROC FREQ offers various tests of association, such as the chi-square test, the Fisher's exact test, and measures of association like Cramer's V. The choice of statistical tests and measures depends on the data's nature and the specific analysis goals. Here is an example where chi-square statistics and Cramer's V measure are included in a crosstabulation analysis:

```
PROC FREQ DATA=envdata.pollution;
   TABLES City * PollutionLevel / CHISQ;
   EXACT CHISQ;
RUN;
```

The CHISQ option requests chi-square statistics, and the EXACT CHISQ statement adds an exact test for chi-square to the analysis, useful especially when expected frequencies are low.

Different formats for presenting the results can provide deeper insights. The OUT= option in the PROC FREQ statement enables the output of frequency counts and percentages to a new SAS dataset for further manipulation or reporting. This functionality is demonstrated below:

```
PROC FREQ DATA=envdata.pollution;
   TABLES City * PollutionLevel / OUT=freqout;
RUN;
```

This command creates a new dataset named freqout containing the counts and percentages for the specified crosstabulation.

For ensuring reproducibility and thorough documentation of the analysis, it is recommended to include a comprehensive range of comments and attributions in the code. The following example showcases best practices for annotating PROC FREQ code:

```
/* Generating frequency distribution for PollutionLevel variable */
PROC FREQ DATA=envdata.pollution;
   TABLES PollutionLevel; /* Get frequency counts and percentages */
RUN;

/* Analyzing frequency distribution across cities */
PROC FREQ DATA=envdata.pollution;
   TABLES City * PollutionLevel / LIST; /* List format for clarity */
RUN;

/* Adding statistical tests to the crosstab analysis */
PROC FREQ DATA=envdata.pollution;
   TABLES City * PollutionLevel / CHISQ; /* Include chi-square test */
   EXACT CHISQ; /* Add exact test for chi-square */
RUN;

/* Output the frequency results to a new dataset */
PROC FREQ DATA=envdata.pollution;
   TABLES City * PollutionLevel / OUT=freqout;
RUN;
```

This comprehensive approach ensures that the analysis is transparent, reproducible, and ready for further scrutiny by peers.

Incorporating PROC FREQ into your data analysis workflow provides a robust mechanism for gaining insights into the frequency distribution of categorical data. The flexibility in the procedure's options facilitates detailed interrogation of data, which is essential for both preliminary data exploration and advanced statistical analysis.

6.6 Basic Statistical Analysis with PROC UNIVARIATE

The PROC UNIVARIATE procedure in SAS is a powerful tool for performing basic statistical analysis on a dataset. This procedure computes descriptive statistics, tests for normality, and produces summary plots of the data. It is an essential component for preliminary data analysis, enabling users to understand the distribution and key characteristics of their data effectively.

To utilize PROC UNIVARIATE, begin by specifying the procedure name followed by the dataset to be analyzed using the DATA option. The basic syntax is as follows:

```
PROC UNIVARIATE DATA=dataset_name;
RUN;
```

By default, PROC UNIVARIATE generates a variety of descriptive statistics, such as mean, median, mode, standard deviation, and percentiles. It also provides tests for normality, including the Shapiro-Wilk, Kolmogorov-Smirnov, Cramér-von Mises, and Anderson-Darling tests. These tests are pivotal for determining if the data follows a normal distribution, which is a key assumption in many statistical methods.

Consider the following example, which demonstrates the use of PROC UNIVARIATE to analyze the weight variable in a dataset named healthdata:

```
PROC UNIVARIATE DATA=healthdata;
   VAR weight;
RUN;
```

Executing this procedure will produce an output with detailed descriptive statistics and normality tests for the weight variable. The results are displayed as follows:

```
                 The UNIVARIATE Procedure
                   Variable: weight

                     Moments
N                     500
Sum Weights               500
Mean                  150.15
Sum                   75075.0
Std Deviation           20.05
Variance               402.00
Skewness                0.12
Kurtosis               -0.63
Uncorrected SS        1135250.0
Corrected SS          200992.0
Coeff Variation         13.36
Std Error Mean           0.90

            Tests for Normality

Test                  Statistic          p Value
Shapiro-Wilk            W= 0.9987          Pr < W    = 0.3234
Kolmogorov-Smirnov        D= 0.0345          Pr > D    > 0.1500
Cramer-von Mises        W-Sq = 0.0247       Pr > W-Sq > 0.2500
Anderson-Darling        A-Sq = 0.4665       Pr > A-Sq > 0.2500
```

The descriptive statistics section provides a thorough summary of the data's central tendency and variability. The normality tests indicate whether the data significantly deviates from a normal distribution, with p-values above 0.05 suggesting that normality cannot be rejected.

PROC UNIVARIATE also allows users to customize their output to focus on specific statistics or graphical representations. The following code illustrates the selection of specific statistics and the request for a histogram and normal probability plot:

```
PROC UNIVARIATE DATA=healthdata PLOT;
   VAR weight;
   HISTOGRAM / NORMAL(COLOR=RED);
   PROBPLOT;
RUN;
```

The HISTOGRAM statement with the NORMAL option overlays a normal curve on the histogram of the weight variable, providing a visual assessment of normality. The PROBPLOT statement generates a normal probability plot, where data points are expected to follow a straight line if the data is normally distributed.

The output for this enhanced procedure includes both graphical plots and additional detailed information about the distribution of the data. Utilizing the PLOT option, the output is as follows:

```
                    The UNIVARIATE Procedure
                      Variable: weight

                   Moments
N                     500
Sum Weights              500
Mean                 150.15
Sum                  75075.0
Std Deviation          20.05
Variance              402.00
Skewness               0.12
Kurtosis              -0.63

               Tests for Normality

Test                   Statistic          p Value
Shapiro-Wilk             W= 0.9987          Pr < W    = 0.3234
Kolmogorov-Smirnov         D= 0.0345          Pr > D    > 0.1500
Cramer-von Mises         W-Sq = 0.0247       Pr > W-Sq > 0.2500
Anderson-Darling         A-Sq = 0.4665      Pr > A-Sq > 0.2500

               (Graphical Output Omitted)
```

The histogram and probability plots offer significant insights into the data distribution, complementing the numerical results.

For more advanced analysis, PROC UNIVARIATE supports the calculation of robust measures of scale such as the interquartile range (IQR), as well as the ability to handle specialized statistical requirements through various options and statements:

```
PROC UNIVARIATE DATA=healthdata ROBUSTSCALE;
  VAR weight;
RUN;
```

This structure equips users with extensive capabilities to explore and evaluate their data thoroughly.

6.7 Creating Tabular Reports with PROC TABULATE

The PROC TABULATE procedure in SAS offers a powerful way to create tabular reports which allow for multi-dimensional summarizations of data. This procedure is particularly useful for displaying descriptive statistics, frequencies, and formatted summaries in a matrix-like structure. We shall now explore the syntax, options, and practical applications of PROC TABULATE.

```
proc tabulate data=your_dataset;
  class variable1 variable2;
  var numeric_variable;
  table variable1, variable2*numeric_variable*(mean sum);
```

```
run;
```

PROC TABULATE can be broadly described in terms of three essential components: CLASS, VAR, and TABLE statements. Each serves a distinct purpose in the report generation process.

The CLASS statement lists the categorical variables to be used as class variables. These are the grouping variables for which the data summaries are computed. Multiple class variables can be specified, separated by spaces.

```
class variable1 variable2;
```

Quantitative variables, on the other hand, are specified using the VAR statement. These are the variables for which summary statistics are calculated.

```
var numeric_variable;
```

The TABLE statement is where the layout and specific statistics of the desired table are defined. The TABLE statement follows a hierarchical syntax that enables the nesting and cross-tabulation of variables.

Consider the following example, where we aim to produce a table displaying the mean and sum of a numeric variable (salary) across combinations of two categorical variables (gender and department):

```
proc tabulate data=employees;
   class gender department;
   var salary;
   table gender, department*salary*(mean sum);
run;
```

This code segment will generate a table where for each gender, the mean and sum of salary are presented for each department. Here, gender is placed in the row dimension, and department combined with salary (along with the statistics mean and sum) is placed in the column dimension.

To enhance the readability and format:

```
proc tabulate data=employees format=dollar8.;
   class gender department;
   var salary;
   table gender all, department all*salary*(mean sum)*f=dollar10.;
run;
```

The above code now includes a formatting directive format=dollar8. which applies a dollar format to the variable salary. Additionally, the keyword all is incorporated to provide a summary of all categories combined.

By default, PROC TABULATE outputs results to the SAS output window or HTML destinations if specified. For customized styling, ODS (Output Delivery System) can be employed. Here's an example outputting to PDF:

```
ods pdf file="report.pdf";
proc tabulate data=employees;
   class gender department;
   var salary;
   table gender all, department all*salary*(mean sum)*f=dollar10.;
run;
ods pdf close;
```

The close of the ODS PDF destination finalizes the output file. Similarly, other ODS destinations (e.g., HTML, RTF) follow analogous syntax.

The KEYLABEL statement can be used to customize the labels of default summary statistics:

```
keylabel mean='Average' sum='Total';
```

This modifies how mean and sum are displayed in the output, enhancing clarity.

Lastly, consider the BOX and PAGE directives for more advanced formatting. These options provide additional control over report presentation, useful for extensive reports within large datasets.

The flexibility and power of PROC TABULATE make it indispensable for producing clear, concise, and comprehensive data summaries. Proper understanding and effective utilization can greatly enhance report quality and data insight.

6.8 Manipulating Data with PROC SQL

PROC SQL is a powerful procedure for interacting with data using the SQL (Structured Query Language). This section delves into various operations that can be performed using PROC SQL in SAS, including data retrieval, subsetting, joining datasets, creating new variables, and aggregating data.

Basic Syntax of PROC SQL

The basic syntax for PROC SQL begins with the PROC SQL statement and ends with the QUIT statement. Within these boundaries, multiple SQL queries can be executed. Here is an illustration of the structure:

```
proc sql;
   select column1, column2
   from dataset
   where condition;
quit;
```

Retrieving and Subsetting Data

PROC SQL allows for the selection of specific columns and rows from a dataset. Suppose we have a dataset named employees. To retrieve the name and salary columns for employees with a salary greater than $50,000, the following query can be used:

```
proc sql;
   select name, salary
   from employees
   where salary > 50000;
quit;
```

The select clause specifies the columns to be retrieved, and the where clause filters the rows based on the given condition.

Joining Datasets

Joining datasets is a common operation where tables are combined based on a related column. The following example joins two datasets, orders and customers, on the customer_id column:

```
proc sql;
   select a.order_id, a.product_id, b.customer_name
   from orders as a, customers as b
   where a.customer_id = b.customer_id;
quit;
```

Here, the a and b are aliases for the orders and customers datasets, respectively. The where clause specifies the join condition.

Creating New Variables

New variables can be created directly within the PROC SQL procedure. For instance, to calculate a new column annual_salary as salary multiplied by 12 from the employees dataset:

```
proc sql;
   select name, salary, salary*12 as annual_salary
   from employees;
quit;
```

The as keyword assigns an alias to the newly created column.

Aggregating Data

Aggregation involves performing calculations across multiple rows to produce a summarized outcome. Examples include counting the number of records, summing values, and calculating averages. Here is an example of calculating the average salary from the employees dataset:

```
proc sql;
   select avg(salary) as average_salary
   from employees;
quit;
```

Aggregate functions such as avg, sum, count, min, and max are used in the select clause to perform the necessary aggregations.

Grouping Data

Groups of rows can be aggregated together using the group by clause. For example, to calculate the total sales for each product in an orders dataset:

```
proc sql;
   select product_id, sum(sales) as total_sales
   from orders
   group by product_id;
quit;
```

The group by clause allows for the aggregation to be performed separately for each value of product_id.

Having Clause

The having clause is used to filter groups based on aggregate values. For instance, if we want to list products that have total sales greater than $10,000:

```
proc sql;
   select product_id, sum(sales) as total_sales
   from orders
   group by product_id
   having sum(sales) > 10000;
quit;
```

The having clause is similar to the where clause but operates on aggregated data.

Creating Tables and Views

PROC SQL can be used to create new tables and views. A table creates a new dataset, while a view creates a virtual table that does not permanently store the data. Here is an example of creating a new table high_salary_employees that contains employees with salaries over

$70,000:

```
proc sql;
   create table high_salary_employees as
   select name, salary
   from employees
   where salary > 70000;
quit;
```

To create a view instead of a table, the create view statement is used similarly.

Union Operation

The union operator combines the results of two or more select queries. For instance, to combine employees from two departments:

```
proc sql;
   select name, department from employees_sales
   union
   select name, department from employees_marketing;
quit;
```

The union operator eliminates duplicate rows by default.

Ordering Data

Data can be sorted using the order by clause. For example, to sort employees by their salaries in descending order:

```
proc sql;
   select name, salary
   from employees
   order by salary desc;
quit;
```

desc denotes descending order, while asc (ascending) is the default order if not specified.

PROC SQL offers extensive functionality and flexibility for data manipulation, making it an indispensable tool in SAS programming.

6.9 Visualizing Data with PROC SGPLOT

PROC SGPLOT is one of the versatile procedures in SAS that enables the creation of a wide variety of plots for data visualization. This section delves into several essential plot types and the corresponding syntax required to generate them. Each example includes actual code along with explanations of key options and statements.

Basic Syntax of PROC SGPLOT:

Before diving into specific examples, let us examine the foundational structure of the PROC SGPLOT step. The general form is as follows:

```
proc sgplot data=<dataset>;
    plot-type x=<x-variable> y=<y-variable> / options;
run;
```

In this structure:

- data=<dataset> specifies the dataset to be used.
- plot-type indicates the type of plot to generate (e.g., scatter, series, vbar).
- x=<x-variable> and y=<y-variable> represent the variables mapped to the x and y axes.
- options provides additional parameters to customize the plot.

Scatter Plot:

Creating a basic scatter plot to visualize the relationship between two continuous variables:

```
proc sgplot data=sashelp.class;
    scatter x=height y=weight;
run;
```

This command generates a scatter plot that displays the relationship between height and weight from the sashelp.class dataset.

Series Plot:

Generating a series plot to visualize trends over time or another continuous variable:

```
proc sgplot data=sashelp.stocks;
    series x=date y=close;
run;
```

This example creates a series plot showing the closing stock prices over time using the sashelp.stocks dataset.

Bar Chart:

The vertical bar chart is useful for displaying the distribution of categorical data:

```
proc sgplot data=sashelp.heart;
```

```
    vbar cholesterol / response=weight stat=mean;
run;
```

In this bar chart, the mean weight is plotted for each category of cholesterol levels from the sashelp.heart dataset.

Histogram:

Histograms are employed to depict the frequency distribution of a continuous variable:

```
proc sgplot data=sashelp.cars;
    histogram mpg_city;
run;
```

With the above code, the histogram displays the distribution of mpg_city (miles per gallon in city) from the sashelp.cars dataset.

Customizing Plots:

Customization enhances the interpretability and aesthetic aspects of plots. Below is an example integrating multiple elements and customizing a scatter plot:

```
proc sgplot data=sashelp.class;
    scatter x=height y=weight / group=sex markerattrs=(symbol=circlefilled size=12);
    reg x=height y=weight / lineattrs=(color=red thickness=2);
    xaxis label="Height (in inches)";
    yaxis label="Weight (in pounds)";
    title "Scatter Plot of Height vs. Weight";
run;
```

In this customized scatter plot:

- group=sex differentiates points by gender.
- markerattrs=(symbol=circlefilled size=12) modifies the marker type and size.
- reg x=height y=weight adds a regression line with specified attributes.
- xaxis label="Height (in inches)" and yaxis label="Weight (in pounds)" customize the axis labels.
- title "Scatter Plot of Height vs. Weight" adds a title to the plot.

Overlaying Multiple Plot Types:

PROC SGPLOT allows multiple plot types to be overlaid in a single graph. The following example overlays a scatter plot and a series plot:

```
proc sgplot data=sashelp.stocks;
    scatter x=date y=close / markerattrs=(symbol=star size=10);
    series x=date y=close / lineattrs=(color=blue);
    xaxis label="Date";
    yaxis label="Closing Price";
    title "Overlay of Scatter and Series Plot";
run;
```

This composite plot includes:

- A scatter plot with star-shaped markers of size 10.
- A series plot with a blue line.
- Customized x and y axis labels, along with a plot title.

Annotations and Insets:

PROC SGPLOT also supports annotations and insets, adding further context and details to visualizations. Here is an application of data labels in a bar chart:

```
proc sgplot data=sashelp.cars;
    vbar make / response=msrp stat=mean datalabel;
    xaxis label="Car Make";
    yaxis label="Average MSRP";
    title "Average MSRP by Car Make";
run;
```

In this bar chart:

- datalabel annotates each bar with its corresponding mean msrp value.
- The xaxis and yaxis labels, along with the title, enhance readability.

6.10 Advanced Reporting with PROC REPORT

PROC REPORT is a highly effective tool for creating sophisticated reports in SAS. This section delves into advanced features and techniques to harness the full potential of PROC REPORT. We will cover the following topics in detail: custom styling, computed variables, complex summary calculations, and integrating ODS (Output Delivery System) for enhanced report presentation.

Custom Styling

The PROC REPORT procedure allows for extensive customization of the appearance of reports. By using the STYLE option, you can modify the presentation elements, such as fonts, colors, and borders. Below is an example that demonstrates how to customize the styling of a report.

```
proc report data=sashelp.class nowd
    style(header)=[font_weight=bold background=lightgrey color=black]
    style(column)=[font_face=Arial font_size=10pt];
    column name age height weight;
    define name / 'Name' style(column)=[font_weight=bold];
    define age / 'Age' style(column)=[color=blue];
    define height / 'Height';
    define weight / 'Weight' format=8.2;
run;
```

In the example above, the STYLE option is applied globally to headers and columns and specifically to individual columns using the DEFINE statement.

Computed Variables

The PROC REPORT procedure can calculate new variables directly within the report. These computed variables are defined using the COMPUTE block. Here is an example that shows how to create a new variable, BMI, within the report.

```
proc report data=sashelp.class nowd;
    column name age height weight bmi;
    define name / 'Name';
    define age / 'Age';
    define height / 'Height';
    define weight / 'Weight';
    define bmi / computed 'Body Mass Index' format=8.2;

    compute bmi;
        bmi = (weight / (height*height)) * 703;
    endcomp;
run;
```

In this example, BMI is calculated using the formula (weight / (height*height)) * 703 within the COMPUTE block. The ENDCOMP statement concludes the computation.

Complex Summary Calculations

PROC REPORT is equipped to handle complex summary calculations, both at the individual level and the group level. Using the BREAK and RBREAK statements, summary rows can be inserted in the report to display total values or other statistics.

```
proc report data=sashelp.class nowd;
    column sex age height weight;
```

```
    define sex / group 'Gender';
    define age / analysis mean 'Average Age' format=8.2;
    define height / analysis mean 'Average Height' format=8.2;
    define weight / analysis mean 'Average Weight' format=8.2;

    break after sex / summarize style=[background=lightyellow];
    rbreak after / summarize style=[background=lightblue];
run;
```

In this example, the BREAK statement inserts summary statistics after each sex group, while the RBREAK statement inserts a summary for the entire report. The STYLE option modifies the appearance of these summary rows.

Integrating ODS for Enhanced Report Presentation

The Output Delivery System (ODS) in SAS allows you to output reports to various file formats, such as HTML, PDF, and RTF, providing flexibility in how reports are shared and viewed.

```
ods html file="output.html";
ods pdf file="output.pdf";

proc report data=sashelp.class nowd;
    column name age height weight bmi;
    define name / 'Name';
    define age / 'Age';
    define height / 'Height';
    define weight / 'Weight' format=8.2;
    define bmi / computed 'BMI' format=8.2;

    compute bmi;
        bmi = (weight / (height*height)) * 703;
    endcomp;
run;

ods html close;
ods pdf close;
```

In the example above, the ODS statements open HTML and PDF destinations for output and then close them after generating the report. This versatility ensures that your reports can meet various presentation and distribution needs.

PROC REPORT's combination of custom styling, computed variables, complex summary calculations, and ODS integration offers a robust framework for creating advanced and comprehensive reports. By utilizing these features, users can generate informative and visually appealing outputs that can be tailored to meet specific requirements.

6.11 Using PROC IMPORT and PROC EXPORT

The PROC IMPORT and PROC EXPORT procedures in SAS are essential tools for importing data from external sources into SAS datasets and exporting data from SAS datasets to external files. Understanding how to use these procedures efficiently allows seamless data exchange between SAS and various other platforms, such as Excel, CSV, and databases like SQL.

PROC IMPORT Syntax and Options

The basic syntax for the PROC IMPORT procedure is structured as follows:

```
PROC IMPORT DATAFILE="file-path"
            OUT=sas-dataset
            DBMS=file-type
            REPLACE;
   GETNAMES=YES/NO;
   DATAROW=n;
RUN;
```

Here is an explanation of the key components:

- DATAFILE="file-path": Specifies the path to the file that you want to import. This can be a local file path or a network path.
- OUT=sas-dataset: Denotes the name of the SAS dataset that will be created.
- DBMS=file-type: Specifies the type of file being imported (e.g., XLSX for Excel files, CSV for comma-separated values files).
- REPLACE: Indicates that if the output SAS dataset already exists, it will be overwritten.
- GETNAMES=YES/NO: Determines whether the first row of the imported file is to be used as variable names (YES) or not (NO).
- DATAROW=n: Specifies the starting row of the data in the file. This is particularly useful when dealing with header information not relevant to the dataset.

An illustrative example of importing a CSV file:

```
PROC IMPORT DATAFILE="/path/to/datafile.csv"
        OUT=mydata
        DBMS=CSV
        REPLACE;
   GETNAMES=YES;
   DATAROW=2;
RUN;
```

In the above example: - The DATAFILE option points to the CSV file to be imported. - The OUT option names the resulting SAS dataset mydata. - DBMS=CSV indicates that the source file is a CSV file. - REPLACE indicates that if mydata already exists, it will be replaced. - GETNAMES=YES uses the first row of the CSV as variable names. - DATAROW=2 specifies that the actual data starts from the second row.

PROC EXPORT Syntax and Options

The PROC EXPORT procedure allows for the exporting of SAS datasets to external files. Its basic syntax is as follows:

```
PROC EXPORT DATA=sas-dataset
        OUTFILE="file-path"
        DBMS=file-type
        REPLACE;
   PUTNAMES=YES/NO;
RUN;
```

Explanation of key components:

- DATA=sas-dataset: Specifies the SAS dataset that will be exported.
- OUTFILE="file-path": Denotes the path where the external file will be saved.
- DBMS=file-type: Specifies the type of file to export to (e.g., XLSX, CSV).
- REPLACE: Indicates if the destination file already exists, it will be overwritten.
- PUTNAMES=YES/NO: Dictates whether the variable names should be written as the first row of the external file (YES) or not (NO).

An example of exporting a SAS dataset to an Excel file:

```
PROC EXPORT DATA=mydata
          OUTFILE="/path/to/outputfile.xlsx"
          DBMS=XLSX
          REPLACE;
   PUTNAMES=YES;
RUN;
```

Here, - The DATA option specifies that the SAS dataset mydata should be exported. - The OUTFILE option indicates the path to the Excel file that will be created. - DBMS=XLSX specifies that the output file should be in Excel format. - REPLACE ensures that if the file already exists, it will be overwritten. - PUTNAMES=YES writes the variable names as the first row in the Excel file.

Common Use Cases and Examples

Importing an Excel file into SAS:

```
PROC IMPORT DATAFILE="/path/to/excelfile.xlsx"
          OUT=sasdata
          DBMS=XLSX
          REPLACE;
   GETNAMES=YES;
RUN;
```

Exporting data to a CSV file:

```
PROC EXPORT DATA=sasdata
          OUTFILE="/path/to/exportfile.csv"
          DBMS=CSV
          REPLACE;
   PUTNAMES=YES;
RUN;
```

These commands demonstrate the flexibility of PROC IMPORT and PROC EXPORT in handling common data formats, making it easier to integrate SAS into broader data workflows.

6.12 Debugging and Optimizing SAS Procedures

Debugging and optimization are critical components of efficient SAS programming. Ensuring that your code runs correctly and performs optimally involves various strategies, including understanding common error messages, utilizing the SAS log, and implementing best practices for performance improvement.

First and foremost, thorough debugging starts with the SAS log. The log provides essential information about the execution of your code, including errors, warnings, and notes. It is crucial to make it a habit to review the log after running any SAS program. Error messages, which usually begin with 'ERROR:', indicate issues that prevent the program from running correctly. Warnings, prefixed by 'WARNING:', may not stop the program from running but flag potential problems. Notes, designated with 'NOTE:', provide additional details about the execution that can be useful for debugging.

Consider a common example where a syntax error occurs in the DATA step:

```
DATA example;
  INPUT name $20. age height;
  DATALINES;
John Smith 30 70
Jane Doe 28 65
;
RUN;
```

If there is a typo in the variable name, such as hight instead of height, the SAS log will capture this error:

```
ERROR: Variable hight not found.
```

Here, the solution is to correct the typographical error and re-run the program.

When dealing with larger datasets or complex procedures, ensuring efficient execution involves optimizing code. Below are some strategies for optimization:

1. **Use WHERE Statements Instead of IF Statements:** Filtering data early in the process streamlines data handling and can significantly reduce processing time. WHERE statements are processed before data is read into the program data vector.

```
PROC PRINT DATA=example;
  WHERE age > 25;
RUN;
```

2. **Keep Dataset Sizes Small:** Remove unnecessary variables or observations before conducting analysis to reduce the size of datasets.

```
DATA smaller_example;
  SET example (KEEP=name age);
RUN;
```

3. **Leverage Indexing:** Create indexes for large datasets to speed up data retrieval processes.

```
PROC DATASETS LIBRARY=work;
  MODIFY example;
  INDEX CREATE age;
QUIT;
```

4. **Optimize Memory Usage:** Use appropriate data types and lengths to conserve memory.

```
DATA optimized_example;
  LENGTH name $20.;
  SET example;
RUN;
```

5. **Proc Sort to Remove Duplicates Efficiently:**

```
PROC SORT DATA=example NODUPKEY;
  BY name;
RUN;
```

Additionally, utilizing the fullstimer system option provides insights into system resources used by your programs:

```
OPTIONS FULLSTIMER;
```

This will output information about CPU time, memory usage, and I/O operations in the SAS log, enabling targeted optimizations.

Optimization and debugging are iterative processes. Regularly reviewing the SAS log and implementing best practices tailored to your specific datasets and procedures will lead to more efficient and reliable SAS programs. This section elaborates on essential techniques and must be integrated continuously into programming workflows to ensure code efficacy and performance.

Chapter 7

Error Handling and Debugging

This chapter covers essential techniques for error handling and debugging in SAS. It begins with an overview of common error types and the interpretation of log messages. Readers will learn to use the PUT statement and other debugging tools such as the ERROR, WARNING, and OPTIONS statements. The chapter also addresses handling data errors, conditional error handling, and debugging macro programs, offering best practices for error prevention and ensuring robust program execution.

7.1 Introduction to Error Handling

Error handling is a fundamental aspect of SAS programming that ensures the reliability and robustness of your code. Proper error handling mechanisms allow programmers to identify, diagnose, and rectify errors efficiently. This section introduces essential concepts and tools for error handling in SAS, providing a strong foundation for more advanced techniques discussed later in the chapter.

Errors in SAS can broadly be categorized into three types: syntax errors, data errors, and logical errors. Understanding these categories helps in diagnosing the errors quickly and applying the appropriate fixes.

Syntax errors occur when the SAS code does not conform to the language syntax rules. These errors typically result in immediate termination of the affected data step or procedure and the generation of error messages in the SAS log. An example of a syntax error is missing a semicolon at the end of a statement:

```
data example;
    set dataset
    where age > 30;
run;
```

Here, the missing semicolon after set dataset causes a syntax error, which will be evident from the log messages.

Data errors happen when data values do not meet the expected format or constraints, leading to issues during data processing. For instance, attempting to perform arithmetic operations on character variables will result in data errors. Consider the following example:

```
data example;
    set dataset;
    total = price * quantity;
run;
```

If price or quantity contains non-numeric values, SAS will generate data error messages in the log.

Logical errors are the most challenging to detect as they arise from incorrect logic in the code, leading to unexpected results rather than explicit error messages. An example of a logical error is using the wrong conditional operator in an if statement:

```
data example;
    set dataset;
    if age = 30 then do;
        output;
    end;
run;
```

If the intention was to filter records where age is greater than 30, the correct operator should be $>$ instead of $=$.

Effective error handling involves several steps:

- **Error Detection:** Identifying the presence of an error through log messages or unexpected output.
- **Error Diagnosis:** Understanding the nature and cause of the error using debugging tools and techniques.
- **Error Correction:** Implementing fixes to eliminate the error and

verify that the code produces the correct results.

The SAS log is a critical resource for error detection and diagnosis. It contains detailed messages about the execution of SAS programs, including errors, warnings, and notes. By carefully reading the log, you can pinpoint the location and nature of errors. For example, the log entry for a missing semicolon might look like this:

```
ERROR 22-322: Syntax error, expecting one of the following: a name, a quoted string, a
        numeric constant, a datetime constant, an expression.
```

Debugging tools such as the PUT statement can assist in diagnosing errors. The PUT statement allows you to print the values of variables and expressions to the log, providing insight into the state of the program at different points during execution. Here's an example:

```
data example;
   set dataset;
   put 'Price=' price 'Quantity=' quantity;
   total = price * quantity;
run;
```

The PUT statement outputs the values of price and quantity to the log, helping to identify any unexpected values that might cause data errors.

Additionally, the OPTIONS statement allows you to control various aspects of the SAS environment that can aid in debugging. Setting OPTIONS OBS=0 limits the number of observations processed, enabling you to test your program without processing entire datasets:

```
options obs=0;
run;
```

Another useful option is MPRINT, which displays the generated code from macro execution, making it easier to trace errors within macro programs:

```
options mprint;
run;
```

Effective error handling not only addresses existing errors but also involves adopting best practices to prevent errors from occurring. Writing clear and structured code, validating input data, and using defensive programming techniques are essential strategies for minimizing errors.

Understanding error handling in SAS is crucial for developing reliable and efficient programs. By mastering these concepts, you will be better equipped to handle errors gracefully, ensuring that your SAS programs run smoothly and produce accurate results.

7.2 Types of Errors in SAS

Understanding the types of errors that can occur in SAS is crucial for effective debugging and error handling. The primary categories of errors in SAS include syntax errors, data errors, and logical errors. Recognizing these errors and interpreting their messages will allow users to develop robust and efficient SAS programs.

Syntax errors occur when the code does not conform to the rules of the language. These errors are usually detected by the SAS compiler and result in the termination of the step or even the entire program. Examples include missing semicolons, misspelled keywords, or incorrect usage of options. Below is an example of a simple syntax error involving a missing semicolon.

```
data example
  set sashelp.class
run
```

The correct code should end each statement with a semicolon:

```
data example;
  set sashelp.class;
run;
```

When a syntax error is present, SAS typically generates a message in the log file indicating the error's nature and position. The log message for the erroneous code might look like this:

```
ERROR 22-322: Syntax error, expecting one of the following: a name, a quoted string, a numeric constant, a datetime constant,
a datetime24.2 constant, an integer constant, a decimal constant.
NOTE: The SAS System stopped processing this step because of errors.
```

Data errors occur when the data do not match the expected format or constraints, such as non-numeric values in numeric variables or out-of-range dates. These errors are often detected at runtime during the DATA step or PROC step processing. An example of a data error might occur in the case of an attempted division by zero:

```
data result;
  set example;
  result = var1 / var2;
run;
```

If var2 equals zero for any observation, this operation will result in a data error. SAS generates messages indicating that invalid data have been encountered, as seen in the following log file snippet:

```
NOTE: Division by zero detected at line 3 column 8.
sample instance data set to missing at line 3 column 8 in computation of result.
```

Logical errors, being the most insidious, occur when the program runs to completion but produces incorrect results. These errors are not detected by the compiler or at runtime but become apparent through erroneous output. For instance:

```
data example;
  set sashelp.class;
  if age > 15 then category = 'adult';
  else category = 'child';
run;
```

Suppose the intention was to classify observations where age is greater than or equal to 18 as 'adult' and others as 'child'. The incorrect logical condition results in erroneous categorizations.

To mitigate logical errors, users should implement thorough testing and validation of their code, incorporating validation checks and debugging outputs using the PUT statement. Leveraging SAS's extensive logging capabilities can also aid in identifying logical discrepancies.

By correctly identifying the types of errors encountered, SAS programmers can take the necessary corrective measures to ensure more accurate and reliable outcomes. Focusing on syntax errors with careful code inspection, addressing data errors through input data validation, and mitigating logical errors with comprehensive testing are essential practices for proficient SAS programming.

7.3 Reading and Interpreting Log Messages

In SAS, the log is a vital resource for understanding how programs execute and for diagnosing issues. Each step of a SAS program is echoed in the log, often with additional notes, warnings, or errors that provide crucial insight into the program's behavior. Properly reading and interpreting log messages is indispensable for effective error handling and debugging.

SAS Log Messages provide feedback about the program execution and have several key components:

- NOTE: Informational messages that typically summarize the actions performed by each step.

- WARNING: Indications of potential issues that may not stop execution but could affect the results.

- ERROR: Serious issues that prevent statements or steps from executing properly and often terminate the program or step.

Example of a SAS Log:

```
data test;
  set sample;
  where age > 30;
run;
```

```
NOTE: There were 50 observations read from the data set WORK.SAMPLE.
NOTE: The data set WORK.TEST has 50 observations and 5 variables.
WARNING: The data set WORK.SAMPLE does not contain a variable named Gender.
ERROR: File WORK.SAMPLE.DATA not found.
```

This sample log includes a NOTE, a WARNING, and an ERROR, each serving a different purpose. Understanding each one is critical.

NOTE Messages are primarily informational. They confirm successful steps and provide execution details. For instance:

```
NOTE: There were 50 observations read from the data set WORK.SAMPLE.
NOTE: The data set WORK.TEST has 50 observations and 5 variables.
```

Here, SAS indicates that it successfully read 50 observations from WORK.SAMPLE and created WORK.TEST with the same number of observations and five variables.

WARNING Messages alert the programmer to potential problems. They do not usually stop the processing but suggest there may be unexpected results or inefficiencies:

```
WARNING: The data set WORK.SAMPLE does not contain a variable named Gender.
```

This warning informs the user that the specified dataset (WORK.SAMPLE) does not have a variable (Gender) that might have been needed.

ERROR Messages indicate significant problems that need immediate attention. These messages stop the step or the entire program, depending upon the severity:

```
ERROR: File WORK.SAMPLE.DATA not found.
```

This error shows that the dataset WORK.SAMPLE was expected but not found. As a result, the step failed, and SAS was unable to execute the intended task.

Reading a Log Involves:

- Start by locating ERROR messages as they indicate the step that needs immediate correction.

- Next, address any WARNING messages to ensure there are no hidden issues that could impact the results.
- Finally, review NOTE messages to understand the execution flow and verify correct actions.

Handling Common Log Issues

When encountering issues in the log, follow these strategies to troubleshoot them effectively:

1. **Incorrect Dataset Name:** - Ensure the dataset exists and is correctly spelled:

```
libname mylib 'path-to-library';
data mylib.test;
    set mylib.sample; /* Verify sample dataset exists */
    where age > 30;
run;
```

2. **Missing Variables:** - Check if the variable exists in the dataset and is correctly spelled:

```
proc contents data=mylib.sample; /* List all variables in the dataset */
run;
```

3. **Syntax Errors:** - Carefully review the code for misplaced semicolons or unmatched parentheses:

```
data mylib.test;
    /* Correct syntax */
    set mylib.sample;
    where age > 30;
run;
```

Properly interpreting SAS log messages facilitates efficient debugging and error resolution, ensuring that programs run correctly and produce reliable results.

7.4 Using the PUT Statement for Debugging

The PUT statement in SAS is an essential tool for debugging programs by providing insights into the data and control flow during the execution of a DATA step. By displaying variable values, text, and conditional output in the SAS log, the PUT statement aids in identifying and correcting errors. This section delves into the various uses of the PUT statement for effective debugging.

The basic syntax of the PUT statement is straightforward. Here is an example:

```
DATA _NULL_;
    SET my_data;
    PUT "The current value of var1 is: " var1;
RUN;
```

Executing the above code results in an output in the SAS log that displays the text along with the current value of var1 for each observation:

```
The current value of var1 is: 42
The current value of var1 is: 35
The current value of var1 is: 56
...
```

The PUT statement can handle multiple variables and literal text integrations in a single line for concise, informative log outputs. Consider the following example:

```
DATA _NULL_;
    SET my_data;
    PUT "Record: " _N_ " var1=" var1 " var2=" var2;
RUN;
```

This code uses _N_ to output the record number along with the values of var1 and var2, helping trace which records might be causing issues:

```
Record: 1 var1=42 var2=8
Record: 2 var1=35 var2=10
Record: 3 var1=56 var2=12
...
```

To enhance readability, SAS allows custom formats. For instance, when debugging dates or large numbers, appropriate formats can make log outputs more understandable:

```
DATA _NULL_;
    SET my_data;
    PUT "Date: " date MMDDYY10. " Amount: " amount DOLLAR10.2;
RUN;
```

Resulting in:

```
Date: 04/25/2023 Amount: $1,500.00
Date: 05/03/2023 Amount: $1,850.00
...
```

Conditional PUT statements enable targeted debugging by checking conditions before printing. This is illustrated as follows:

```
DATA _NULL_;
   SET my_data;
   IF var1 > 50 THEN PUT "var1 exceeds threshold: " var1;
RUN;
```

Only values that meet the condition appear in the log, reducing the volume of log messages and focusing on crucial information:

```
var1 exceeds threshold: 56
var1 exceeds threshold: 78
...
```

The PUT statement can also be integrated within loops or complex conditional structures, helping debug such logic effectively. For example:

```
DATA _NULL_;
   SET my_data;
   ARRAY values[3] a1-a3;
   DO i = 1 TO 3;
      IF values[i] < 0 THEN PUT "Negative value found for variable:" values[i];
   END;
RUN;
```

Here, the PUT statement checks each element of the array for a negative value and logs it, assisting in identifying problematic data.

Moreover, using the PUT statement within custom formats can provide flexible debugging solutions. A format can be defined to output specific information when certain conditions are met:

```
PROC FORMAT;
   VALUE highval
      LOW - 50 = 'LOW'
      51 - 100 = 'MEDIUM'
      101 - HIGH = 'HIGH';
RUN;

DATA _NULL_;
   SET my_data;
   PUT "var1 is in the " var1 highval.;
RUN;
```

This outputs:

```
var1 is in the MEDIUM
var1 is in the LOW
...
```

In addition, pairing the PUT statement with the FILE statement can redirect the output to external files, concentrating log messages in a manageable format outside the SAS environment. This pair helps in maintaining a clean and less cluttered log file within SAS:

```
DATA _NULL_;
    SET my_data;
    FILE 'debug_output.txt';
    PUT "var1: " var1 " var2: " var2;
RUN;
```

It writes the output directly to debug_output.txt file:

```
var1: 42 var2: 8
var1: 35 var2: 10
...
```

Another important use of the PUT statement is within IF-THEN/ELSE structures and DATA step flow control, offering fine-grained debugging:

```
DATA _NULL_;
    SET my_data;
    IF MISSING(var1) THEN PUT "var1 is missing for record " _N_;
    ELSE IF var1 < 0 THEN PUT "var1 is negative for record " _N_;
    ELSE PUT "var1 is valid for record " _N_;
RUN;
```

Providing clear and concise log information based on conditions aids immensely in identifying and resolving issues related to missing values or invalid data:

```
var1 is negative for record 4
var1 is missing for record 7
var1 is valid for record 1
...
```

Overall, mastering the PUT statement for debugging within the SAS programming environment mitigates errors and enhances the reliability and efficiency of data processing scripts.

7.5 Common Syntax Errors and Solutions

Understanding and resolving common syntax errors is crucial for effective SAS programming. Syntax errors occur when the code written does not conform to the rules of the SAS language. These errors can halt the execution of your program and produce error messages in the SAS log. Here we will thoroughly explore typical syntax errors and provide solutions to help you recognize and correct them efficiently.

One of the frequent syntax errors is related to mismatched or missing quotation marks. Consider the following example:

```
data test;
  name = "John;
run;
```

The error here is that the opening quote for the name variable's value does not have a corresponding closing quote. To fix this, ensure that all quotation marks are properly matched:

```
data test;
  name = "John";
run;
```

Another common error involves missing semicolons. In SAS, semicolons are used to terminate statements. Omitting a semicolon can cause multiple statements to be concatenated into a single, invalid statement. For example:

```
data test
  name = "John";
  age = 30
run;
```

The age assignment statement is missing a semicolon, leading to an error. The corrected version would be:

```
data test;
  name = "John";
  age = 30;
run;
```

Errors in variable names also occur frequently. SAS variable names must start with a letter or underscore and can be followed by letters, numbers, or underscores. Using invalid characters or formats can result in syntax errors. For example:

```
data test;
  2name = "John";
run;
```

The variable name 2name is invalid because it starts with a number. The corrected version should start with a letter or an underscore, such as:

```
data test;
  name2 = "John";
run;
```

Another common issue is the improper use of keywords. Keywords have specific meanings in SAS and using them as variable names or inappropriately within code can cause errors. For instance:

```
data test;
  input = "John";
run;
```

The word input is a SAS keyword used for reading data. Using it as a variable name will cause an error. To resolve this, choose a different variable name:

```
data test;
  name_input = "John";
run;
```

Additionally, mismatches in the DATA and PROC steps can produce errors. DATA steps are used for manipulating data, while PROC steps analyze data. Ending a DATA step without a matching run; statement leads to issues. For example:

```
data test;
  name = "John";

proc print data=test;
run;
```

This will produce an error because the DATA step is not properly terminated. The solution is to add a run; statement at the end of the DATA step:

```
data test;
  name = "John";
run;

proc print data=test;
run;
```

A more subtle error can occur with the missing format or informat specifications in data steps. For example:

```
data test;
  input name $;
  datalines;
John
run;
```

The mistake here is minor but can disrupt the program. The correct termination for the data lines must be preceded by datalines;, as shown:

```
data test;
  input name $;
  datalines;
John
;
run;
```

One must also be cautious with parentheses and brackets, which should always be matched. For instance:

```
data test;
  if (age > 18 then status = "Adult";
run;
```

The error here is due to the if condition's missing closing parenthesis. The corrected if statement should be:

```
data test;
  if (age > 18) then status = "Adult";
run;
```

Lastly, improper merging or joining of datasets could lead to syntax errors. Consider an example where two datasets are merged without specifying the by statement properly:

```
data merged;
  merge dataset1 dataset2;
run;
```

If the datasets were supposed to be merged based on a common variable such as id, the proper syntax would include the by statement:

```
data merged;
  merge dataset1 dataset2;
  by id;
run;
```

Addressing these common syntax errors by paying close attention to the log messages and adhering to the syntax rules of the SAS language will significantly enhance the robustness of your code. Proper use of quotation marks, semicolons, valid variable names, appropriate termination of DATA and PROC steps, correct conditional syntax, and accurate merge and join statements will avert most syntax-related issues.

7.6 Handling Data Errors

In SAS programming, data errors can arise from various sources and manifest in multiple ways, depending on the nature of the data and the specific operations being performed. Proper handling of data errors is crucial to maintain the integrity of your results and ensure robust program execution. This section will delve into various strategies and techniques to identify, handle, and mitigate data errors in SAS.

Data errors typically fall into two main categories: input data errors and computation errors. Input data errors occur at the point of reading data into SAS, whereas computation errors occur during data manipulation or transformation.

Identifying Input Data Errors

Input data errors commonly arise when the data being imported into SAS does not conform to expected formats or values. SAS provides several tools and statements to identify and manage such errors. The INPUT statement is one of the fundamental constructs used to read data. Consider an example where data is being read from an external file:

```
data sales;
    infile 'sales_data.txt';
    input ID $ Date : mmddyy10. SalesAmount supplier $;
run;
```

In this example, if the Date field contains values that do not conform to the mmddyy10. format, SAS will write notes in the log and may set the Date variable to missing for those records. Special care must be taken to ensure that all data fields comply with the expected formats.

To better handle and debug input data errors, we can use the MISSOVER or TRUNCOVER options in the infile statement. The MISSOVER option prevents SAS from advancing to a new input line if it does not find values for all the variables in the current line. The TRUNCOVER option allows SAS to read the remaining values in the line, even if they are shorter than expected.

```
data sales;
    infile 'sales_data.txt' missover;
    input ID $ Date : mmddyy10. SalesAmount supplier $;
run;
```

Using these options helps in managing unexpected data lengths and ensures that the program does not skip lines of data silently.

Detecting and Handling Missing Values

Missing values are a common type of data error, which can significantly impact the outcomes of analyses. SAS provides various functions and options to detect and handle missing values appropriately. The NMISS and CMISS functions are used to count missing values for numeric and character variables, respectively.

Consider the following data step:

```
data sales;
    set sales;
```

```
    MissingCount = nmiss(SalesAmount, supplier);
run;
```

In this case, MissingCount will contain the number of missing values in the SalesAmount and supplier variables for each observation. You can then apply conditional logic to handle these missing values, such as imputing default values or excluding records with missing information.

```
data sales_clean;
    set sales;
    if MissingCount > 0 then delete;
run;
```

This code snippet removes any observations with missing values, ensuring that the cleaned dataset sales_clean contains only complete records.

Handling Data Errors During Computation

Data errors can also arise during data manipulations, such as arithmetic operations, merges, and transformations. SAS writes notes, warnings, or errors in the log to flag these issues. A common example is division by zero, which generates a note and results in a missing value for that particular computation.

```
data results;
    set sales;
    UnitPrice = SalesAmount / Quantity;
run;
```

If Quantity contains zero or missing values, the division operation will fail, resulting in notes in the log and missing values for UnitPrice. To handle such scenarios, conditionally check the divisor before performing the operation:

```
data results;
    set sales;
    if Quantity > 0 then UnitPrice = SalesAmount / Quantity;
    else UnitPrice = .;
run;
```

This conditional approach ensures that only valid divisions are carried out, reducing potential errors in the dataset.

Error Handling in Data Merging

When merging datasets, mismatched keys or improperly sorted data can lead to errors. SAS will generate warnings if there are issues in the merge process. To ensure error-free merging, always sort the datasets on the key variable(s) before merging.

```
proc sort data=sales;
    by ID;
run;

proc sort data=customers;
    by ID;
run;

data sales_customers;
    merge sales customers;
    by ID;
run;
```

This practice avoids issues related to unsorted data and ensures that the merge operation is performed correctly.

By employing these strategies and techniques, you can effectively manage and mitigate data errors in your SAS programs, ensuring the reliability and accuracy of your analysis results.

7.7 Using the ERROR and WARNING Statements

In SAS programming, the proper use of ERROR and WARNING statements is crucial for effective error detection and debugging. These statements are employed to generate custom error and warning messages in the SAS Log, which aids in the identification and correction of code or data issues. By mastering these statements, programmers can proactively manage potential errors and improve the robustness of their programs.

The ERROR Statement

The ERROR statement is utilized to generate error messages under specific conditions. An error message produced using the ERROR statement immediately terminates the DATA step in which it occurs. This is particularly useful in scenarios where encountering a specific condition should halt further data processing. Here is the syntax for the ERROR statement:

```
ERROR message;
```

message is a string literal that describes the error encountered. Below is an example that demonstrates the use of the ERROR statement:

```
DATA example;
    SET dataset;
```

```
    IF missing(var1) THEN
        ERROR 'ERROR: Variable var1 is missing.';
RUN;
```

In this example, the ERROR statement is triggered if the variable var1 is missing. The error message "ERROR: Variable var1 is missing." will then be written to the SAS Log, and the DATA step will terminate. This helps identify missing values that are critical for subsequent data operations.

The WARNING Statement

Unlike the ERROR statement, the WARNING statement generates a warning message without halting the DATA step. This is useful for alerting the programmer to conditions that are concerning but not severe enough to stop program execution. The syntax for the WARNING statement is:

```
WARNING message;
```

As with the ERROR statement, message is a descriptive string. Here is an example using the WARNING statement:

```
DATA example;
    SET dataset;
    IF missing(var1) THEN
        WARNING 'WARNING: Variable var1 is missing.';
RUN;
```

In this instance, if the variable var1 is missing, the warning "WARNING: Variable var1 is missing." will be logged. The DATA step will continue processing the dataset, but the presence of the warning message can guide the programmer in verifying data completeness.

Combining ERROR and WARNING Statements with Conditional Logic

The ERROR and WARNING statements can be effectively combined with conditional logic to enforce complex data validation rules. The following example integrates both statements within nested conditions:

```
DATA example;
    SET dataset;
    IF missing(var1) THEN DO;
        IF var2 < 0 THEN
            ERROR 'ERROR: Missing var1 and var2 is negative.';
        ELSE
            WARNING 'WARNING: Missing var1.';
    END;
RUN;
```

In this code, if var1 is missing and var2 is negative, an error is triggered, halting the DATA step. If only var1 is missing, a warning is generated, and the program continues. This allows for detailed handling of various conditions within the same data validation block.

Practical Usage with Macro Variables

When working with macro variables, the ERROR and WARNING statements can be dynamically constructed, offering flexibility in error handling. Consider the following example:

```
%LET threshold = 10;

DATA example;
   SET dataset;
   IF var3 < &threshold THEN DO;
      ERROR "ERROR: var3 below threshold of &threshold.";
   END;
   ELSE IF var3 = &threshold THEN DO;
      WARNING "WARNING: var3 equals the threshold.";
   END;
RUN;
```

Here, the threshold macro variable defines a runtime condition. The ERROR and WARNING statements dynamically incorporate the threshold value, enabling context-sensitive messaging. This approach aids in maintaining configurable and adaptable error handling mechanisms.

Interpreting Log Messages

Messages generated by the ERROR and WARNING statements appear in the SAS Log, providing insights into the nature and location of problems. Consistent formatting and clear descriptions facilitate swift debugging. Below is an example of a SAS Log excerpt resulting from the previous usage of the ERROR statement:

```
DATA example;
  SET dataset;
  IF var3 < 10 THEN DO;
    ERROR
    "ERROR: var3 below threshold of 10.";
  END;
  ELSE IF var3 = 10 THEN DO;
    WARNING
    "WARNING: var3 equals the threshold.";
  END;
RUN;

ERROR: var3 below threshold of 10.
NOTE: The SAS System stopped processing this step because of the errors.
WARNING: var3 equals the threshold.
```

The log messages precisely indicate the conditions causing errors and warnings, allowing programmers to directly trace and rectify issues within the code.

Applying the ERROR and WARNING statements judiciously ensures that critical conditions are flagged appropriately, enabling robust error handling and comprehensive debugging processes in SAS programming.

7.8 Conditional Error Handling

Conditional error handling in SAS allows for the interception of specific conditions during program execution, enabling the programmer to manage them effectively. This capability is vital for ensuring programs run smoothly, even when encountering unexpected data or situations. Utilizing conditional error handling means setting up the program to check for specific criteria and take appropriate actions based on those criteria.

One primary tool for conditional error handling in SAS is the IF-THEN/ELSE statement. This control structure evaluates conditions and routes the program flow accordingly. Here is a simple example demonstrating the use of IF-THEN/ELSE for conditional error handling:

```
data _null_;
    set mydata;
    if age < 0 then do;
        put 'ERROR: Invalid age value --' age;
        call symput('error_flag', '1');
    end;
    else do;
        call symput('error_flag', '0');
    end;
run;
```

This code evaluates the age variable and checks if it is less than zero, printing an error message if the condition is true and setting a macro variable error_flag to 1. If the condition is false, the error_flag is set to 0.

Another mechanism for conditional error handling is using the ERROR statement within a DATA step. The ERROR statement allows explicit signaling of an error condition based on specific criteria:

```
data _null_;
    set mydata;
    if age < 0 then do;
        error 'ERROR: Invalid age value --' age;
    end;
```

```
run;
```

This code not only prints an error message but also generates an error condition that can be detected and handled using SAS tools.

SAS also provides the ABORT statement to stop the current step's execution immediately when an error occurs. This is particularly useful in scenarios where the erroneous condition makes continued execution undesirable:

```
data _null_;
    set mydata;
    if age < 0 then do;
        put 'ERROR: Invalid age value --' age;
        abort;
    end;
run;
```

Use the ABORT statement with caution as it will terminate the execution of the current DATA step immediately and release any resources associated with it.

Nested conditional error handling allows for more complex decision-making processes during debugging. Using nested IF-THEN/ELSE constructs, a program can address multiple error conditions sequentially:

```
data _null_;
    set mydata;
    if age < 0 then do;
        put 'ERROR: Invalid age value --' age;
    end;
    else if height < 0 then do;
        put 'ERROR: Invalid height value --' height;
    end;
    else if weight < 0 then do;
        put 'ERROR: Invalid weight value --' weight;
    end;
run;
```

In this example, each conditional block checks for a different error condition, ensuring that all potential data issues are handled.

For more sophisticated error handling, consider combining conditional structures with SAS functions like N() and CMISS(). These functions can aid in identifying missing values or outliers and handling them appropriately:

```
data _null_;
    set mydata;
    if n(age, height, weight) < 3 then do;
        put 'ERROR: Missing values in the dataset at record number ' _n_;
    end;
```

```
run;
```

In this code, the N() function counts the number of non-missing numeric values among the specified variables. If any are missing, an error message is printed.

Handling errors conditionally extends beyond simple data validation. In the context of macro programming, conditional error handling involves the use of macro variables, functions, and conditional constructs %IF-%THEN/%ELSE. This allows macros to dynamically adapt their behavior based on the occurrence of errors.

```
%macro check_age(age);
    %if &age. < 0 %then %do;
        %put ERROR: Invalid age value -- &age.;
        %let error_flag = 1;
    %end;
    %else %do;
        %let error_flag = 0;
    %end;
%mend;

%check_age(-5);
```

In this macro, the %IF statement checks the age parameter and sets a flag accordingly. Utilizing this technique allows macros to manage control flow based on conditions encountered during execution.

Finally, conditional error handling in SAS can be augmented with custom warning and informational messages using the PUT statement accompanied by NOTE: or WARNING:

```
data _null_;
    set mydata;
    if age < 0 then do;
        put 'ERROR: Invalid age value --' age;
    end;
    else if age = . then do;
        put 'WARNING: Missing age value.';
    end;
    else do;
        put 'NOTE: Processing record with valid age value --' age;
    end;
run;
```

This approach helps provide detailed and descriptive log messages, facilitating easier debugging and error diagnosis. Combining these powerful techniques enables the creation of robust, error-resistant SAS programs capable of handling various data irregularities encountered during execution.

7.9 Debugging with the LINESIZE and PAGESIZE Options

Debugging SAS programs can often be facilitated through the use of various system options that affect the way output is formatted and displayed. Two particularly useful options for debugging are the LINESIZE and PAGESIZE options. These options control the width and length of the lines in the output, respectively, which can help in visualizing the data more effectively and identifying issues more efficiently.

LINESIZE Option

The LINESIZE option sets the number of characters per line of the SAS output. By default, SAS sets the LINESIZE to 80 characters, but this can be modified according to the requirements of your debugging process to better fit the data being analyzed or diagnose formatting issues.

Example:

```
options linesize=120;
```

In this example, the linesize is set to 120, allowing for wider lines in the output. This can help in situations where data fields are being truncated or where longer lines can present the information more clearly.

PAGESIZE Option

The PAGESIZE option determines the number of lines in each page of the SAS output. A higher PAGESIZE can reduce the frequency of page breaks, making it easier to follow the logical flow and relationships within the data on the screen or printed output.

Example:

```
options pagesize=40;
```

Here, the pagesize is set to 40 lines per page. This adjustment can help in creating a more manageable output that fits better in the debugging environment and provides greater continuity when assessing large logs or datasets.

Using LINESIZE and PAGESIZE Together

Both LINESIZE and PAGESIZE options can be used in conjunction to optimize the output for specific debugging needs. Consider the following code:

```
options linesize=100 pagesize=50;
```

In this example, the output is formatted with a line length of 100 characters and a page length of 50 lines. This setting can help in debugging by ensuring that more data or log information is visible on a single screen or page, reducing the need to scroll or navigate through multiple pages.

Practical Applications

LINESIZE and PAGESIZE options are particularly beneficial in the following scenarios:

- **Wide Datasets:** When dealing with datasets that have many columns, adjusting the linesize can prevent data from wrapping onto multiple lines, which can obscure relationships and make debugging more complex.
- **Log Examination:** When analyzing SAS log files, setting an appropriate pagesize can help in viewing entire sections of the log without frequent breaks, making it easier to trace errors and warnings through the log's progression.
- **Data Inspection:** For extensive raw data or intermediate results, the LINESIZE and PAGESIZE options can provide a more continuous view, facilitating error detection related to data formatting, alignment, or truncation.

Adjusting Dynamically

It is often necessary to adjust these settings dynamically within a program. SAS allows for on-the-fly changes to linesize and pagesize using OPTIONS within different parts of the code. This flexibility aids in tailoring the output format according to the specific debugging needs at various stages of program execution. Example:

```
data _null_;
    length var1 $ 100;
    input var1 $;
    put var1;
    if _n_ = 5 then do;
        options linesize=200;
        put var1;
    end;
    else put var1;
datalines;
A very long string that might benefit from a larger linesize setting
Another long string that could also fit better with adjusted linesize
Yet another example string to illustrate linesize usage dynamically
Additional string data for testing linesize adjustment
```

```
Fifth string in the dataset where linesize changes
Continued string examples post-linesize change
Additional testing strings
;
run;
```

In this example, the linesize is temporarily changed when the dataset's fifth line is reached, demonstrating real-time adjustments based on data characteristics encountered during execution.

Understanding and utilizing the LINESIZE and PAGESIZE options can significantly enhance the ability to debug SAS programs effectively by providing better data visibility and log management. These options help to create a customized and clearer output that aligns with the specific requirements of the debugging task at hand.

7.10 Using the OPTIONS Statement for Debugging

The OPTIONS statement in SAS is a powerful tool for enhancing the debugging process by adjusting system options that control the environment of SAS sessions. This section explores various options and their configurations, which can be leveraged for diagnosing, tracing, and debugging errors in SAS programs. Understanding these options will enable programmers to fine-tune their debugging approach effectively.

The OPTIONS statement syntax can be illustrated as follows:

```
OPTIONS option1=value1 option2=value2 ... optionN=valueN;
```

Each option can be set to a specific value or turned on/off by using appropriate parameters. Several options are specifically useful for debugging:

- **MPRINT**
  The MPRINT option enables the printing of SAS statements generated by macro execution in the SAS log. This is particularly beneficial when diagnosing issues within macro programs. When MPRINT is enabled, the SAS log will display the resolved macro code, offering visibility into the underlying operations.

```
OPTIONS MPRINT;
```

Suppose you have a macro named mymacro that generates a series of DATA steps:

```
%macro mymacro;
    data sample;
        set sashelp.class;
        where age > 12;
    run;
%mend mymacro;
%mymacro;
```

With MPRINT enabled, you would observe output similar to the following in the SAS log:

```
MPRINT(MYMACRO):  data sample;
MPRINT(MYMACRO):  set sashelp.class;
MPRINT(MYMACRO):  where age > 12;
MPRINT(MYMACRO):  run;
```

- **SYMBOLGEN**
  The SYMBOLGEN option prints the resolution of macro variables in the log, aiding in troubleshooting issues related to variable resolution.

```
OPTIONS SYMBOLGEN;
```

For example, consider a macro variable &threshold used in a DATA step condition:

```
%let threshold = 15;
data sample;
    set sashelp.class;
    where age > &threshold;
run;
```

With SYMBOLGEN enabled, the SAS log would display:

```
SYMBOLGEN:  Macro variable THRESHOLD resolves to 15
```

- **MLOGIC**
  The MLOGIC option tracks the flow of macro execution, displaying information about macro invocation and completion, as well as the values of macro parameters.

```
OPTIONS MLOGIC;
```

When used within the macro mymacro:

```
%macro mymacro(param);
    %put Parameter value is &param;
    data sample;
        set sashelp.class;
```

```
    where age > &param;
  run;
%mend mymacro;
%mymacro(12);
```

The SAS log would show detailed macro execution flow:

```
MLOGIC(MYMACRO): Beginning execution.
MLOGIC(MYMACRO): Parameter PARAM has value 12.
MLOGIC(MYMACRO): %PUT Parameter value is &param.
Parameter value is 12
MLOGIC(MYMACRO): Ending execution.
```

- **ERRORABEND**
  The ERRORABEND option can be set to force SAS to terminate after encountering an error. This can be useful in batch processing environments where continuation upon error is undesirable.

```
OPTIONS ERRORABEND;
```

- **OBS, FIRSTOBS**
  The OBS and FIRSTOBS options control the number of observations processed. These can be useful when debugging large datasets by limiting the number of rows read.

```
OPTIONS OBS=10 FIRSTOBS=5;
```

  In this example, SAS will process observations 5 through 14. This can help isolate issues in a manageable subset of data.

- **NOTES, ERRORS, SOURCE, SOURCE2**
  The NOTES option controls whether notes are printed to the log. The ERRORS option limits the number of error messages printed. The SOURCE and SOURCE2 options control whether original SAS statements and macro-generated statements, respectively, are printed.

```
OPTIONS NOTES ERRORS=2 SOURCE SOURCE2;
```

  The above configuration ensures that notes are shown, limits error messages to two, and prints both original and macro-generated statements for better traceability.

Full Example Demonstrating Multiple Options
Below is an example illustrating the effect of combining multiple options for comprehensive debugging:

```
OPTIONS MPRINT SYMBOLGEN MLOGIC;

%let threshold = 10;
%macro filter_data;
    %put Filtering data for age > &threshold;
    data filtered;
        set sashelp.class;
        where age > &threshold;
    run;
%mend filter_data;
%filter_data;
```

Upon execution, the SAS log provides a detailed trace together with valuable information from the MPRINT, SYMBOLGEN, and MLOGIC options:

```
SYMBOLGEN:  Macro variable THRESHOLD resolves to 10
MLOGIC(FILTER_DATA):  Beginning execution.
MPRINT(FILTER_DATA):   %put Filtering data for age > &threshold;
Filtering data for age > 10
MPRINT(FILTER_DATA):   data filtered;
MPRINT(FILTER_DATA):   set sashelp.class;
MPRINT(FILTER_DATA):   where age > 10;
MPRINT(FILTER_DATA):   run;
MLOGIC(FILTER_DATA):  Ending execution.
```

This integrated approach to utilizing the OPTIONS statement significantly enhances the diagnostic capabilities available within SAS, enabling effective problem resolution and ensuring program reliability.

7.11 Tracing Errors in Macro Programs

In SAS, macro programs provide a powerful mechanism for automating repetitive tasks and enhancing the dynamic capabilities of data analysis. However, debugging macro programs introduces a unique set of challenges due to their complexity and abstraction layers. To effectively trace errors in macro programs, it is crucial to understand both the macro language and the tools available for diagnosing issues.

1. Leveraging the MPRINT, MLOGIC, and SYMBOLGEN System Options

The MPRINT, MLOGIC, and SYMBOLGEN system options provide vital insights into the execution of macro programs. By enabling these options, you can generate detailed log messages that reveal the internal workings of your macros.

MPRINT displays the SAS code generated by macro execution, which helps in understanding what the macro %'s actually executing.

```
options mprint;
%mymacro;
```

In the log, MPRINT will output the standard SAS code, facilitating the identification of syntactical and logical errors.

MLOGIC writes detailed messages about macro execution decisions, such as conditional logic (%IF-%THEN-%ELSE) and loop processing (%DO-%END).

```
options mlogic;
%mymacro;
```

Activating MLOGIC allows tracking the decision-making process within macros, aiding in diagnosing logical errors.

SYMBOLGEN displays the values of macro variables as they are resolved, providing visibility into symbol resolution.

```
options symbolgen;
%mymacro;
```

Using SYMBOLGEN, you can confirm that macro variables contain expected values at different points in the macro's execution.

2. Implementing %PUT Statements

The %PUT statement is an essential tool for macro debugging. It allows printing custom messages and macro variable values to the SAS log. Strategic placement of %PUT statements in your macro code can pinpoint stages where errors originate.

For example, to display the value of a macro variable:

```
%let myvar = 10;
%put The value of myvar is &myvar;
```

This will output to the log:

```
The value of myvar is 10
```

To diagnose more complex scenarios, you can include conditional %PUT statements:

```
%if &myvar > 5 %then %put &myvar is greater than 5;
```

Such diagnostic statements allow you to track the flow of execution and the logical conditions within your macro.

3. Using the SYSFUNC Function for Enhanced Debugging

The SYSFUNC function can evaluate macro expressions and functions, which can be outputted using %PUT for real-time debugging.

For instance, to calculate and display the current date and time:

```
%put Current Date and Time is %sysfunc(datetime(), datetime.);
```

The log will display:

```
Current Date and Time is 10NOV22:10:15:22
```

4. Error Handling with %IF-%THEN and %GOTO

Integrating conditional checks within macros using %IF-%THEN directives helps handle unexpected scenarios gracefully. Implementing %GOTO for error conditions allows controlled exits from macro execution.

For instance:

```
%macro checkdiv(a, b);
    %if &b = 0 %then %do;
        %put ERROR: Division by zero encountered.;
        %goto exit;
    %end;
    %let result = %eval(&a / &b);
    %put The result of division is &result;
%exit:
%mend checkdiv;

%checkdiv(10, 0);
```

The SAS log displays:

```
ERROR: Division by zero encountered.
```

5. Comprehensive Error Handling with %ABORT

For more severe error conditions requiring termination of macro execution, the %ABORT statement can be used:

```
%macro criticalcheck(x);
    %if &x < 0 %then %do;
        %put ERROR: x must be non-negative.;
        %abort cancel;
    %end;
    %put The value of x is valid: &x;
%mend criticalcheck;

%criticalcheck(-5);
```

This produces:

```
ERROR: x must be non-negative.
NOTE: Macro criticalcheck will not execute further statements.
```

Effectively tracing errors in macro programs requires a keen understanding of macro diagnostic tools and strategic placement of debugging statements. Leveraging the MPRINT, MLOGIC, SYMBOLGEN options, coupled with the intelligent use of %PUT, %SYSFUNC, %GOTO, and %ABORT, provides a robust framework for identifying and resolving macro errors.

7.12 Best Practices for Error Prevention

Efficient error prevention in SAS programming requires a combination of proactive coding practices, robust validation checks, and diligent adherence to coding standards. The following best practices can significantly mitigate the risk of errors and improve the reliability of SAS programs.

1. Use of Commenting

Including comments in your code enhances readability and serves as a guide for others (or yourself at a later time) who might need to understand or modify the code. Use the * symbol or the %% to add comments in SAS code.

```
* This is a single-line comment;
data example;
    set dataset;
    /* This block comment explains the
    purpose of the data step */
    if age > 18 then adult = 1;
    else adult = 0;
run;
```

2. Modularize Code

Break down complex programs into smaller, manageable subprograms or macros. Modularization improves debug-ability and allows testing of individual components separately.

```
%macro process_data(data=, out=);
    data &out.;
        set &data.;
        /* Data processing steps */
    run;
%mend;
```

```
%process_data(data=input_dataset, out=output_dataset);
```

3. Consistent Naming Conventions

Adhere to a consistent naming convention for variables, datasets, and macros to avoid confusion. For example, use descriptive names and follow a pattern such as var_name for variables and dataset_name for datasets.

```
data work.patient_data_set;
    set source.raw_data;
    patient_id = id;
    /* further data processing */
run;
```

4. Validate Assumptions and Inputs

Validate data assumptions and inputs before processing to prevent unexpected errors. Use the PROC CONTENTS and PROC MEANS procedures to examine data attributes.

```
proc contents data=input_dataset;
run;

proc means data=input_dataset;
    var age height weight;
run;
```

5. Implement Error and Warning Statements

Explicitly use ERROR and WARNING statements within the code to handle and flag erroneous conditions as they occur.

```
data output;
    set input;
    if age < 0 then do;
        ERROR 'Age cannot be negative: ' age=;
        stop;
    end;
run;
```

6. Regular Code Review and Refactoring

Periodically review and refactor code to identify and eliminate potential sources of error. Leverage version control systems like Git for managing changes and maintaining code history.

7. Use of OPTIONS Statement for Debugging

Utilize the OPTIONS statement to set system options that help identify and trace errors more effectively. Adjust LINESIZE, PAGESIZE, and other relevant options to provide detailed log information.

```
options linesize=120 pagesize=60 mergenoby=error;
```

8. Maintain Comprehensive Test Cases

Develop and maintain a suite of test cases that cover a wide range of scenarios, including edge cases. Automated testing frameworks can augment this process, ensuring that changes do not introduce new errors.

9. Adequate Data Type and Length Management

Ensure that variables are assigned appropriate data types and lengths to prevent data truncation or conversion errors.

```
data work.cleaned_data;
    length name $50. age 8.;
    set work.raw_data;
    if find(name, 'invalid_substring') then delete;
run;
```

10. Use Robust Macros with Parameter Checks

When writing macros, check for parameter validity to avoid unintended behavior. For example, validate that necessary parameters are not missing.

```
%macro subset_data(data=, var=);
    %if %length(&data.) = 0 or %length(&var.) = 0 %then %do;
        %PUT ERROR: Both parameters for macro subset_data must be specified.;
        %RETURN;
    %end;

    data subset;
        set &data.;
        if &var. ne .;
    run;
%mend;

%subset_data(data=input, var=age);
```

These best practices, when applied consistently, can significantly reduce the likelihood of errors, thereby improving the stability and reliability of SAS programs. The practices emphasize proactive measures, proper coding standards, and the use of SAS-specific error handling capabilities to maintain robust and error-free code.

Chapter 8

Data Visualization with SAS

This chapter introduces the graphical capabilities of SAS for data visualization. It covers the use of procedures like PROC GCHART for creating bar and pie charts, PROC GPLOT for line plots, and PROC SGSCATTER for scatter plots. Readers will learn to customize graphics with ODS Graphics and visualize data using PROC SGPLOT and PROC SGPANEL. The chapter also includes techniques for creating maps with PROC GMAP, interactive visualization methods, and best practices for effective data presentation.

8.1 Introduction to Data Visualization

Data visualization plays a crucial role in the interpretation and communication of data. It involves the representation of data in a graphical format, facilitating the understanding of complex datasets by revealing patterns, trends, and correlations that might not be apparent in raw data. SAS provides robust tools for creating a wide range of visualizations, offering various procedures designed to handle different types of graphical representations.

Data visualization in SAS entails utilizing specialized procedures that transform raw data into visual formats. Among the most widely used procedures are PROC GCHART, PROC GPLOT, PROC SGSCATTER, PROC SGPLOT, and PROC SGPANEL. Each of these procedures has unique capabilities and is tailored to produce specific types of charts and plots.

Understanding the basics of these procedures is essential for effective data visualization. For instance, PROC GCHART is used to create bar charts and pie charts that summarize categorical data. PROC GPLOT focuses on generating line plots suitable for depicting trends over time. PROC SGSCATTER enables the creation of scatter plots, which are ideal for showing relationships between numeric variables.

Customization is a vital aspect of data visualization, ensuring that graphics are not only informative but also visually appealing. SAS's ODS Graphics framework offers extensive options for customizing graphical elements such as titles, labels, legends, and color schemes. This flexibility aids in creating publication-quality graphics that adhere to specific aesthetic and functional requirements.

```
proc sgplot data=sashelp.class;
  scatter x=height y=weight;
  title "Height vs Weight of Students";
  xaxis label="Height (inches)";
  yaxis label="Weight (pounds)";
run;
```

This example demonstrates the use of PROC SGPLOT to create a scatter plot. The data parameter specifies the dataset, while the scatter statement defines the variables for the x and y axes. The title, xaxis label, and yaxis label statements illustrate how to customize the plot.

Further, SAS introduces advanced procedures such as PROC SGPANEL, which can generate panelled plots allowing for the comparison of multiple categories within a single visualization framework. This capability is particularly useful when dealing with multilayered data structures that require comparison across different groups or conditions.

```
proc sgpanel data=sashelp.iris;
  panelby species;
  scatter x=sepalwidth y=sepallength;
  title "Sepal Dimensions of Iris Species";
  colaxis label="Sepal Width (cm)";
  rowaxis label="Sepal Length (cm)";
run;
```

In this PROC SGPANEL example, the panelby statement divides the scatter plot into panels based on the species variable. This facilitates the visualization of sepal dimensions across different species of the Iris dataset.

The use of maps to represent geographical data is another powerful aspect of SAS data visualization, achieved through PROC GMAP. This procedure allows users to create detailed maps that display data geographically, which is particularly useful in fields such as epidemiology, marketing, and environmental studies.

```
proc gmap data=maps.us map=maps.us;
  id state;
  choro population / levels=5;
  title "Population Distribution by State";
run;
```

Here, PROC GMAP is employed to map the population distribution across different states. The id statement specifies the variable representing geographical boundaries, while the choro statement defines the shading of the map based on population levels.

Interactive visualization further enhances data exploration by allowing users to interact with the data points, facilitating deeper insights. SAS supports interactive visualizations through tools such as SAS Visual Analytics and JMP.

Integrating visualizations into a broader data analysis workflow can significantly improve the clarity and impact of the communicated results. By leveraging the powerful visualization capabilities of SAS, analysts can create effective and engaging graphical representations of data, making complex information accessible and comprehensible to diverse audiences.

8.2 Overview of SAS Graph Procedures

SAS offers a robust suite of procedures specifically designed for data visualization. These graphical procedures empower users to transform raw data into meaningful graphics, facilitating better comprehension and analysis. The principal SAS graph procedures include PROC GCHART, PROC GPLOT, PROC SGSCATTER, PROC SGPLOT, PROC SGPANEL, and PROC GMAP. Each of these procedures serves distinct purposes and excels in different types of data representation.

PROC GCHART is employed primarily for generating bar charts and pie charts. These visual tools are essential for categorical data representation, whereby different categories can be illustrated with bars or slices to show proportions or counts. This procedure is straightforward and enables customization through various options and statements. Below is an example of a basic PROC GCHART usage to create a bar chart.

```
proc gchart data=sashelp.class;
    vbar age / discrete;
run;
quit;
```

The above code generates a vertical bar chart of the age variable within the sashelp.class dataset, explicitly specifying the bars to be discrete with the discrete option.

Moving forward, PROC GPLOT is targeted at producing line plots. Line plots are highly valuable for illustrating trends over continuous variables, such as time-series data. Users can plot multiple series on the same graph to compare different data streams. An elementary example of PROC GPLOT follows:

```
proc gplot data=sashelp.class;
    plot height*age;
run;
quit;
```

This code plots height against age from the sashelp.class dataset, generating a simple line plot.

For scatter plots, PROC SGSCATTER provides a versatile approach. Scatter plots are indispensable when exploring relationships between two continuous variables. They allow for the identification of correlations, clusters, and outliers. An example illustrating the use of PROC SGSCATTER is shown below:

```
proc sgscatter data=sashelp.class;
    plot height*weight;
run;
quit;
```

In this instance, the scatter plot visualizes the relationship between weight and height.

The PROC SGPLOT procedure offers a more modern and flexible approach for creating various types of plots, including bar charts, line plots, scatter plots, and more. This procedure supersedes older graphics procedures by providing a unified syntax and modern graphical capabilities with enhanced aesthetics. Below is a sample code to create a scatter plot using PROC SGPLOT:

```
proc sgplot data=sashelp.class;
    scatter x=weight y=height;
```

```
run;
quit;
```

This command generates a scatter plot with weight on the x-axis and height on the y-axis.

For more complex graphical layouts, PROC SGPANEL enables the division of data into panels based on one or more classification variables, facilitating multi-faceted visual analysis. An example of utilizing PROC SGPANEL is as follows:

```
proc sgpanel data=sashelp.class;
    panelby sex;
    scatter x=weight y=height;
run;
quit;
```

The plot created by this code segments the data by the sex variable, generating a scatter plot for each gender.

Finally, PROC GMAP is tailored for producing geographical maps. It merges data with map datasets to visualize data distribution across different regions, such as states or countries. An example of mapping with PROC GMAP is provided below:

```
proc gmap data=mymap_data map=maps.us;
    id state;
    choro population;
run;
quit;
```

Here, the PROC GMAP procedure generates a choropleth map of the United States, illustrating population distribution across states based on the mymap_data dataset.

These SAS graph procedures collectively provide a comprehensive toolkit for data visualization, catering to various analytic needs. Proper understanding and application of these procedures enable users to derive and convey insights effectively through graphical representations.

8.3 Creating Bar Charts with PROC GCHART

The PROC GCHART procedure in SAS is extensively utilized for creating various types of bar charts. These bar charts can represent categorical data effectively, providing a visual representation that facilitates comparisons across different categories. By leveraging

PROC GCHART, users can produce vertical, horizontal, stacked, and grouped bar charts with customized aesthetics.

Below is a detailed explanation of the syntax, options, and examples for constructing bar charts using PROC GCHART.

Basic Syntax and Usage

The basic syntax for PROC GCHART is straightforward. It includes the proc gchart statement followed by the vbar or hbar statement to specify the type of bar chart (vertical bar chart or horizontal bar chart, respectively).

```
proc gchart data=dataset;
    vbar variable / options;
    hbar variable / options;
run;
```

variable is the categorical variable representing the categories for which the bars will be plotted.

Examples of Vertical and Horizontal Bar Charts

The following examples illustrate how to create vertical and horizontal bar charts with PROC GCHART.

```
proc gchart data=sashelp.class;
    vbar age;
run;
```

This example creates a vertical bar chart for the age variable from the sashelp.class dataset.

```
proc gchart data=sashelp.class;
    hbar age;
run;
```

This example generates a horizontal bar chart for the age variable.

Enhancing Bar Charts with Options

PROC GCHART offers a wide range of options to customize bar charts. These options include specifying colors, adding labels, controlling bar widths, and arranging chart elements.

Example: Adding Titles and Axis Labels

```
proc gchart data=sashelp.class;
    title "Distribution of Age in Class";
    vbar age / discrete;
    label age = "Age in Years";
run;
```

In this example, title sets the chart title, label changes the axis label, and discrete ensures that every value is treated as a separate category.

Example: Grouped Bar Charts

To create grouped bar charts for additional variables, use the group option.

```
proc gchart data=sashelp.class;
    vbar age / group=sex discrete;
run;
```

Here, the group option illustrates the age distribution by sex.

Example: Stacked Bar Charts

For stacking bars, the subgroup option is used.

```
proc gchart data=sashelp.class;
    vbar age / subgroup=sex discrete;
run;
```

This creates a stacked bar chart with sex as the subgroup within each age bar.

Bar Width Control

The width option modifies the bar width in the chart.

```
proc gchart data=sashelp.class;
    vbar age / width=10 discrete;
run;
```

In this example, the bars have a width of 10 units.

Bar and Background Color Customization

Colors contribute to the visual appeal and clarity of bar charts. The cbarline, cfill, and caxis options customize bar lines, fills, and axes, respectively.

```
proc gchart data=sashelp.class;
    vbar age / cbarline=black cfill=blue caxis=gray;
run;
```

This example produces a bar chart with black bar lines, blue bar fills, and gray axes.

Example: Adding Statistical Summary Info

Add tooltip information or values directly on the bars for more insight.

```
proc gchart data=sashelp.class;
    vbar age / sumvar=weight type=mean discrete;
run;
```

Here, the sumvar option specifies the variable for summarization (for example, calculating the mean weight per age group).

Advanced Customizations

For more advanced users, options such as annotate, pattern, and minor can provide more customization capabilities.

Example: Using Annotate Data Set

Annotate data sets can add custom text, lines, or markers to bar charts.

```
data anno;
    retain xsys '2' ysys '2';
    length function $8 color $8;
    function='label';
    x=2; y=15;
    text='Highest';
    color='red';
    output;
run;

proc gchart data=sashelp.class;
    vbar age / annotate=anno discrete;
run;
```

This example uses an annotate data set to add a "Highest" label at the specified coordinates.

The PROC GCHART procedure provides robust functionality for creating and tailoring bar charts, ensuring that the visuals effectively communicate the underlying data. Its extensive options facilitate both basic and advanced customizations, adapting the charts to various requirements and specifications.

8.4 Generating Pie Charts with PROC GCHART

The PROC GCHART procedure in SAS is a powerful tool for creating pie charts, which are effective for displaying the proportional distribution of categorical data. This section delves into the capabilities and customization options of PROC GCHART for generating pie charts, providing a detailed explanation and examples to ensure clarity and understanding.

A basic pie chart can be created using the PIE statement within PROC

GCHART. Consider the following SAS code that produces a pie chart from a dataset named sales_data:

```
proc gchart data=sales_data;
   pie product / sumvar=sales;
run;
quit;
```

In the above example, product is the categorical variable for which the pie chart is created, and sales is the numerical variable that determines the size of each slice.

Customizing Pie Charts

PROC GCHART offers numerous options for customizing pie charts to improve readability and aesthetic appeal. Key customization features include specifying slice labels, applying patterns, and adding titles.

- Slice Labels: Labels provide essential information about each slice. By default, SAS labels slices with the category name. However, you can enhance the labels with additional information, such as percentages or values, using the value option.

Example:

```
proc gchart data=sales_data;
   pie product / sumvar=sales value=inside percent=inside;
run;
quit;
```

- Applying Patterns: Patterns and colors can help differentiate slices. Using pattern statements allows you to define specific patterns or colors for each slice.

Example:

```
pattern1 color=blue;
pattern2 color=green;
pattern3 color=red;

proc gchart data=sales_data;
   pie product / sumvar=sales;
run;
quit;
```

- Adding Titles: Titles are vital for providing context to the graphs. Titles and footnotes can be added using title and footnote statements.

Example:

```
title "Sales Distribution by Product";
footnote "Data Source: FY2023 Sales Records";

proc gchart data=sales_data;
   pie product / sumvar=sales;
run;
quit;
```

Exploding Slices

Exploding slices is a technique used to emphasize particular slices of the pie chart. This is done by separating a slice from the rest of the pie. The explode option is used to specify which slice(s) to explode.

Example:

```
proc gchart data=sales_data;
   pie product / sumvar=sales explode="ProductA";
run;
quit;
```

PROC GCHART also supports exploding multiple slices by specifying multiple categories in the explode option.

Pie Charts with Subgrouping

Subgrouping allows users to create pie charts with additional layers of information by segmenting each slice further based on another categorical variable. The subgroup option helps achieve this.

Example:

```
proc gchart data=sales_data;
   pie product / sumvar=sales subgroup=region;
run;
quit;
```

In this example, the pie slices for product are further divided by region, providing a more detailed view of the data distribution.

Creating 3D Pie Charts

Three-dimensional pie charts add a visual depth to the chart, making them more appealing. The couter value=outside options in conjunction with the pie3d statement can be used to generate 3D pie charts.

Example:

```
proc gchart data=sales_data;
   pie3d product / sumvar=sales value=outside;
run;
quit;
```

Additional Features

PROC GCHART includes several other less commonly used but powerful options for further customization and control over the appearance of pie charts:

- angle: Specifies the angle of the first slice.
- percent: Displays percentage values on the chart.
- other=label: Groups small slices into an "Other" category for clarity.
- legend: Adds a legend for better slice identification.

Example utilizing additional features:

```
proc gchart data=sales_data;
   pie3d product / sumvar=sales angle=90 percent=inside other=5 legend=legend1;
run;
quit;
```

This example demonstrates various options to enhance the pie chart's utility and readability.

Displaying a pie chart is a pivotal task in data visualization that enables a clear understanding of categorica

8.5 Drawing Line Plots with PROC GPLOT

PROC GPLOT is a versatile procedure in SAS that allows for the creation of line plots, which are essential for visualizing trends and patterns in data over continuous intervals. Line plots are particularly useful in time series analysis, scientific research, and any domain where understanding the progression of data points over intervals is crucial. This section delves into the technical details of employing PROC GPLOT to generate and customize line plots effectively.

To begin with, a basic line plot can be created using the following structure:

```
proc gplot data=sashelp.class;
    plot weight*height;
run;
quit;
```

In this example, the dataset sashelp.class contains information about students, including their weight and height. The plot statement specifies that we wish to plot weight on the Y-axis against height on the X-axis.

```
        The SAS System                  12:14 Friday, October 27, 2023

                          Plot of Weight vs Height


                        Height
60 ---------------------------------------------
   |                    *                      W
   | *                   +                     W+ +
   |   *                                                  +
   |    *                                                ++
   |        *  *        *                   *
   |           *         *                         *
   |            *       +   *** *
   |    *   * * **    *     ** *
   |   *
0 ---------------------------------------------
Height
```

The result is a simple scatter plot connecting the points with lines. For a more customized and sophisticated line plot, additional options and statements are available.

SYMBOL statements are utilized to define the attributes of the plotted lines or markers. Here is an example of customizing the line type, color, and symbols:

```
symbol1 interpol=join value=dot color=blue line=1;

proc gplot data=sashelp.class;
    plot weight*height / vaxis=axis1 haxis=axis2;
    axis1 label=(angle=90 "Weight (lbs)");
    axis2 label=("Height (inches)");
run;
quit;
```

In this code, symbol1 specifies that the data points are connected by a line (interpol=join), the points should be marked with dots (value=dot), and the line color is set to blue (color=blue) with a solid line type (line=1). Additionally, axis1 and axis2 statements are used to customize the vertical and horizontal axes with labels.

To further enhance the line plot's aesthetic, multiple SYMBOL statements can be defined for different plots within the same procedure. For instance, plotting multiple groups can be achieved by the following:

```
symbol1 interpol=join value=plus color=red line=2;
symbol2 interpol=join value=star color=green line=1;

proc gplot data=sashelp.class;
    plot weight*height=sex / overlay;
    axis1 label=(angle=90 "Weight (lbs)");
```

```
    axis2 label=("Height (inches)");
run;
quit;
```

In this scenario, weight against height is plotted separately for each sex (assuming sex is a variable in the dataset), with lines for one group plotted in red using plus symbols, and green stars for the alternative group. The overlay option combines these plots into a single graph.

Advanced customization options include using different interpolation methods, adding reference lines, and annotating the graph for clarity. Below is an advanced example with these features:

```
symbol1 interpol=spline line=2 color=blue;
symbol2 interpol=spline line=1 color=green;

proc gplot data=sashelp.class;
    plot weight*height=sex / overlay;
    axis1 label=(angle=90 "Weight (lbs)") order=(50 to 150 by 10);
    axis2 label=("Height (inches)") order=(50 to 75 by 5);
    title "Line Plot of Weight vs Height by Sex";
    footnote "Data Source: sashelp.class";
run;
quit;
```

Here, the interpol=spline option uses a spline interpolation for a smooth curve. The axis1 and axis2 statements provide explicit axis scales and labels. The title and footnote statements enhance the plot with descriptive information.

Further, annotations can add specific details on the graph for emphasis:

```
data annotations;
    length function color $8;
    xsys = '2';
    ysys = '2';
    x = 60;
    y = 85;
    function = 'label';
    text = 'Sample Point';
    color = 'black';
run;

proc gplot data=sashelp.class;
    plot weight*height / annotate=annotations;
    symbol1 interpol=join value=circle color=red line=1;
    axis1 label=(angle=90 "Weight (lbs)") order=(50 to 150 by 10);
    axis2 label=("Height (inches)") order=(50 to 75 by 5);
    title "Annotated Line Plot of Weight vs Height";
run;
quit;
```

In this example, a separate dataset annotations is created and used in the annotate option to label a specific point on the plot, illustrating how annotations can be incorporated to highlight important data features.

Each parameter and option within PROC GPLOT allows fine-tuning and tailoring of plots to better interpret and present data, demonstrating the procedure's capacity to handle various visualization needs in SAS programming. The ability to identify trends and patterns in datasets visually is enhanced significantly by utilizing the customized features of PROC GPLOT.

8.6 Creating Scatter Plots with PROC SGSCATTER

PROC SGSCATTER is a versatile procedure in SAS utilized for generating scatter plots. Scatter plots are essential tools for visualizing relationships between two continuous variables. In this section, we will examine the syntax and functionality of PROC SGSCATTER, various options for customizing scatter plots, and the interpretation of results.

To generate a basic scatter plot using PROC SGSCATTER, the fundamental syntax is:

```
proc sgscatter data=<dataset_name>;
  plot <y_variable>*<x_variable>;
run;
```

This code generates a scatter plot of texttty_variable against texttt x_-variable using the dataset specified in texttt<dataset_name>. Below is an example using a hypothetical dataset named texttmydata, where we aim to visualize the relationship between texttWeight and texttHeight:

```
proc sgscatter data=mydata;
  plot Weight*Height;
run;
```

This code produces a basic scatter plot with texttWeight on the y-axis and texttHeight on the x-axis. To enhance the visualization and make it more informative, PROC SGSCATTER allows various additional options.

- GROUP=: To differentiate groups within the data.
- GRID: To add grid lines to the plot.
- LOESS or REG: To add fit lines.

- MARKERATTRS: To customize marker attributes such as color and size.

For instance, if we want to differentiate points by a categorical variable textttGender, add grid lines, and include a regression line, the code is:

```
proc sgscatter data=mydata;
  plot Weight*Height / group=Gender grid reg;
run;
```

Here, textttGROUP=Gender differentiates the points by gender, GRID adds grid lines for better readability, and REG includes a regression fit line to discern trends.

Visualizing Multiple Scatter Plots

PROC SGSCATTER also supports the generation of multiple scatter plots simultaneously. This is particularly useful when visualizing relationships between several pairs of variables. The plot statement is repeated for each pair of variables:

```
proc sgscatter data=mydata;
  plot (Weight Height)*Age;
run;
```

This code generates scatter plots of textttWeight versus textttAge and textttHeight versus textttAge within the same output pane. To add customized attributes to these scatter plots, the options discussed earlier can be applied similarly.

Scatter Plot Matrix

A scatter plot matrix is a grid of scatter plots used to visualize potential correlations among multiple variables. PROC SGSCATTER facilitates the creation of scatter plot matrices using the Matrix statement:

```
proc sgscatter data=mydata;
  matrix Weight Height Age;
run;
```

This will generate a matrix of scatter plots showcasing pairwise relationships between textttWeight, textttHeight, and textttAge.

Customization Options for Scatter Plot Matrix

Customization options can also be applied to scatter plot matrices. For instance, adding grid lines and grouping by textttGender:

```
proc sgscatter data=mydata;
  matrix Weight Height Age / group=Gender grid;
run;
```

Legend and Layout Adjustments

To improve the interpretability of scatter plots, adjusting legends and layout settings can be crucial. The legend and layout options facilitate these enhancements:

```
proc sgscatter data=mydata;
  plot Weight*Height / group=Gender grid reg markerattrs=(symbol=CircleFilled);
  keylegend / position=right across=1;
run;
```

In this example, markerattrs=(symbol=CircleFilled) customizes the plot markers, and keylegend / position=right across=1 adjusts the legend to the right side with a single column layout.

Interpretation of Scatter Plots

The interpretation of scatter plots involves analyzing the spread and pattern of data points. Key aspects to observe include:

- **Correlation:** Whether there is a visible linear or non-linear relationship.
- **Outliers:** Identification of any points that deviate significantly from the trend.
- **Trends:** Understanding how one variable affects the other.

By leveraging the full capabilities of PROC SGSCATTER, intricate relationships between variables can be visualized effectively, offering valuable insights into the data.

Ensuring scatter plots are well-labeled, appropriately scaled, and visually clear is paramount to convey accurate information. The diverse customization options provided by PROC SGSCATTER facilitate the creation of tailored, insightful scatter plots suitable for comprehensive data analysis.

8.7 Customizing Graphs with ODS Graphics

In this section, we will explore how to customize graphs using the Output Delivery System (ODS) Graphics in SAS. ODS Graphics provides a rich set of tools for customizing the appearance and layout of graphs, allowing for detailed and professional-grade visualizations. We will cover customizing graph styles, templates, and options that can be applied across various SAS graph procedures.

Graph Styles: ODS Graphics supports various predefined styles that control the overall appearance of graphs, including elements like colors, fonts, and line styles. These styles can be applied easily by specifying them in the ODS statement.

```
ods graphics / reset noborder;
ods listing style=journal;
```

The above code resets the current ODS graphics settings and applies the journal style, which is a clean, publication-ready style.

ODS Graphics supports a multitude of built-in styles such as statistical, htmlblue, listing, and more. Users can preview and choose from these styles based on their requirements.

Graph Templates: Graph templates provide a mechanism to define the layout and appearance of plots in SAS. Using the Graph Template Language (GTL), complex plots can be designed with precision.

Below is a simple example of a GTL template for a scatter plot.

```
proc template;
  define statgraph scatterTemplate;
    begingraph;
      layout overlay;
        scatterplot x=xvar y=yvar / markerattrs=(symbol=circlefilled size=12);
      endlayout;
    endgraph;
  end;
run;
```

This code defines a template named scatterTemplate, which creates a scatter plot with circular markers sized at 12 points. Once defined, this template can be referenced in PROC SGRENDER to create a plot.

```
proc sgrender data=mydata template=scatterTemplate;
  dynamic xvar="age" yvar="height";
run;
```

Customizing Graph Elements: Individual elements within a graph can be customized using attributes such as colors, line styles, and marker types. For instance, one can adjust the appearance of a series plot as follows:

```
proc sgplot data=mydata;
  series x=year y=sales / lineattrs=(color=red pattern=solid thickness=2);
  scatter x=year y=sales / markerattrs=(symbol=starfilled color=blue size=8);
run;
```

In this example, the series plot displays sales data over years with a solid red line that is two points thick. The overlaying scatter plot uses blue star markers of size 8.

ODS Graphics also allows for advanced customizations such as annotation, creating multi-panel layouts, and utilizing the SGANNO data set for detailed annotations which can be applied in PROC SGPLOT and others.

Here is how you can add annotations:

```
data anno;
  set mydata;
  x1='5JUN2020'd;
  y1=600;
  function='text';
  text='Peak Sales';
  drawspace='datavalue';
  position='top';
run;

proc sgplot data=mydata sganno=anno;
  series x=date y=sales / lineattrs=(color=green pattern=dashed);
run;
```

The annotation dataset anno is used here to add the text "Peak Sales" at the specified data coordinate. The sganno option in PROC SGPLOT applies this annotation to the graph.

Titles, Footnotes, and Legends: Proper labeling is crucial for the clear communication of information in visualizations. Titles, footnotes, and legends can be customized to improve the readability and aesthetics of graphs.

```
title "Yearly Sales Data";
footnote "Data source: Company Database";

proc sgplot data=mydata;
  series x=year y=sales / lineattrs=(color=purple);
  keylegend / location=inside position=topright across=1;
run;
```

The above code sets a title and a footnote for the graph, while the keylegend statement customizes the legend to be positioned inside the plot area at the top-right corner.

Exporting Customized Graphs: Finally, exporting customized graphs for reporting and publication is straightforward. Different formats such as PNG, PDF, and SVG can be specified in the ODS statement.

```
ods graphics / outputfmt=png;
ods html file="output_graph.html";
```

```
proc sgplot data=mydata;
  series x=year y=sales / lineattrs=(color=black);
run;

ods html close;
```

This code generates a PNG file within an HTML document storing the formatted graph.

Consistency and precision are key to professional-grade graphics. With ODS Graphics, templates, styles, and extensive customization options are available to create crisp and informative visualizations, enhancing the communication of data insights.

8.8 Visualizing Data with PROC SGPLOT

The PROC SGPLOT procedure in SAS provides a versatile and powerful way to create various types of graphs for data visualization. It supports a wide range of plot types including scatter plots, line plots, bar charts, histograms, box plots, and more. This section will delve into the syntax, options, and examples to effectively use PROC SGPLOT for producing quality visualizations.

PROC SGPLOT begins with the declaration of the procedure and is followed by the specification of the plot types, along with any required options. The basic syntax for PROC SGPLOT is as follows:

```
PROC SGPLOT DATA=dataset;
   plot-type x-axis-variable = y-axis-variable / options;
RUN;
```

We will explore different plot types supported by PROC SGPLOT.

Scatter Plots

Scatter plots are useful for visualizing the relationship between two continuous variables. To create a scatter plot, you use the SCATTER statement within PROC SGPLOT.

```
PROC SGPLOT DATA=sashelp.class;
   SCATTER x=height y=weight / markerattrs=(symbol=circlefilled);
RUN;
```

A scatter plot uses the x= and y= options to designate the x and y axes respectively. The markerattrs option allows for customizing the appearance of the markers.

Line Plots

Line plots are used to display data points connected by straight lines, often used for time series data. The following example demonstrates a basic line plot using PROC SGPLOT.

```
PROC SGPLOT DATA=sashelp.air;
    SERIES x=date y=air / lineattrs=(pattern=solid);
RUN;
```

Here, the SERIES statement is used, and the lineattrs option allows customization of the line pattern.

Bar Charts

Bar charts are another common visualization type that can be easily created with PROC SGPLOT. The VBAR statement is used for vertical bar charts.

```
PROC SGPLOT DATA=sashelp.class;
    VBAR age / response=weight stat=mean;
RUN;
```

In this example, the VBAR statement creates a vertical bar chart displaying the mean weight for each age group. The response option specifies the response variable, and the stat option specifies the statistic to be used.

Histograms

Histograms are used to visualize the distribution of a single variable. The HISTOGRAM statement provides a straightforward way to create histograms.

```
PROC SGPLOT DATA=sashelp.cars;
    HISTOGRAM horsepower;
RUN;
```

This example creates a histogram of the variable horsepower from the sashelp.cars dataset.

Box Plots

Box plots are useful for summarizing the distribution of a variable and identifying outliers. The VBOX statement creates vertical box plots.

```
PROC SGPLOT DATA=sashelp.class;
    VBOX height / category=age;
RUN;
```

The VBOX statement generates a box plot for the variable height, categorized by age.

Customizing Graphs

Customization is an integral aspect of creating effective visualizations. PROC SGPLOT offers numerous options to customize plots. For instance, the TITLE and FOOTNOTE statements can add titles and footnotes.

```
PROC SGPLOT DATA=sashelp.iris;
    SCATTER x=sepalLength y=petalLength / group=species;
    TITLE "Scatter Plot of Iris Data";
    FOOTNOTE "Source: SASHELP.IRIS dataset";
RUN;
```

This example also demonstrates the use of the group option to color the points by species.

ODS GRAPHICS options can be used to further enhance the appearance of the plots. To change the size or resolution of the output graphics, you can use:

```
ODS GRAPHICS / WIDTH=5in HEIGHT=3in IMAGENAME="plot";
PROC SGPLOT DATA=sashelp.iris;
    SCATTER x=sepalLength y=petalLength / group=species;
RUN;
ODS GRAPHICS / RESET;
```

Re-setting the ODS GRAPHICS options ensures that the settings apply specifically to this graph and do not affect subsequent plots.

Combining Multiple Plots

Using the PROC SGPLOT procedure, multiple plot types can be combined within a single graph. For instance, combining a series plot and a scatter plot can be achieved as follows:

```
PROC SGPLOT DATA=sashelp.stocks;
    SERIES x=date y=close / group=stock;
    SCATTER x=date y=high / group=stock;
RUN;
```

In this example, the SERIES plot and SCATTER plot are overlays, utilizing the same x= and y= variables.

The PROC SGPLOT procedure facilitates the creation of diverse, customizable, and publication-ready plots suitable for a variety of data types and analysis needs. By leveraging its robust set of options, users can tailor their visualizations to convey their data effectively and efficiently.

8.9 Advanced Graphics with PROC SGPANEL

PROC SGPANEL is a powerful procedure in SAS that facilitates creating advanced graphical representations by displaying multiple plots simultaneously. This approach enhances the comprehensibility of complex data sets by segregating data into panels based on categorical variables. To use PROC SGPANEL effectively, one must comprehend key elements such as PANELBY statement, CATEGORY statement, and other customizations available in the procedure. The syntax for this procedure allows extensive customization to enhance readability and presentation quality of graphical outputs.

The PROC SGPANEL syntax begins typically with defining the dataset and specifying the variables for panels, categories, and response variables. Here is a basic example:

```
proc sgpanel data=sashelp.cars;
   panelby make;
   vbar type / response=horsepower stat=mean;
run;
```

In this example, the dataset sashelp.cars is utilized. The panelby make statement specifies that each distinct value of the variable make will create a different panel. The vbar type / response=horsepower stat=mean statement generates vertical bar charts in each panel representing the mean horsepower for different type values.

It is essential to explore more intricate customizations and variations to maximize the efficacy of PROC SGPANEL. Below is an in-depth exploration of the components and their customizations.

The PANELBY statement is fundamental:

```
panelby variable1 (options) / options;
```

Here, variable1 can be any categorical variable in the dataset. The options within parentheses apply to individual panels, while those following the slash (/) apply to all panels. A specific configuration example might look like this:

```
proc sgpanel data=sashelp.cars;
   panelby make / columns=3 spacing=5;
   vbar type / response=horsepower stat=mean;
run;
```

This code creates a panel grid with three columns, and a spacing of 5 units between each panel.

Another significant statement is LOESS, which performs local regression smoothing:

```
proc sgpanel data=sashelp.cars;
   panelby make / layout=columnlattice;
   loess x=weight y=mpg_city / nomarkers smooth=0.5;
run;
```

This example demonstrates how to create a panel where each panel is a columnlattice layout, applying a LOESS smoothing function to weight versus mpg_city without displaying markers and with a smoothing parameter of 0.5.

Each type of chart (e.g., VBAR, HBAR, SCATTER, SERIES) has its syntax for customization. Here is a deeper dive into a scatter plot within panels:

```
proc sgpanel data=sashelp.iris;
   panelby species;
   scatter x=sepallength y=sepalwidth / group=species;
   rowaxis label='Sepal Width';
   colaxis label='Sepal Length';
run;
```

This example uses the iris dataset and creates separate scatter plots for each species, grouping data points by species as well. Labels for rowaxis and colaxis enhance the readability of the graph.

To provide a cohesive and professional look to the panels, use options such as TITLE and FOOTNOTE:

```
proc sgpanel data=sashelp.cars;
   title "Mean Horsepower by Car Make and Type";
   footnote "Source: SASHELP.CARS dataset";
   panelby make;
   vbar type / response=horsepower stat=mean;
run;
```

This addition places a title at the top and a footnote at the bottom of the graphics output, offering context to the viewers.

Adjusting for better visual separation and clarity, consider spacing and layout options:

```
proc sgpanel data=sashelp.cars;
   panelby make / rows=2 columns=3 spacing=5;
   histogram msrp / binwidth=2000 transparency=0.5;
   rowaxis label='Frequency';
   colaxis label='MSRP';
run;
```

Here, setting the rows=2 and columns=3 neatly organizes six panels with equal spacing, improving visual distribution.

An advanced feature is the usage of INSET statement to add textual information inside the panels which might be particularly relevant for detailed analysis:

```
proc sgpanel data=sashelp.cars;
   panelby make;
   scatter x=weight y=horsepower / group=type;
   rowaxis label='Horsepower';
   colaxis label='Weight';
   inset "Model: &sysver" / position=topleft;
run;
```

This snippet incorporates an inset at the top-left position indicating the version of SAS being used.

Other customization includes modifying plot attributes like markers and line styles. An extensive command set provides ultimate control over the graphical appearance:

```
proc sgpanel data=sashelp.cars;
   panelby make;
   series x=weight y=mpg_highway / lineattrs=(pattern=solid thickness=2);
   scatter x=weight y=mpg_highway / markerattrs=(symbol=circlefilled size=8);
run;
```

This example illustrates how to adjust the series line's pattern and thickness, and customize the scatter plot markers' symbols and sizes, ensuring each data point and trend line is visually distinct and clear.

Employing PROC SGPANEL can significantly enhance data visualization by effectively display multiple plots, facilitating deeper insights and clearer communication of data patterns. The array of customization options allows for professional and tailored visual outputs.

8.10 Creating Maps with PROC GMAP

PROC GMAP is a powerful procedure in SAS for creating geographic maps that visualize data in a spatial context. This procedure can represent data geographically by overlaying data values on a map of a particular region, such as a country, state, or other predefined boundary.

To use PROC GMAP, you must have a map dataset that contains the geometric boundaries of the area to be mapped and a response dataset that includes the data to be visualized on the map.

Basic Syntax

The basic syntax for PROC GMAP is as follows:

```
proc gmap data=<response dataset> map=<map dataset>;
    id <id variable(s)>;
    choro <response variable>;
run;
```

In the above syntax, <response dataset> is the dataset that contains the data to be mapped, and <map dataset> is the dataset containing the geometric boundaries. The id statement is used to specify the vari able(s) in both datasets that link the boundaries to the data, and the choro statement is used to specify the variable to be mapped (choropleth map).

Example: Visualizing Population Data

Suppose you have data on the population of different states in the United States, and you want to visualize this population data on a map. You would use a map dataset such as maps.us provided by SAS, which contains the boundaries of US states.

The response dataset might look like this:

```
data pop_data;
    input state_code $ population;
    datalines;
AL 4779736
AK 710231
AZ 6392017
...
;
run;
```

To visualize this data, you would use the following code:

```
proc gmap data=pop_data map=maps.us;
    id state_code;
    choro population;
run;
```

The resulting map will display each state of the United States shaded according to its population, with darker shades representing higher population values.

Customizing the Map

You can customize the appearance of the map by using additional options in the choro statement, such as the levels option to specify the number of color levels, and the legend statement to customize the map legend.

For instance, to create a map with 5 levels and to modify the legend, you can use the following code:

```
proc gmap data=pop_data map=maps.us;
    id state_code;
    choro population / levels=5;
    legend1 label=("Population Levels");
run;
```

This code will produce a map with the population data visualized in 5 different shades, and a legend that is labeled "Population Levels".

Working with Annotated Maps

You can add annotations to your maps to provide additional information such as labels or markers. To do this, you need an annotation dataset that contains the details of what to add to the map.

For example, to annotate the map with the names of the states, create an annotation dataset as follows:

```
data anno;
    length function $8 color $8;
    retain xsys '2' ysys '2' color 'black';
    input state_code $ x y text $;
    function = 'label';
    size = 1; /** label size **/
    position = '5'; /** center the text **/
    datalines;
AL 0.5 0.5 Alabama
AK 0.1 0.9 Alaska
AZ 0.2 0.2 Arizona
...
;
run;
```

Use PROC GMAP with the annotate option:

```
proc gmap data=pop_data map=maps.us;
    id state_code;
    choro population / annotate=anno;
    legend1 label=("Population Levels");
run;
```

This will add the state names at the specified coordinates on the map.

Creating Drill-Down Maps

PROC GMAP also allows the creation of drill-down maps for web-based interactive applications. By generating HTML output, users can click regions of the map to navigate to more detailed maps or additional information.

To create a drill-down map, you must output the map to an HTML file using the ODS HTML statement:

```
ods html file="map_output.html" path=".";

proc gmap data=pop_data map=maps.us;
    id state_code;
    choro population / html=html_variable;
run;

ods html close;
```

In this code, the html option of the choro statement uses a variable that links to detailed information or another map. For the drill-down functionality, the html_variable should include the URL of the link.

Using PROC GMAP enables the effective visualization of spatial data, enhancing the interpretability and impact of geographic patterns and trends. Customizing and annotating maps, combined with ODS tools for generating interactive output, supports a wide range of data visualization needs in various applications.

8.11 Interactive Visualization Techniques

Interactive visualization techniques in SAS provide a powerful means to explore and understand data dynamically. Such techniques enhance traditional static visualizations by allowing users to interact with charts and graphs, adjust parameters, and gain deeper insights into their data. This section discusses methods and tools available in SAS for creating interactive visualizations, focusing on the use of SAS Visual Analytics and the PROCs suitable for interactive usage.

SAS Visual Analytics is a sophisticated tool designed to facilitate advanced data exploration and visualization. It allows for the creation of highly interactive reports and dashboards, which can be shared across an organization. The primary components include the Visual Analytics Hub, Visual Analytics Designer, and Visual Data Builder. Together, they enable users to perform actions like drill-downs, filtering, and parameter adjustments in real-time.

To illustrate, here is an example of creating an interactive dashboard in SAS Visual Analytics. Imagine we have a dataset named sales_data containing sales figures, regions, and time periods. The steps typically involve uploading the dataset, creating visualizations, and then combining them into a dashboard.

```
proc import datafile="&path./sales_data.csv" out=work.sales_data dbms=csv replace;
    getnames=yes;
run;
```

Once the data is uploaded, we can proceed by creating various interactive visualizations, such as bar charts and line plots, using the Visual Analytics Designer. To integrate these visualizations into a cohesive dashboard, one might employ actions like filtering a bar chart based on the selected region in a list table.

Here is a more technical example utilizing SAS code to create interactive visualizations via the ODS HTML5 destination. This allows generating HTML files with embedded JavaScript, providing interactive capabilities.

```
ods html5 path="&path" (url=none) file="interactive.html" options(svg_mode="
    embed");

proc sgplot data=sashelp.class;
   scatter x=height y=weight / datalabel=name;
   title "Interactive Scatter Plot of Height vs. Weight";
run;

ods html5 close;
```

In this example, the sgplot procedure is used to create an interactive scatter plot. By setting the output destination to html5, the resulting file (interactive.html) can be viewed in a web browser, where users can hover over points to see data labels or zoom in and out of the plot.

Another popular method for interactive visualizations in SAS is the use of the SGRENDER procedure in conjunction with the ODS HTML destination. This approach provides extensive control over the graphical output through the use of Graph Template Language (GTL).

```
proc template;
   define statgraph scattertemplate;
      begingraph;
         entrytitle "Height vs Weight of Class Data";
         layout overlay;
            scatterplot x=height y=weight / datalabel=name;
         endlayout;
      endgraph;
   end;
run;

ods html path="&path" (url=none) file="scatter.html";

proc sgrender data=sashelp.class template=scattertemplate;
run;

ods html close;
```

This code defines a scatter plot template and renders it with the sgrender procedure. The interactive output allows user actions such as hovering over data points to view details, making it a powerful tool for dynamic data exploration.

Interactive visualization techniques in SAS not only facilitate better data understanding but also improve user engagement. By seamlessly combining different visual elements and allowing real-time interaction, users can derive more meaningful insights and make data-driven decisions more effectively.

8.12 Best Practices for Data Visualization

Effective data visualization is essential for interpreting complex datasets and communicating findings clearly. This section elaborates on established best practices to ensure that graphical representations are both informative and comprehensible. Employing these practices will enhance the clarity, accuracy, and impact of your visualizations.

Choosing the Right Chart Type

The first step in creating an effective visualization is selecting the appropriate chart type. Each type of chart is suited to specific kinds of data and analysis objectives. It is important to align the choice of graph with the nature of the data and the message intended to be communicated. For example:

- **Bar Charts:** Ideal for comparing discrete categories or groups. Use horizontal bars for long category names that may clutter the vertical space.
- **Line Plots:** Best suited for showing trends over time. Ensure that time is plotted on the x-axis to intuitively represent progression.
- **Pie Charts:** Most useful for representing parts of a whole. Limit the number of slices to avoid complexity and ensure slices are ordered consistently.
- **Scatter Plots:** Suitable for showing relationships between two continuous variables. Highlight clusters or outliers for deeper insights.
- **Box Plots:** Efficient for displaying the distribution of a dataset by showing the data's quartiles and median.

Ensuring Clarity and Simplicity

Clarity and simplicity in design prevent misinterpretation and enhance readability. Follow these guidelines to achieve clear and simple visualizations:

- **Limit the Number of Variables:** Visualizations with too many variables can overwhelm the viewer. Focus on key variables that effectively communicate the essential message.
- **Consistent Scales:** Use consistent scales across multiple charts to facilitate comparisons. Avoid dual y-axes unless absolutely necessary and clearly label them.
- **Minimize Non-Data Ink:** Remove unnecessary gridlines, backgrounds, and borders to keep the focus on the data.
- **Readable Text:** Use legible fonts and appropriate sizes for titles, labels, and annotations. Ensure color contrasts used in text are accessible.
- **Color Usage:** Employ colors purposefully. Use a consistent color scheme and avoid colors that are hard to distinguish. Consider colorblind-friendly palettes.

Avoiding Misleading Visualizations

A visualization must represent data accurately to avoid misleading the audience. Here are some practices to avoid misinterpretation:

- **Correct Axis Scaling:** Ensure that the axes start at zero to avoid exaggerated differences. Use appropriate scaling to represent data variations truthfully.
- **Appropriate Data Aggregation:** Aggregate data responsibly to avoid hiding critical details or showing misleading trends.
- **Contextual Information:** Provide necessary context such as units of measurement, time periods, and explanatory notes to make the data comprehensible.
- **Avoid Overplotting:** When plotting large datasets, overplotting can obscure patterns. Utilize techniques like jitter or alpha blending to manage density.

Leveraging Annotative Elements

Annotations can significantly enhance the interpretability of visualizations. Key annotative elements include:

- **Titles and Subtitles:** A concise, informative title and a subtitle can provide context and clarify the purpose of the graph.
- **Axis Labels:** Clearly label the x-axis and y-axis to define what is being measured. Include units where applicable.
- **Data Labels:** Where appropriate, label data points directly rather than relying on a legend alone.
- **Text Annotations:** Use text annotations to highlight key findings, trends, or anomalies within the graph.

Incorporating Best Practices with SAS

SAS offers extensive capabilities for creating high-quality visualizations. Utilizing tools and procedures such as PROC SGPLOT, PROC SGSCATTER, and PROC SGPANEL, you can adhere to best practices effectively. Consider the following example which demonstrates the creation of a clear and accurate bar chart:

```
proc sgplot data=sashelp.cars;
  vbar make / response=mpg_city
       stat=mean
       datalabel
       fillattrs=(color=steelblue);
  xaxis label="Car Make";
  yaxis label="Average City MPG"
        grid;
  title "Average City MPG for Various Car Makes";
run;
```

The above code produces a bar chart comparing the average city miles per gallon (MPG) for different car makes. It adheres to several best practices such as clearly labeled axes, an informative title, the use of a consistent color, and gridlines for better readability.

The strategic application of best practices in data visualization ensures that the resultant graphs convey accurate, clear, and actionable insights.

Chapter 9

Advanced Data Step Techniques

This chapter delves into sophisticated data manipulation methods within the SAS data step. It covers using the SET statement with multiple datasets, interleaving data with the BY statement, and creating and using indexes. Readers will explore hash objects, advanced merging techniques, and the use of First. and Last. variables. The chapter also addresses programming with DO loops, retaining values with the RETAIN statement, generating summary statistics, efficient data handling with the MODIFY statement, and advanced array processing.

9.1 Introduction to Advanced Data Step Techniques

The aim of this chapter is to extend your understanding of the SAS Data Step, leveraging advanced techniques to handle complex data manipulation tasks. By mastering these methods, you will be able to perform intricate operations with greater efficiency and precision. We will systematically explore the intricacies of the Data Step beyond basic data manipulation, including the integration of multiple datasets, the use of indexes for quick data retrieval, and the implementation of hash objects for data storage and lookup. This section sets the foundation for these advanced techniques by elucidating the core principles that underpin sophisticated Data Step programming.

At the outset, it's imperative to grasp the fundamental structure and functionality of the Data Step, which includes reading, transforming, and outputting dataset observations. We will systematically progress to advanced constructs by building on established concepts. The key topics covered will include:

- Using the SET statement for combining multiple datasets.
- Interleaving data with the BY statement to achieve sorted merges.
- Creating and utilizing indexes to enhance data retrieval performance.
- Employing hash objects for efficient data lookups and storage.
- Implementing advanced data merging techniques for sophisticated data integration.
- Utilizing First. and Last. variables for identifying group boundaries within BY groups.
- Programming with DO loops and DO WHILE statements for iterative operations.
- Retaining variables across iterations with the RETAIN statement.
- Generating summary statistics within the Data Step.
- Efficient dataset modification with the MODIFY statement.
- Advanced array processing for handling multiple variables simultaneously.

The SET statement, often used for reading datasets, is extended to combine multiple datasets efficiently. Consider the following example, where we integrate dataset1 and dataset2 using the SET statement:

```
data combined;
   set dataset1 dataset2;
run;
```

In this example, the observations from dataset1 and dataset2 are concatenated sequentially into the combined dataset. Attention must be paid to ensuring variable consistency across datasets to avoid data anomalies.

Interleaving with the BY statement comes into play when datasets are already sorted by a common key, allowing for a merged dataset that maintains the sorted order. The syntax for this operation is as follows:

```
data interleaved;
    set dataset1 dataset2;
    by common_key;
run;
```

Identifying and utilizing indexes can dramatically improve data retrieval times, especially with large datasets. Indexes create a direct path to rows of interest, bypassing the need for sequential searches. To create an index on a variable key_var, use the proc datasets procedure:

```
proc datasets lib=work;
    modify large_dataset;
    index create key_var;
quit;
```

Hash objects, introduced in SAS 9, offer an advanced method for temporarily storing and retrieving data within the Data Step, akin to dictionaries in other programming languages. The following example illustrates a hash object for the demo dataset:

```
data _null_;
    if 0 then set demo;
    declare hash h(dataset:'demo');
    h.defineKey('id');
    h.defineData('name', 'age');
    h.defineDone();
run;
```

This code snippet initializes a hash object from demo, defining id as the key and name and age as data fields.

Advanced data merging encompasses intricate scenarios where multiple datasets are linked based on complex conditions. These techniques ensure the creation of comprehensive datasets for robust analysis. An illustrative example of merging with a conditional check is shown below:

```
data merged;
    merge dataset1(in=a) dataset2(in=b);
    by id;
    if a and b;
run;
```

Variables such as First. and Last. are particularly useful when working with BY groups, as they help you ascertain the start and end of a group. Consider this code snippet where we count observations within groups:

```
data grouped;
   set dataset;
   by group_var;
   if First.group_var then count=0;
   count+1;
   if Last.group_var then output;
run;
```

To handle repetitive tasks, DO loops and DO WHILE statements become indispensable. For instance, an incremental summation over a specified range can be achieved as follows:

```
data sum_loop;
   total = 0;
   do i = 1 to 10;
      total + i;
   end;
run;
```

The RETAIN statement plays a crucial role in preserving variable values across iterations of the Data Step. Here is an example that uses RETAIN to carry forward a previous value:

```
data retain_example;
   set dataset;
   retain previous;
   if _N_ = 1 then previous = 0;
   difference = current - previous;
   previous = current;
run;
```

Generating summary statistics, such as sums or averages, can be efficiently performed within the Data Step. This code calculates the total sales for each group:

```
data summary;
   set sales;
   by product_id;
   if First.product_id then total_sales = 0;
   total_sales + amount;
   if Last.product_id then output;
run;
```

The MODIFY statement offers a powerful way to perform in-place data updates without creating new datasets, enhancing memory efficiency. An application of the MODIFY statement is:

```
data update;
   modify dataset_up;
   if condition then variable = new_value;
run;
```

Advanced array processing allows for simultaneous operations on multiple variables, as shown here where we standardize a set of scores:

```
data standardized;
    set scores;
    array score_vars{*} score1-score5;
    do i = 1 to dim(score_vars);
        score_vars{i} = (score_vars{i} - mean(score_vars{i})) / std(score_vars{i});
    end;
run;
```

These sophisticated Data Step techniques will empower you to handle complex data scenarios, enhancing your proficiency and efficiency in SAS programming.

9.2 Using the SET Statement for Multiple Datasets

The SET statement in the SAS data step is pivotal for reading and combining multiple datasets. This section explores how to efficiently use the SET statement to achieve complex data manipulations and explains various scenarios where it becomes indispensable.

The basic form of the SET statement to read multiple datasets is straightforward. Consider two datasets, data1 and data2, each containing similar structures:

```
DATA combined;
    SET data1 data2;
RUN;
```

In this example, SAS will read all observations from data1 followed by all observations from data2. The combined dataset will contain the concatenated rows of both data1 and data2.

A crucial aspect to remember when using the SET statement is the alignment of variable definitions across the datasets involved. Variables with the same names in different datasets should ideally have the same type and length to avoid discrepancies in the combined dataset.

When datasets have differing structures, SAS merges the datasets intelligently based on variable names but aligns content by column, which may lead to unintended missing values where the datasets do not align perfectly.

To address such scenarios, one might need to specify RENAME or

DROP statements as follows:

```
DATA combined;
    SET data1 (RENAME=(old_var=new_var)) data2;
RUN;
```

In certain use cases, it is necessary to carry over variables from multiple datasets without loss of integrity. Suppose data1 and data2 contain different but essential variables. You can use a more comprehensive approach:

```
DATA combined;
    SET data1 (KEEP=name age) data2 (KEEP=address phone);
RUN;
```

Here, the KEEP option ensures that only specified variables are read from each dataset, creating a cohesive combined dataset with the selected variables.

An advanced use of the SET statement is interleaving datasets using the BY statement. Interleaving allows for the merging of datasets by a common variable, which is particularly useful for sorted datasets. Suppose data1 and data2 are sorted by id:

```
DATA interleaved;
    SET data1 data2;
    BY id;
RUN;
```

The BY statement facilitates the combined dataset to be sorted by id and maintains logical grouping, an essential requirement for subsequent data analysis.

Pre-processing steps such as sorting the datasets beforehand are mandatory:

```
PROC SORT DATA=data1;
    BY id;
RUN;

PROC SORT DATA=data2;
    BY id;
RUN;
```

For scenario where the datasets have different structures and some preprocessing like reordering or merging data based on conditions is needed, the IF-THEN construct can be utilized. Consider datasets students and teachers:

```
DATA school;
    SET students teachers;
    IF _N_ <= NOBS1 THEN DO;
```

```
        /* Processing for students */
    END;
    ELSE DO;
        /* Processing for teachers */
    END;
RUN;
```

The _N_ variable represents the iteration number within the data step, allowing the conditional logic to differentiate the source dataset. NOBS1 would be obtained by a preliminary SET statement with the NOBS option:

```
DATA _NULL_;
    SET students NOBS=NOBS1;
    CALL SYMPUT('NOBS1', NOBS1);
    STOP;
RUN;
```

Utilize CALL SYMPUT to store the number of observations into a macro variable, facilitating adaptive processing within your data step.

Careful consideration of memory and processing efficiency is essential when working with very large datasets. In such cases, options like OBS=, FIRSTOBS=, and temporary datasets can optimize the performance.

The versatility of the SET statement provides SAS programmers with powerful tools to combine and manipulate datasets seamlessly. Mastering these techniques allows for efficient and robust data preparation workflows, essential for sophisticated analyses.

Building on foundational concepts, this advanced usage enhances your capability to handle complex datasets effectively.

9.3 Interleaving Data with the BY Statement

The BY statement in SAS is a powerful tool used to interleave or combine datasets based on the values of one or more variables. Interleaving is the process of merging datasets in a sorted order, aligning observations from each dataset according to the BY variables.

BY **Statement Syntax**:

```
BY by-variable(s);
```

To utilize the BY statement effectively, the input datasets must be sorted by the BY variable(s) beforehand. The PROC SORT procedure can be utilized prior to the data step to ensure that each dataset is ordered correctly.

Sorting Datasets:

```
proc sort data=dataset1;
    by by-variable;
run;

proc sort data=dataset2;
    by by-variable;
run;
```

Once the datasets have been sorted, the SET statement along with the BY statement can be used within a data step to interleave the datasets. The following example demonstrates this concept:

```
data interleaved_data;
    set dataset1 dataset2;
    by by-variable;
run;
```

Example of Interleaving Datasets: Consider two datasets, dataset1 and dataset2, that contain the same by-variable, representing chronological order dates, and additional data variables.

```
/* Dataset 1 example structure */
data dataset1;
    input date : date9. value1;
    format date date9.;
    datalines;
01JAN2023 10
02JAN2023 20
04JAN2023 30
;
run;

/* Dataset 2 example structure */
data dataset2;
    input date : date9. value2;
    format date date9.;
    datalines;
02JAN2023 100
03JAN2023 200
05JAN2023 300
;
run;

/* Sorting datasets by the variable 'date' */
proc sort data=dataset1;
    by date;
run;

proc sort data=dataset2;
    by date;
run;

/* Interleaving using the BY statement */
```

```
data interleaved_data;
    set dataset1 dataset2;
    by date;
run;
```

The resulting dataset, interleaved_data, will have observations listed in chronological order, combining the rows from both dataset1 and dataset2.

date	value1	value2
01JAN2023	10	.
02JAN2023	20	100
03JAN2023	.	200
04JAN2023	30	.
05JAN2023	.	300

In this output, observing empty cells is significant. They indicate that a corresponding value from one dataset was not present for a specific date. This result is achieved through the alignment of rows based on the BY variable while preserving the order.

To further handle potential issues and provide accurate information across datasets, the IN= data set option can be used. This option creates temporary variables that indicate the source dataset from which each observation originated.

Using IN= to Track Dataset Source:

```
data interleaved_data;
    set dataset1(in=in1) dataset2(in=in2);
    by date;
    if in1 then source='dataset1';
    if in2 then source='dataset2';
run;
```

date	value1	value2	source
01JAN2023	10	.	dataset1
02JAN2023	20	100	dataset1
03JAN2023	.	200	dataset2
04JAN2023	30	.	dataset1
05JAN2023	.	300	dataset2

It is essential to grasp that the ordering of the observations is contingent upon the sorting criteria in the BY variable. Careful attention must be paid to the preprocessing step to ensure valid and meaningful interleaving.

This technique is highly beneficial, especially for consolidating time-series data, merging dataset updates, or combining observations across varied datasets. By harnessing the BY statement, data processing becomes organized and systematic, leveraging SAS's powerful capabilities for data integration.

9.4 Creating and Using Indexes

Indexes in SAS enhance data retrieval speeds, particularly in large datasets. By creating indexes, the user can significantly improve the efficiency of data step operations and PROC steps that involve WHERE clauses. This section will elucidate index creation, types of indexes, and appropriate usage scenarios.

Definition and Purpose of Indexes

An index is a data structure that allows faster retrieval of records from a dataset. It functions similarly to an index in a book, where it helps to quickly locate specific rows based on key values. SAS supports two types of indexes: simple and composite. A simple index is based on a single variable, while a composite index involves multiple variables.

Creating an Index

To create an index in SAS, use the INDEX option in the DATA step or with the PROC DATASETS procedure. Here's an example of creating both simple and composite indexes in a dataset:

```
data work.example;
    input ID Name $ Age Height;
    datalines;
    1 John 25 68
    2 Alice 30 64
    3 Bob 22 71
    ;
run;

/* Creating a simple index on the variable ID */
data work.example (index=(ID));
    set work.example;
run;

/* Creating a composite index on Age and Height */
proc datasets lib=work;
    modify example;
    index create AgeHeight=(Age Height);
quit;
```

In the DATA step, the (index=(ID)) option creates a simple index named ID on the ID variable. The PROC DATASETS procedure with the index create statement generates a composite index named AgeHeight based on the Age and Height variables.

Using Indexes

Indexes streamline data access in operations that use the WHERE clause in DATA step or PROC steps. The following example showcases how the created indexes are used:

```
data work.filtered;
    set work.example;
    where ID = 2; * Uses simple index ID;
run;

proc print data=work.example;
    where Age = 30 and Height = 64; * Uses composite index AgeHeight;
run;
```

In this code, the where clause in both the DATA step and PROC PRINT takes advantage of the existing indexes, thereby minimizing the data access time.

Verifying Index Usage

To ensure SAS is using the indexes, one can use the OPTIONS MSGLEVEL=I statement, which provides messages about the efficiency of the index usage:

```
options msglevel=i;

data work.filtered;
    set work.example;
    where ID = 2;
run;
```

Upon execution, SAS will display messages in the log indicating whether the index has been successfully utilized.

Benefits and Considerations

Using indexes can yield significant performance improvements; however, there are trade-offs involved. Index creation and maintenance introduce additional overhead, particularly during data manipulations like insertions, deletions, and updates. The benefits are most pronounced in read-heavy scenarios with relatively static datasets.

Several factors should be considered before deciding to use an index:

- **Read-Heavy Workloads**: If the dataset undergoes frequent read operations with selective filtering, indexes can greatly enhance performance.
- **Selective Queries**: When queries often retrieve a small subset of rows based on specific criteria, indexes help expedite access.
- **Update Frequency**: Datasets with frequent updates may experience overhead due to index maintenance. Assess the balance between read and write operations.

- **Storage Considerations**: Indexes consume additional storage space. Evaluate the available storage resources against the performance benefits.

SAS provides tools like PROC CONTENTS to display index information for a dataset:

```
proc contents data=work.example;
run;
```

The output lists existing indexes and relevant attributes, aiding in effective index management and optimization of data access patterns. Through judicious use of indexes, users can achieve substantial improvements in data retrieval efficiency, underlining their importance in advanced data step techniques.

9.5 Understanding and Using Hash Objects

In SAS, hash objects provide an efficient way to perform key-value lookups and manipulations directly within the data step. Introduced in SAS 9, hash objects are in-memory data structures that facilitate rapid data retrieval, making them particularly suitable for applications involving large datasets and complex data processing tasks.

To use hash objects, we must understand their declaration, methods, and practical applications. Consider the following key phases in the use of hash objects: initialization, data insertion, and data manipulation.

Initialization

Creating a hash object within a data step requires declaring it and defining the key and data variables. This is typically done using the DECLARE statement:

```
data example;
    if _N_ = 1 then do;
        declare hash h(dataset: "dataset_name");
        h.defineKey('key_variable');
        h.defineData('data_variable1', 'data_variable2');
        h.defineDone();
    end;
run;
```

In the example above, DECLARE initializes a hash object h using data from dataset_name. The defineKey method specifies the key variable, while defineData defines the data variables stored in the hash object.

The defineDone method finalizes the definition.

Data Insertion

Once the hash object is initialized, we can load data into it. If the hash object is based on a SAS dataset (as in the above example), the variables from that dataset are automatically inserted. For a hash object without a predefined dataset, we can explicitly add key-value pairs:

```
data example;
    if _N_ = 1 then do;
        declare hash h();
        h.defineKey('key_variable');
        h.defineData('data_variable1', 'data_variable2');
        h.defineDone();
        h.add(key: 'key1', data: 'value1a', 'value1b');
        h.add(key: 'key2', data: 'value2a', 'value2b');
    end;
run;
```

In this code, individual records are added to the hash object using the add method, associating keys with corresponding data values.

Data Manipulation

Hash objects offer various methods for manipulating and accessing data. Common methods include find, output, and remove. Below, we illustrate these methods with practical examples:

```
data example;
    if _N_ = 1 then do;
        declare hash h();
        h.defineKey('key_variable');
        h.defineData('data_variable1', 'data_variable2');
        h.defineDone();
        h.add(key: 'key1', data: 'value1a', 'value1b');
        h.add(key: 'key2', data: 'value2a', 'value2b');
    end;

    key_variable = 'key1';
    if h.find() = 0 then do;
        put data_variable1=;
        put data_variable2=;
    end;
run;
```

In this code snippet, the find method searches the hash object for the specified key. If the key exists, the corresponding data values are retrieved. The output method allows outputting hash object data to a new dataset, while remove deletes a key-value pair.

Example: Joining Tables Using Hash Objects

As an efficient alternative to traditional joins, hash objects enable rapid data lookups without requiring data to be sorted. Consider the following example where we join two datasets using hash objects:

```
data main;
    input id $ value;
    datalines;
    A 100
    B 200
    C 300
    ;
run;

data lookup;
    input id $ description $;
    datalines;
    A Apple
    B Banana
    C Cherry
    ;
run;

data joined;
    if _N_ = 1 then do;
        declare hash h(dataset: 'lookup');
        h.defineKey('id');
        h.defineData('description');
        h.defineDone();
    end;

    set main;
    if h.find() = 0 then output;
run;

proc print data=joined;
run;
```

The output of this code will be:

Obs	id	value	description
1	A	100	Apple
2	B	200	Banana
3	C	300	Cherry

In this example, the hash object facilitates a join between the main and lookup datasets by loading the lookup dataset into memory and matching records on the id variable.

By leveraging hash objects, SAS programmers gain access to powerful tools for managing complex data relationships, optimizing data retrieval, and improving the efficiency of their data processing workflows. Proper mastery of hash objects enhances one's capability to handle intricate data manipulations seamlessly within the data step.

9.6 Advanced Data Merging Techniques

In SAS, merging datasets is a fundamental operation, especially vital when working with complex data analysis tasks. This section expands on foundational merging techniques to address more advanced scenarios. The effective use of merging ensures that data is combined accurately and efficiently, facilitating robust analysis.

Multiple Key Merging

When merging datasets based on multiple key variables, it is essential to define all the necessary keys in the BY statement. Consider two datasets dataset1 and dataset2, each containing variables id, year, and various other attributes. To merge these datasets by id and year, the following syntax is used:

```
data merged_dataset;
    merge dataset1 dataset2;
    by id year;
run;
```

This approach aligns records precisely when both key variables match across the datasets, ensuring that only appropriate rows are combined.

Merging with IN= Option

The IN= option in the MERGE statement is instrumental in discerning which dataset(s) contribute to the merged output. This boolean variable flags the presence of observations in specific datasets, allowing for conditional processing post-merge. For example:

```
data merged_dataset;
    merge dataset1 (in=a) dataset2 (in=b);
    by id;
    if a and b then source='both';
    else if a then source='dataset1';
    else if b then source='dataset2';
run;
```

The variables a and b will be TRUE (1) for records from dataset1 and dataset2, respectively. This capability is crucial for tasks that require tracking the origin of data.

Handling Many-to-Many Merges

A complex scenario arises when many-to-many relationships exist between datasets. SAS does not support direct many-to-many merges within the DATA step due to the ambiguity in record matching. Instead, SQL procedures or explicit duplication through PROC SQL are recommended:

```
proc sql;
    create table merged_dataset as
    select a.*, b.*
    from dataset1 as a
    inner join dataset2 as b
    on a.id = b.id and a.year = b.year;
quit;
```

SQL join operations handle many-to-many relationships by generating Cartesian products of matching rows, ensuring no information is inadvertently excluded or inaccurately combined.

Merging with Conditional Logic

Conditional logic within a merge alters the resulting dataset based on specific criteria, essential for nuanced data integration tasks. Employing the IF-THEN construct in combination with the IN= option allows for granular control over the merge output:

```
data conditional_merged;
    merge dataset1 (in=a) dataset2 (in=b);
    by id;
    if a and b then do;
        combined_var = var1 + var2;
    end;
    else if a then do;
        combined_var = var1;
    end;
    else if b then do;
        combined_var = var2;
    end;
run;
```

Such flexibility ensures that the merged dataset meets complex analytical needs and adheres to specific business logic.

Using the RENAME= and DROP= Options

To prevent naming conflicts and streamline datasets during merges, the RENAME= and DROP= options can be used to control variable names and their inclusion. Renaming variables to avoid overlap is necessary when datasets share common variable names with different semantics:

```
data merged_dataset;
    merge dataset1 (rename=(weight=weight1)) dataset2 (rename=(weight=weight2));
    by id;
    total_weight = weight1 + weight2;
    drop weight1 weight2;
run;
```

This technique ensures clarity in the resultant dataset, preventing ambiguity and facilitating straightforward analysis.

Merging Large Datasets

Handling large datasets efficiently during merge operations requires considering system memory and processing time. Utilizing indexes can significantly speed up the merge process. First, create an index on key variables in both datasets:

```
proc datasets lib=work;
    modify dataset1;
    index create id;
    modify dataset2;
    index create id;
run;
```

An indexed merge operation performs more efficiently, leveraging binary search mechanisms to reduce computational complexity.

Advanced data merging techniques in SAS empower users to undertake robust data integration tasks, essential for comprehensive data analysis projects. Understanding and applying these methods ensures data is merged precisely, maintaining integrity and facilitating insightful analytical outcomes.

9.7 Using First. and Last. Variables

First. and Last. variables, also known as indicator variables, are automatic variables created by the BY statement during data step processing. These variables are instrumental in controlling and manipulating grouped data within a dataset. This section discusses the concept, usage, and practical examples of First. and Last. variables.

When a BY statement is specified in a data step, SAS automatically creates two variables for each variable listed in the BY statement: First.variable and Last.variable. These variables are Boolean indicators that denote the first and last observation within a group, as defined by the BY statement. First.variable is set to 1 for the first observation in a group and 0 for all others. Correspondingly, Last.variable is set to 1 for the last observation in a group and 0 for all others.

A common use case of First. and Last. variables involves computing summary statistics for grouped data. Consider the dataset sales shown below:

sales

```
-----------------
Month  Sales
-----------------
Mar    100
Mar    150
Mar    200
Apr    300
Apr    350
May    400
May    450
May    500
```

Assume we want to calculate the total sales for each month. This can be efficiently achieved using First. and Last. variables, as demonstrated in the following SAS code:

```
data total_sales;
  set sales;
  by Month;
  if first.Month then total_sales = 0;
  total_sales + Sales;
  if last.Month then output;
run;
```

```
total_sales
---------------
Month  Total_Sales
---------------
Mar    450
Apr    650
May    1350
```

In this example:

- The by Month statement tells SAS to process the data by the value of the Month variable.
- if first.Month then total_sales = 0; initializes the cumulative total_sales at the start of a new month.
- The statement total_sales + Sales; accumulates the sales within each month.
- if last.Month then output; writes the sum for the month when the last observation for a month is reached.

Another advanced technique involves using First. and Last. variables to identify and isolate groups of duplicate records. Consider a dataset where we have multiple records for customers, and we aim to keep only the first and last record for each customer.

```
data unique_customers;
  set customers;
  by CustomerID;
  if first.CustomerID or last.CustomerID then output;
run;
```

This code retains only the first and last observations for each CustomerID, thus reducing redundancy.

We can also use First. and Last. variables to perform tasks such as tagging the start or end of groups, generating sequence numbers within groups, and sub-setting data efficiently. The following example illustrates generating sequence numbers within groups:

```
data seq_numbers;
  set customers;
  by CustomerID;
  if first.CustomerID then seq_num = 0;
  seq_num + 1;
run;
```

For each CustomerID, seq_num resets to 0 at the start and increments for each subsequent record within the same CustomerID group, providing a sequence number within each group.

Through these examples, it becomes evident that understanding and utilizing the First. and Last. variables provides a powerful mechanism for managing grouped data effectively within the SAS environment. These constructs facilitate precise control over data transformation and aggregation tasks, contributing significantly to advanced data step techniques.

9.8 Programming with DO Loops and DO WHILE Statements

The usage of DO loops and DO WHILE statements significantly enhances the efficiency and capability of data step processing in SAS. These looping mechanisms allow for repetitive execution of a code block, which is fundamental in various data manipulation and computational tasks.

A DO loop in SAS is used to execute a block of code a fixed number of times. It can also iterate over a specified set of values. The basic syntax of a DO loop is as follows:

```
DO index-variable = start TO stop <BY increment>;
```

```
    /* Code to be executed repeatedly */
END;
```

index-variable serves as a loop control variable, start and stop specify the range of the loop, and increment provides the step size between iterations.

Consider an example where you need to create a dataset containing squares of numbers from 1 to 10. The following code demonstrates this:

```
DATA squares;
    DO i = 1 TO 10;
        square = i * i;
        OUTPUT;
    END;
RUN;
```

In this snippet, the DO loop iterates from 1 to 10, computing the square of each value and writing the result to the squares dataset.

Another form of the DO loop allows iteration over a specific set of values. For instance:

```
DATA custom_squares;
    DO i = 2, 4, 6, 8, 10;
        square = i * i;
        OUTPUT;
    END;
RUN;
```

Here, the loop iterates over the specified values (2, 4, 6, 8, and 10) only.

DO WHILE statements provide additional control by allowing the repetition of a block of code based on a condition. The syntax for a DO WHILE loop is given by:

```
DO WHILE (condition);
    /* Code to be executed while the condition is true */
END;
```

The loop executes as long as the condition is true. For illustration, consider the following example where we want to sum consecutive numbers until the sum exceeds 50:

```
DATA sum_numbers;
    total = 0;
    i = 1;
    DO WHILE (total <= 50);
        total + i; /* shorthand for total = total + i */
        i + 1;
        OUTPUT;
```

```
    END;
RUN;
```

In this example, the DO WHILE loop continues to iterate and sum the numbers while the total is less than or equal to 50.

A DO UNTIL loop is similar but checks the condition after the loop body executes, ensuring that the loop runs at least once:

```
DO UNTIL (condition);
    /* Code to be executed until the condition becomes true */
END;
```

Using a DO UNTIL loop, we can achieve similar functionality but with a guarantee of at least one execution:

```
DATA sum_numbers_until;
    total = 0;
    i = 1;
    DO UNTIL (total > 50);
        total + i;
        i + 1;
        OUTPUT;
    END;
RUN;
```

Complex looping scenarios often involve nested DO loops, where one loop operates inside another. An example is generating a multiplication table:

```
DATA multiplication_table;
    DO i = 1 TO 10;
        DO j = 1 TO 10;
            product = i * j;
            OUTPUT;
        END;
    END;
RUN;
```

This nested loop structure iterates over all combinations of i and j to generate the products for a 10x10 multiplication table.

Efficiency in reading and processing large datasets can be achieved by using DO loops in combination with the SET statement. Here, an example demonstrates reading multiple datasets and processing them iteratively:

```
DATA combined_data;
    SET dataset1
        dataset2
        dataset3;
    DO i = 1 TO N; /* N represents the number of rows in the current dataset */
        /* Processing code */
        OUTPUT;
```

```
    END;
RUN;
```

DO loops and DO WHILE statements provide robust mechanisms for iterative processing within the DATA step. Understanding and utilizing these constructs is essential for efficient and advanced data manipulation tasks in SAS. Their versatility enables diverse applications, from simple iterations to complex nested operations, streamlining data management and computational tasks.

9.9 Retaining Values Across Iterations with the RETAIN Statement

In SAS programming, the RETAIN statement provides a mechanism to persist the values of variables across multiple iterations of the data step. Unlike the default behavior, where variable values are reset to missing at the beginning of each iteration, the RETAIN statement allows certain variables to remember their values from one iteration to the next.

The primary application of the RETAIN statement is to accumulate values, create running totals, or maintain the state of a variable across data step iterations. This section will elucidate the syntax and intricacies of the RETAIN statement, supplemented by examples to demonstrate its utility in data manipulation.

Basic Syntax:

The RETAIN statement is straightforward in syntax:

```
RETAIN variable-list initial-value-list;
```

- variable-list: A list of one or more variables whose values are to be retained.
- initial-value-list: Optional initial values for the retained variables. If omitted, variables are initialized to missing or 0 in the case of numeric variables.

Example 1: Accumulating a Running Total

Consider a dataset sales containing daily sales amounts. We aim to create a running total of sales:

```
DATA sales;
    INPUT day sales_amount;
    DATALINES;
    1 100
    2 200
    3 150
    4 175
    ;
RUN;

DATA running_total;
    SET sales;
    RETAIN total_sales 0;
    total_sales + sales_amount;
RUN;
```

day	sales_amount	total_sales
1	100	100
2	200	300
3	150	450
4	175	625

In this example, total_sales retains its value across iterations, allowing us to compute a cumulative total. The sum statement total_sales + sales_amount; adds sales_amount to total_sales for each observation.

Example 2: Carrying Forward the Last Non-Missing Value

The RETAIN statement can also maintain the last non-missing value of a variable. Consider the following dataset temperature with some missing temperature measurements:

```
DATA temperature;
    INPUT day temperature;
    DATALINES;
    1 22.5
    2 .
    3 23.1
    4 .
    5 24.0
    ;
RUN;

DATA forward_fill;
    SET temperature;
    RETAIN last_temp;
    IF NOT MISSING(temperature) THEN last_temp = temperature;
    ELSE temperature = last_temp;
RUN;
```

day	temperature	last_temp
1	22.5	22.5
2	22.5	22.5
3	23.1	23.1
4	23.1	23.1
5	24.0	24.0

Here, last_temp retains the last non-missing value encountered. In cases where temperature is missing, the data step assigns the last recorded value to temperature.

Interaction with BY-Group Processing

When processing data by groups using the BY statement, it may be necessary to reset retained variables at the start of each new group. This can be achieved in conjunction with FIRST. and LAST. variables.

```
DATA sales_by_region;
    INPUT region $ day sales_amount;
    DATALINES;
    North 1 100
    North 2 200
    North 3 150
    South 1 175
    South 2 125
    South 3 100
    ;
RUN;

DATA cumulative_sales;
    SET sales_by_region;
    BY region;
    RETAIN total_sales 0;
    IF FIRST.region THEN total_sales = 0;
    total_sales + sales_amount;
RUN;
```

region	day	sales_amount	total_sales
North	1	100	100
North	2	200	300
North	3	150	450
South	1	175	175
South	2	125	300
South	3	100	400

In this code, the total_sales variable is reset to zero at the beginning of each region group, as indicated by the FIRST.region conditional. This ensures that cumulative sales totals are calculated within each region independently.

The RETAIN statement is a powerful feature in the SAS data step, enabling complex data manipulations and state management across iterations. By using RETAIN, it is possible to create running totals, handle missing values, and manage group-wise data effectively.

9.10 Generating Summary Statistics in the Data Step

Generating summary statistics within the SAS data step is an essential skill for data manipulation and analysis. The process involves creating descriptive statistics such as sums, means, counts, maximums, and minimums to derive meaningful insights from the data. This section illustrates detailed methods and techniques for effectively calculating these statistics using the data step.

To begin with, consider using the retain statement to hold values across iterations of the data step. Retaining values is fundamental when calculating running totals or cumulative statistics.

```
data summary_stats;
    set original_data;
    retain total_sales count_sales max_sales min_sales mean_sales;

    if _N_ = 1 then do;
        total_sales = 0;
        count_sales = 0;
        max_sales = .;
        min_sales = .;
    end;

    total_sales + sales;
    count_sales + 1;
    if sales > max_sales or max_sales = . then max_sales = sales;
    if sales < min_sales or min_sales = . then min_sales = sales;

    if count_sales > 0 then mean_sales = total_sales / count_sales;
run;
```

The _N_ variable is used to initialize the retained variables only once at the beginning of the data step. This setup ensures that the accumulating variables, such as total_sales, count_sales, max_sales, and min_sales, maintain their values across data step iterations.

The addition operator + is applied in an accumulating context, so total_sales + sales; adds the current sales value to total_sales. Similarly, count_sales + 1; increments the count of records processed.

max_sales = sales; and min_sales = sales; are conditional statements ensuring the maximum and minimum values are updated appropriately. The mean is calculated using a conditional statement to avoid division by zero errors.

For more complex summary statistics, consider using the summary procedure in tandem with the data step. For instance, when dealing with grouped data, the BY statement is indispensable. Here is an example to illustrate calculating grouped summary statistics:

```
proc sort data=original_data;
    by group_variable;
run;

data grouped_summary;
    set sorted_data;
    by group_variable;
    retain total_sales count_sales mean_sales;

    if first.group_variable then do;
        total_sales = 0;
        count_sales = 0;
    end;

    total_sales + sales;
    count_sales + 1;

    if last.group_variable then do;
        mean_sales = total_sales / count_sales;
        output;
    end;
run;
```

In this example, the by statement is used to specify the grouping variable (group_variable). The first. and last. variables are pivotal for resetting and outputting the summary statistics respectively. When first.group_variable is true, the retained variables are initialized to zero. Throughout the group, the statistics accumulate, and upon reaching last.group_variable, the mean is calculated, and the record is outputted.

An alternative method involves the proc means or proc summary procedures, which can simplify the calculation of summary statistics while offering flexibility to output to datasets:

```
proc means data=original_data noprint;
    by group_variable;
    var sales;
    output out=summary_stats
        sum=total_sales
        mean=mean_sales
        max=max_sales
        min=min_sales
        n=count_sales;
run;
```

In this procedure, the noprint option is specified to suppress printed output, the by group_variable; indicates that summary statistics are computed for each group, and the var sales; denotes the variable for which statistics are calculated. The output statement directs the procedure to create a new dataset (summary_stats) containing the desired statistics (total_sales, mean_sales, max_sales, min_sales, and count_sales).

This comprehensive approach ensures that summary statistics are calculated accurately and efficiently, leveraging both the data step and SAS procedures. By combining these techniques, one can optimize data processing, gain deep insights, and ensure robust analytical capabilities.

9.11 Efficient Data Handling with the MODIFY Statement

The MODIFY statement in SAS provides capabilities for updating and managing data efficiently within the Data Step. Unlike the SET statement, which reads data sequentially, the MODIFY statement offers the flexibility to update observations in place, minimizing the need for creating intermediate datasets and reducing I/O operations. This feature is particularly useful for large datasets where performance and resource management are critical.

To understand the operational aspects of the MODIFY statement, let's examine its syntax and practical usage scenarios. The basic form of the MODIFY statement is as follows:

```
MODIFY dataset-name;
```

Here, dataset-name refers to the name of the dataset that needs to be modified. Unlike the SET statement, no new datasets are created. Instead, the observations in the dataset are directly updated based on conditions specified within the Data Step.

Key Features of the MODIFY Statement:

- Efficient Updating: Directly update observations without creating a new dataset.
- Integration with Key Variables: Use key variables to locate and update specific observations.
- Reduced I/O Operations: Minimize read/write operations, leading to improved performance.
- Enhanced Control Over Data: Conditions and expressions can determine which observations are updated.

Example: Updating Observations with Key Variables

Consider a scenario where we have a dataset containing employee information. We want to update the salaries of employees based on their employee ID. We can use the MODIFY statement with a BY statement to achieve this.

```
data employees;
    modify employees;
    by EmpID;
    if EmpID = 102 then Salary = 75000;
    else if EmpID = 205 then Salary = 85000;
run;
```

In this example, the dataset employees is modified directly. The BY statement ensures that the dataset is processed by the key variable EmpID, allowing specific observations to be located and updated efficiently.

Using the MODIFY Statement with a Transaction Dataset

A common use case for the MODIFY statement involves updating a master dataset with changes specified in a transaction dataset. The master dataset represents the current state of data, while the transaction dataset contains new updates.

```
data master;
    input EmpID $ Name $ Salary;
    datalines;
    101 John 50000
    102 Jane 60000
    103 Jim 55000
;
run;

data transactions;
    input EmpID $ NewSalary;
    datalines;
    102 75000
    103 70000
;
run;

data master;
    modify master transactions;
    by EmpID;
    if _IORC_ = 0 then Salary = NewSalary;
    else output;
run;
```

In this code, the MODIFY statement processes both the master and transactions datasets based on the EmpID key variable. The _IORC_-automatic variable facilitates the identification of matches between the master and transaction datasets. When _IORC_ = 0, an observation in the master dataset is found, and the NewSalary is updated accordingly.

Error Handling with MODIFY Statement

Handling missing or unmatched key values gracefully is essential to prevent errors during data updates. Utilizing the _ERROR_ and _IORC_ variables, we can manage these conditions effectively.

```
data master;
    modify master transactions;
    by EmpID;
    if _IORC_ = %sysrc(_SOK) then do;
        Salary = NewSalary;
        _ERROR_ = 0;
    end;
    else do;
        put "ERROR: Employee ID not found - " EmpID;
    end;
run;
```

In this example, the _IORC_ variable is compared against the macro variable %sysrc(_SOK), which indicates a successful match. If no match is found, an error message is written to the log, and further action can be taken as needed.

Combining MODIFY Statement with UPDATE and DELETE Actions

Beyond simple updates, the MODIFY statement can be used with the REPLACE and REMOVE commands to achieve more complex data manipulation.

```
data master;
    modify master;
    by EmpID;
    if EmpID = 102 then do;
        Salary = 80000;
        replace;
    end;
    else if EmpID = 103 then do;
        remove;
    end;
run;
```

In this example, the REPLACE statement updates the salary for the employee with ID 102, while the REMOVE statement deletes the observation for the employee with ID 103. These actions illustrate the versatility of the MODIFY statement in managing data changes.

Best Practices for Using MODIFY Statement

- Always backup your dataset before performing modifications.
- Test the MODIFY operations on a subset of data to ensure cor-

rectness.

- Use key variables wisely to ensure intentional and accurate updates.
- Manage errors and unexpected conditions using _ERROR_ and _IORC_ variables.
- Monitor the log for messages to ensure operations execute as expected.

The MODIFY statement empowers SAS programmers to handle data updates effectively while minimizing resource usage. When used appropriately, it significantly enhances data processing efficiency and robustness.

9.12 Advanced Array Processing

Advanced array processing in SAS provides powerful capabilities for managing and manipulating data efficiently within the DATA step. Arrays in SAS allow users to perform repetitive calculations, transform data, and manage complex datasets efficiently. This section presents advanced techniques in array processing, including the use of multidimensional arrays, dynamic arrays, and leveraging array processing for conditional logic.

Multidimensional Arrays

Multidimensional arrays can be defined to organize data in a matrix structure. This structure can simplify operations that involve rows and columns. To declare a multidimensional array, define the array name and specify the dimensions:

```
data multidim_example;
   array matrix[3, 3] m1-m9; /* Declares a 3x3 multidimensional array */

   /* Initialize the array */
   do i = 1 to 3;
      do j = 1 to 3;
         matrix[i, j] = i * j; /* Assigns the product of indices to the array elements */
      end;
   end;

   /* Output the data for verification */
   do k = 1 to 3;
      do l = 1 to 3;
         output;
```

```
        end;
    end;
run;

proc print data=multidim_example;
run;
```

In this example, matrix[3, 3] declares a 3x3 array. The nested DO loops initialize each element with the product of its indices, allowing for efficient data manipulation and output.

Dynamic Arrays

Dynamic arrays offer flexibility by letting the size of the array be determined during execution. This can be particularly useful when the number of elements is not known beforehand. Dynamic arrays in SAS can be created using the _TEMPORARY_ keyword:

```
data dynamic_array_example;
    array scores[*] _temporary_; /* Dynamic array */
    retain count 0;

    do i = 1 to 10;
        scores[i] = i * 10; /* Assign values to the dynamic array */
        count + 1;
    end;

    /* Output each element of the dynamic array */
    do j = 1 to count;
        score = scores[j];
        output;
    end;
run;

proc print data=dynamic_array_example;
run;
```

Here, the scores[*] array uses _TEMPORARY_ to create a dynamic array where the elements are assigned values and later accessed for output.

Advanced Conditional Logic in Arrays

Utilizing arrays can simplify conditional logic operations. For instance, when processing threshold values across multiple variables, arrays allow for concise and readable code:

```
data threshold_check;
    array measurements[5] temp1-temp5;
    array results[5] _temporary_;

    do i = 1 to 5;
        if measurements[i] > 50 then
            results[i] = 1; /* Flag as above threshold */
        else
            results[i] = 0; /* Flag as below threshold */
```

```
    end;

    /* Create output dataset with flags */
    do j = 1 to 5;
        temp_id = j;
        result = results[j];
        output;
    end;
run;

proc print data=threshold_check;
run;
```

The arrays measurements[5] and results[5] streamline the process of flagging temperatures that exceed a specified threshold.

Performing Operations Across Arrays

Arrays in SAS can also be used to perform operations across multiple arrays simultaneously. This is particularly useful for tasks like vector addition:

```
data array_operations;
    array a[3] a1-a3 (1, 2, 3);
    array b[3] b1-b3 (4, 5, 6);
    array c[3] c1-c3;

    do i = 1 to 3;
        c[i] = a[i] + b[i]; /* Perform element-wise addition */
    end;

    /* Output the resultant array */
    output;
run;

proc print data=array_operations;
run;
```

In this example, arrays a[3] and b[3] contain predefined values. The DATA step computes the element-wise sum and stores the result in array c[3].

Using Arrays with BY-Groups

Arrays can interact with BY-groups for performing grouped operations efficiently. Consider the following example where we calculate the mean of test scores grouped by student ID:

```
data test_scores;
    input student_id test1-test5;
    datalines;
1 90 85 88 92 94
2 78 84 80 82 76
;
/* Further data lines */

data mean_scores;
```

```
    array scores[5] test1-test5;
    mean_score = mean(of test1-test5);
    output;
run;

proc sort data=test_scores;
    by student_id;
run;

proc means data=test_scores noprint;
    by student_id;
    var test1-test5;
    output out=mean_scores mean=mean_score;
run;

proc print data=mean_scores;
run;
```

The mean(of test1-test5) simplifies the calculation of the mean score for each student by utilizing the array scores.

Integrating these advanced array processing techniques into your SAS programs can enhance performance and maintainability, fostering efficient and powerful data manipulation capabilities. The use of multidimensional and dynamic arrays, combined with conditional logic and grouped operations, provides a robust toolkit for tackling complex data scenarios.

Chapter 10

Introduction to SAS Macros

This chapter introduces the SAS macro facility, focusing on dynamic code generation and automation. It covers macro variables, creating and using them, and employing macro functions and expressions. Readers will learn to define macros with %MACRO and %MEND, pass parameters, and utilize conditional execution with %IF-%THEN-%ELSE. The chapter also explores iterative processing with %DO loops, debugging macros, best practices for writing efficient macros, advanced macro techniques, and methods for storing and reusing macro code.

10.1 Introduction to SAS Macros

The SAS macro facility enables dynamic code generation and automation within the SAS environment. This facility is crucial for creating reusable, parameterized code that can adapt to varying requirements without the need for extensive manual rewriting. The emphasis on automation significantly enhances productivity, especially in repetitive tasks involving data manipulation and analysis.

Macros in SAS are composed of macro variables and macro programs. Macro variables store text strings that can be inserted into SAS code, fostering a dynamic coding approach.

Macro variables may be created with a \$ prefix and referenced by preceding the variable name with an ampersand (&), such as \$myvar="Hello" and referenced as &myvar. The macro processor evaluates these variables before passing the generated SAS statements to the compiler.

```
%let name = world;
%put Hello, &name.;
```

```
Hello, world
```

In this example, \$name is a macro variable containing the string "world" and is referenced within the %put statement using &name.. The macro processor substitutes &name with "world" before the %put statement executes, resulting in "Hello, world" being printed.

The macro facility also introduces powerful constructs for conditional and iterative execution, dramatically extending SAS programming capabilities. The primary mechanisms include:

- **Macro Definitions**: Defined using %MACRO and terminated with %MEND, macro definitions allow users to encapsulate code logic that can be invoked as needed.
- **Parameters**: Macro definitions can accept parameters, enhancing reusability by enabling variable input handling.
- **Conditional Execution**: %IF-%THEN-%ELSE constructs facilitate conditional logic within macros.
- **Iterative Processing**: %DO loops allow for repetitive execution of code blocks, controlled by macro variables.

For example, consider the simple macro definition below:

```
%macro greeting(name);
   %put Hello, &name.;
%mend greeting;

%greeting(SAS Programmer);
```

```
Hello, SAS Programmer.
```

In this macro, %macro greeting(name); introduces a macro named greeting with one parameter, name. The %put statement uses the parameter to print a greeting message. When %greeting(SAS Programmer); is invoked, it outputs "Hello, SAS Programmer."

The integration of conditional execution using %IF-%THEN-%ELSE constructs allows for decisions to be made within macro code, as demonstrated below.

```
%macro check_value(x);
   %if &x > 5 %then %do;
      %put &x is greater than 5;
   %end;
   %else %do;
      %put &x is 5 or less;
   %end;
%mend check_value;

%check_value(10);
```

```
10 is greater than 5
```

In this example, the macro check_value examines the input parameter x. If x is greater than 5, it prints "&x is greater than 5". Otherwise, it prints "&x is 5 or less."

Iterative processing within macros utilizes %DO loops, which can execute a code block multiple times based on a specified criterion. Example:

```
%macro repeat_action(n);
   %do i=1 %to &n;
      %put This is iteration &i;
   %end;
%mend repeat_action;

%repeat_action(3);
```

```
This is iteration 1
This is iteration 2
This is iteration 3
```

The repeat_action macro runs the code block inside the %DO loop three times, as specified when %repeat_action(3); is called, resulting in multiple output lines indicating each iteration.

Macros can also be stored and reused across different SAS sessions using libraries or auto-call facilities. This chapter will unfold various methods and practices for optimal storage, reuse, and documentation of macro code.

To summarize, SAS macros provide a robust mechanism to automate and dynamically generate SAS code, significantly enhancing coding efficiency, reusability, and maintainability. Understanding the fundamentals introduced here sets a solid foundation for mastering more advanced techniques and practices in SAS macro programming.

10.2 Understanding Macro Variables

Macro variables in SAS are foundational elements in the SAS Macro Facility, enabling dynamic and flexible coding. They store text strings which can be substituted into SAS code during execution. The ability to define, store, and reuse these values across different parts of a program greatly enhances code efficiency and manageability. Macro variables are categorized into two types: automatic and user-defined.

Automatic Macro Variables are predefined by the SAS system and provide information about the SAS session and operating environment. These variables are readily available upon session initiation and do not require explicit definition. Examples include $\$\_N$, $\$\_VOKR$, $\$SYSDATE$, and $\$SYSJOBID$. Utilization of these variables allows users to dynamically insert system-specific information into their code. For instance:

```
data _null_;
  put "Current SAS System date: &SYSDATE Current SAS job id: &SYSJOBID";
run;
```

The output of the above code demonstrates the insertion of the system date and job ID at runtime.

```
Current SAS System date: 17OCT2023 Current SAS job id: 12345
```

User-Defined Macro Variables, on the other hand, are created by users to store specific values needed within their programs. These variables can be defined in various ways, including the %LET statement, functions such as symput, and during data step execution. The %LET statement assigns a value to a macro variable as follows:

```
%let city=New York;
%let population=8419000;
```

Subsequently, these macro variables can be utilized within the SAS program:

```
data _null_;
  put "City: &city Population: &population";
run;
```

This produces the following output:

```
City: New York Population: 8419000
```

Scope of Macro Variables is essential to understand for their efficient utilization. Macro variables have two scopes: local and global. Local macro variables are confined to the macro in which they are defined, while global macro variables are accessible throughout the entire SAS session. Without explicit scoping, variables defined using %LET are considered global. For instance:

```
%macro demo_scope;
   %let localvar=This is a local variable;
   %put NOTE: Inside Macro -> &localvar;
%mend demo_scope;

%demo_scope;

%put NOTE: Outside Macro -> &localvar;
```

Running this code will result in:

```
NOTE: Inside Macro -> This is a local variable
NOTE: Outside Macro -> Localvar Macro Variable Not Resolved
```

The above output illustrates that $localvar is inaccessible outside the demo_scope macro, confirming its local scope.

Creating Local Macro Variables within a macro can be performed using:

```
%local local_macro_var;
```

Whereas **Creating Global Macro Variables** is done by:

```
%global global_macro_var;
```

Consider the scenario where one needs to define a macro variable within a data step. Using the call symput routine allows data step values to be assigned to macro variables:

```
data _null_;
   call symput('avg_salary', '50000');
run;

%put Average Salary is &avg_salary;
```

Expected output is:

```
Average Salary is 50000
```

Understanding macro variables is paramount for proficient SAS programming. They offer powerful capabilities to store, manipulate, and dynamically substitute values within a SAS program. Grasping the various ways to define, utilize, and scope these variables significantly aids in crafting responsive and streamlined SAS code.

10.3 Creating and Using Macro Variables

Macro variables in SAS serve as essential components for dynamic code generation and automation. Macro variables store text and can be resolved or substituted during the execution of macro code. Understanding how to create and utilize macro variables effectively is critical for leveraging the full power of SAS.

Macro variables can be defined in multiple ways. One of the simplest methods is by utilizing the %LET statement. For example, consider the following:

```
%LET name = John;
```

This statement creates a macro variable named name with the value John. To use the value stored in a macro variable, precede its name with an ampersand (&). For example:

```
%PUT &name;
```

The above statement will output:

```
John
```

Macro variables can also be created using the CALL SYMPUT routine within a DATA step. CALL SYMPUT assigns a value to a macro variable based on the values of dataset variables. For instance:

```
DATA _NULL_;
    SET mydata;
    CALL SYMPUT('var_name', var_value);
RUN;
```

In this example, the value of var_value in the dataset mydata is assigned to the macro variable var_name for each observation in the dataset.

To dynamically assign unique values to macro variables, the CALL SYMPUTX can be used. It automatically trims leading and trailing blanks from the value before assigning it, enhancing the precision and usability of the macro variables.

Consider the following example:

```
DATA _NULL_;
    SET mydata;
    CALL SYMPUTX('var_name', TRIM(var_value));
RUN;
```

Furthermore, the PROC SQL step can also be utilized to create macro variables. PROC SQL enables querying and processing dataset information while creating macro variables simultaneously. Here is an example:

```
PROC SQL;
    SELECT avg(salary) INTO :avg_salary FROM employees;
QUIT;
```

This SQL statement calculates the average salary from the employees table and assigns it to the macro variable avg_salary. The macro variable can then be used as follows:

```
%PUT &avg_salary;
```

The output will be the calculated average salary value.

Here is an advanced use case that demonstrates creating and using multiple macro variables in a loop. This example will loop through a dataset, retrieving specific column values into macro variables:

```
DATA _NULL_;
    SET employees;
    CALL SYMPUTX(cats('emp_id_', _N_), ID);
    CALL SYMPUTX(cats('emp_name_', _N_), Name);
    CALL SYMPUTX(cats('emp_salary_', _N_), Salary);
RUN;
```

In this example, the CALL SYMPUTX function dynamically creates macro variables for each row in the employees dataset, naming them with the format emp_id_#, emp_name_#, and emp_salary_#, where # is the row number.

It is crucial to be aware of the scope of macro variables. By default, macro variables created using %LET are global, meaning they can be accessed from anywhere in the SAS session. Conversely, macro variables created within a macro or via a DATA step as illustrated may have local scope, accessible only within the specific macro.

Efficient use of macro variables can be exemplified through iterative processes. For instance, consider this scenario where macro variables are used to automate the generation of multiple reports:

Algorithm 2: Automating Report Generation Using Macro Variables

```
Data: Dataset sales_data
Result: Generated Reports for Each Region
%LET regions = North South East West ;
foreach region in North South East West do
    PROC REPORT DATA=sales_data
    WHERE Region="\&region";
    RUN;
```

In this example, the macro variable regions stores a list of regions. The %DO loop iterates over each region, generating a custom report for each one. This approach demonstrates the utility of macro variables in reducing repetitive code and enhancing code readability.

Through the examples and techniques outlined, it is evident that mastering macro variables in SAS lends significant advantages in terms of code efficiency, dynamic programming capabilities, and automation. Moreover, understanding the scope and application of macro variables ensures robust and maintainable SAS programs.

10.4 Macro Functions and Expressions

SAS macro functions provide a powerful way to manipulate and transform macro variables. They enable more complex operations within your macro code, facilitating the creation of dynamic and flexible SAS programs. This section explores a variety of SAS macro functions, illustrating how to use them effectively in different scenarios.

Macro functions in SAS operate similarly to data step functions but are explicitly designed for use within the macro environment. They can perform tasks such as string manipulation, arithmetic operations, date and time calculations, and conditional logic.

String Manipulation Functions

String manipulation is a common requirement in macros, and SAS provides several functions to handle strings dynamically. Let's start with some fundamental string functions:

- \%LEFT: Removes leading blanks from a string.
- \%TRIM: Removes trailing blanks from a string.

- \%UPCASE: Converts all characters in a string to uppercase.
- \%SUBSTR: Extracts a substring from a string.

Consider the following example that demonstrates the use of these functions:

```
%let str = SAS Macros ;
%put %left(&str);
%put %trim(&str);
%put %upcase(&str);
%put %substr(&str, 5, 6);
```

The output of these macro variable manipulations is as follows:

```
SAS Macros
  SAS Macros
SAS MACROS
Macros
```

Here, %LEFT removes the leading blanks, %TRIM removes trailing blanks, %UPCASE converts the entire string to uppercase, and %SUBSTR extracts a substring starting from position 5 and spanning 6 characters.

Arithmetic Functions

Arithmetic functions enable mathematical calculations within macros. Some frequently used arithmetic functions include:

- \%EVAL: Evaluates arithmetic and logical expressions.
- \%SYSEVALF: Evaluates arithmetic expressions with floating-point arithmetic.
- \%SUM: Computes the sum of values.

Here is an example illustrating these functions:

```
%let num1 = 10;
%let num2 = 5;
%let result1 = %eval(&num1 + &num2);
%let result2 = %sysevalf(&num1 / 3);
%let result3 = %sum(&num1, &num2);

%put &result1;
%put &result2;
%put &result3;
```

This produces the following output:

```
15
3.3333333
15
```

In this example, %EVAL calculates the sum of num1 and num2, %SYSEVALF performs floating-point division, and %SUM sums the values of num1 and num2.

Date and Time Functions

Date and time functions are crucial for handling temporal data within macros. Common date and time functions include:

- \%SYSFUNC: Allows the use of a SAS function within a macro.
- \%QSYSFUNC: Same as \%SYSFUNC, but prevents resolution of macro variables within the argument.

An example of using date and time functions is as follows:

```
%let today = %sysfunc(today());
%let current_year = %sysfunc(year(&today));
%let current_month = %sysfunc(month(&today));

%put 'Todays date: &today;
%put Current Year: &current_year;
%put Current Month: &current_month;
```

The output of this macro code section is:

```
Today's date: 22777
Current Year: 2023
Current Month: 3
```

In this example, %SYSFUNC is used to call the today(), year(), and month() functions, which return the current date in SAS date value format, the current year, and the current month, respectively.

Conditional Logic Functions

Conditional logic is essential for controlling the flow of macro execution. SAS provides conditional macro functions such as:

- \%IF ...\%THEN ...\%ELSE: Enables conditional branching within macros.
- \%STR: Masks special characters within macro expressions during conditional evaluation.

An example of using conditional logic functions is:

```
%let x = 15;

%if &x < 20 %then %do;
    %put The value of x is less than 20.;
```

```
%end;
%else %do;
   %put The value of x is 20 or more.;
%end;
```

The output generated is:

```
The value of x is less than 20.
```

In this case, the %IF ...%THEN ...%ELSE construct evaluates the value of x and executes the corresponding block of code based on the condition.

Macro Expressions

Macro expressions in SAS extend the power of macro functions, allowing the execution of complex conditional logic and arithmetic directly within the macro facility. They can utilize logical operators (<, >, =, etc.) and arithmetic operators (+, -, *, etc.) to form more sophisticated expressions.

Here is an example demonstrating a macro expression:

```
%let a = 10;
%let b = 20;

%if %eval(&a + &b > 25) %then %do;
   %put The sum of a and b is greater than 25.;
%end;
```

The output for this example is:

```
The sum of a and b is greater than 25.
```

This example showcases how %EVAL is combined with logical operators to form a macro expression evaluated by the %IF statement.

Understanding and effectively utilizing macro functions and expressions are crucial for mastering SAS macros, significantly enhancing the flexibility and robustness of macro programs. This knowledge allows for the creation of more dynamic, efficient, and readable code, ultimately leading to better automation and customization in SAS programming.

10.5 Defining Macros with %MACRO and %MEND

SAS macros are central to automating repetitive code and structuring dynamic SAS programs. Macros begin with the %MACRO statement and terminate with the %MEND statement. The general form of a macro definition is:

```
%MACRO macro-name;
  macro-text
%MEND macro-name;
```

The macro-name is a valid SAS name and refers to the macro when invoked. The macro-text encompasses the SAS code intended for execution.

%MACRO and %MEND define macro boundaries, enabling the inclusion of complex SAS code within these bounds. Consider the following example:

```
%MACRO greet;
  %PUT Hello, World!;
%MEND greet;
```

To execute the above macro, invoke it by name, prefixed with a percent sign:

```
%greet
```

The output in the SAS log will be:

```
Hello, World!
```

Macros accept parameters to make them dynamic. Parameters are specified within parentheses immediately after the macro's name in the %MACRO statement. Here is an example:

```
%MACRO greet_user(name);
  %PUT Hello, &name!;
%MEND greet_user;
```

The macro can be called with:

```
%greet_user(Mary)
```

The resulting output is:

```
Hello, Mary!
```

Here, name is a positional parameter. The value Mary is assigned to name, and the &name token resolves to Mary. The %PUT statement then prints the greeting.

For more complex cases, keyword parameters are beneficial. Keyword parameters allow default values and are defined using the equal sign within the parameter list. Consider the following macro:

```
%MACRO greet_users(greet=Hello, name);
  %PUT &greet, &name!;
%MEND greet_users;
```

Invocation examples are:

```
%greet_users(name=John)
%greet_users(greet=Hi, name=Emily)
```

With corresponding log outputs:

```
Hello, John!
Hi, Emily!
```

If no value is provided for greet, it defaults to "Hello". Keyword parameters enable versatility and default assignment in macros.

Macros often integrate conditional code execution via macro statements. Employing %IF-%THEN-%ELSE facilitates conditional logic within macros. For example:

```
%MACRO greet_with_time(name, time_of_day);
  %IF &time_of_day = morning %THEN %DO;
    %PUT Good morning, &name!;
  %END;
  %ELSE %IF &time_of_day = evening %THEN %DO;
    %PUT Good evening, &name!;
  %END;
  %ELSE %DO;
    %PUT Hello, &name!;
  %END;
%MEND greet_with_time;
```

Execution examples:

```
%greet_with_time(name=Alice, time_of_day=morning)
%greet_with_time(name=Bob, time_of_day=evening)
%greet_with_time(name=Charlie, time_of_day=)
```

Producing:

```
Good morning, Alice!
Good evening, Bob!
Hello, Charlie!
```

Macros significantly enhance code reusability, maintainability, and clarity. Each macro should be tailored to specific, repeated tasks, thus optimizing the programming workflow. Mastery of %MACRO and %MEND sets the foundation for sophisticated SAS programming practices. Understanding the subtleties of parameters and conditional constructs refines macro utility, aligning with best practices for efficient, readable, and adaptable code.

10.6 Passing Parameters to Macros

One powerful feature of the SAS macro facility is the ability to pass parameters to macros. This capability enhances flexibility, enabling the creation of more dynamic and reusable code. Parameters can be passed both positionally and by keyword, allowing for customizable execution without modifying the macro definition. This section delves into the methods for passing parameters and illustrates their use through examples.

Positional Parameters:

Positional parameters allow arguments to be passed to a macro based on their position in the invocation. When defining a macro, the parameters are listed in the

```
%MACRO example_positional(param1, param2);
  %LET result = %EVAL(&param1 + &param2);
  %PUT The sum of &param1 and &param2 is &result.;
%MEND example_positional;

%example_positional(5,10);
```

The above code defines a macro named example_positional with two positional parameters, param1 and param2. When the macro is called with arguments 5 and 10, these values are passed to the respective parameters, and the result is calculated and printed.

```
The sum of 5 and 10 is 15.
```

Keyword Parameters:

Keyword parameters provide an alternative method for passing arguments to macros, where each parameter is specified by name, allowing more flexibility in the order of parameters.

```
%MACRO example_keyword(param1=, param2=);
  %LET result = %EVAL(&param1 * &param2);
  %PUT The product of &param1 and &param2 is &result.;
%MEND example_keyword;

%example_keyword(param1=4, param2=7);
```

In the macro definition example_keyword, param1 and param2 are defined as keyword parameters. When the macro is invoked, the arguments are passed by naming each parameter and assigning it a value. This method is especially useful when dealing with a large number of parameters or when the order of parameters might change.

```
The product of 4 and 7 is 28.
```

Default Values for Keyword Parameters:

Keyword parameters allow setting default values, eliminating the need to specify every parameter during the macro call. If a parameter is not provided, the macro uses the default value.

```
%MACRO example_defaults(param1=1, param2=2);
  %LET result = %EVAL(&param1 ** &param2);
  %PUT &param1 raised to the power of &param2 is &result.;
%MEND example_defaults;

%example_defaults(param1=3);
%example_defaults();
```

In this macro, param1 defaults to 1 and param2 defaults to 2 if not specified. The first invocation of example_defaults sets param1 to 3, while the second invocation uses the default values for both parameters.

```
3 raised to the power of 2 is 9.
1 raised to the power of 2 is 1.
```

Combining Positional and Keyword Parameters:

A macro may combine both positional and keyword parameters, providing greater flexibility and control over the macro invocation.

```
%MACRO example_combined(param1, param2=5, param3=10);
  %LET sum = %EVAL(&param1 + &param2 + &param3);
  %PUT Sum of &param1, &param2, and &param3 is &sum.;
%MEND example_combined;

%example_combined(6);
%example_combined(6, param2=8);
%example_combined(6, param2=8, param3=12);
```

Here, example_combined uses a positional parameter, param1, and two keyword parameters, param2 and param3, with default values. Different combinations of arguments are passed, demonstrating the flexibility in specifying values.

```
Sum of 6, 5, and 10 is 21.
Sum of 6, 8, and 10 is 24.
Sum of 6, 8, and 12 is 26.
```

Best Practices for Passing Parameters:

When designing macros, it is crucial to consider readability and maintainability. Follow these best practices:

- Use keyword parameters for macros with multiple arguments, enhancing clarity.
- Provide default values where appropriate, simplifying macro calls.

- Document the use and expected values of parameters within the macro definition.
- Validate parameter values within the macro to ensure correct usage.

Adequate design and documentation of macros with parameters improve code robustness and reusability, making it easier for others to understand and use the macros effectively.

10.7 Conditional Execution with %IF-%THEN-%ELSE

The %IF-%THEN-%ELSE statements in SAS macros allow conditional logic to be introduced within macro programs. This enables the execution of code branches based on certain conditions, enhancing the flexibility and decision-making capability of your macros. Understanding how to correctly implement these statements ensures that your macros can handle a variety of scenarios dynamically.

To effectively utilize the %IF-%THEN-%ELSE construct, it is important to comprehend its syntax and operational mechanism. The logical flow within the conditional execution must be planned meticulously to ensure that the macro executes the intended code paths under specific conditions.

```
%macro example_macro(var);
    %if &var = 1 %then %do;
        %put The value of var is 1;
    %end;
    %else %if &var = 2 %then %do;
        %put The value of var is 2;
    %end;
    %else %do;
        %put The value of var is neither 1 nor 2;
    %end;
%mend example_macro;

%example_macro(1);

%example_macro(3);
```

Executing the above macro calls produces the following output:

```
The value of var is 1
The value of var is neither 1 nor 2
```

In this macro, %IF statements evaluate the value of the macro variable var. If var equals 1, the first branch executes, printing a message that var is 1. If var equals 2, the second branch executes, indicating that var is 2. For any other value of var, the %ELSE branch executes, indicating the variable is neither 1 nor 2.

Understanding and using logical operators enhances the power of %IF-%THEN constructs. Examples of such operators include:

- =, = or NE, EQ
- > or GT, < or LT
- Logical AND (&) and OR (|)

Consider an example where conditions involve multiple logical expressions:

```
%macro check_value(x);
    %if &x > 10 and &x < 20 %then %do;
        %put The value &x is between 10 and 20;
    %end;
    %else %if &x >= 20 or &x <= 10 %then %do;
        %put The value &x is outside the range 10 to 20;
    %end;
%mend check_value;

%check_value(25);

%check_value(15);
```

The corresponding output would be:

```
The value 25 is outside the range 10 to 20
The value 15 is between 10 and 20
```

%IF-%THEN-%ELSE statements can also be nested to handle more complex logical conditions. When nesting conditional statements, attention must be paid to the scopes of %DO and %END blocks to ensure that the internal logic is correctly executed.

Here is an example of nesting %IF-%THEN-%ELSE statements:

```
%macro nested_check(y);
    %if &y >= 0 %then %do;
        %if &y < 5 %then %do;
            %put The value &y is between 0 and 5;
        %end;
        %else %do;
            %put The value &y is 5 or greater but non-negative;
        %end;
    %end;
    %else %do;
        %put The value &y is negative;
    %end;
```

```
%mend nested_check;

%nested_check(3);

%nested_check(-2);

%nested_check(7);
```

The execution of this macro will produce:

```
The value 3 is between 0 and 5
The value -2 is negative
The value 7 is 5 or greater but non-negative
```

The nesting ensures that only the appropriate block of code is executed based on the value of y. Such nested constructs are powerful tools in developing dynamic and responsive macros.

Proper handling of null and missing values is crucial while using %IF-%THEN-%ELSE constructs. Macros often need to account for scenarios where input values may be missing or null, requiring explicit checks to avoid unintended behavior.

```
%macro handle_nulls(z);
    %if &z = %then %do;
        %put The value is missing or null;
    %end;
    %else %do;
        %put The value is &z;
    %end;
%mend handle_nulls;

%handle_nulls();

%handle_nulls(42);
```

The output will be:

```
The value is missing or null
The value is 42
```

This ensures the macro responds appropriately to missing input by checking if the variable z is null before continuing with further logic.

Mastering the %IF-%THEN-%ELSE constructs in SAS macros allows for sophisticated decision making and flexibility in macro programming, making your code adaptive to various conditions dynamically.

10.8 Iterative Processing with %DO Loops

Iterative processing in SAS macros is facilitated through the use of %DO loops. These loops enable the execution of a block of code repeatedly based on specified conditions and can be immensely useful for tasks that involve repetitive operations. The %DO statement is used to begin the loop, and it ends with the %END statement.

To illustrate the application of %DO loops, consider the following basic structure of a %DO loop in a SAS macro:

```
%macro example_do_loop;
   %do i = 1 %to 5;
      %put Iteration: &i;
   %end;
%mend example_do_loop;

%example_do_loop;
```

In this example, the macro example_do_loop prints the iteration number from 1 to 5. The macro variable i is initialized at 1 and incremented by 1 in each iteration until it reaches 5.

```
Iteration: 1
Iteration: 2
Iteration: 3
Iteration: 4
Iteration: 5
```

It is important to note that the macros created inside a %DO loop utilize the macro variable in their logic. Now, let's delve deeper into the parameters of the %DO loop and explore variations that make %DO loops even more versatile.

Controlling the Increment Value

By default, the increment value is 1, but you can control it by specifying a value for the by parameter. For example:

```
%macro do_loop_with_step;
   %do i = 1 %to 10 %by 2;
      %put Step Iteration: &i;
   %end;
%mend do_loop_with_step;

%do_loop_with_step;
```

```
Step Iteration: 1
Step Iteration: 3
Step Iteration: 5
Step Iteration: 7
Step Iteration: 9
```

Iterating Through Macro Variables

Another powerful feature is iterating through a list of values stored in macro variables. This can be particularly useful for dynamically generating code based on a set of parameters. Consider the following example:

```
%let list = A B C;

%macro iterate_list;
   %let count = %sysfunc(countw(&list));
   %do i = 1 %to &count;
      %let item = %scan(&list, &i);
      %put Item &i: &item;
   %end;
%mend iterate_list;

%iterate_list;
```

In this example, the macro iterate_list iterates through the list of items stored in the macro variable list. The function countw returns the number of items in the list, and scan extracts each item during the iteration.

```
Item 1: A
Item 2: B
Item 3: C
```

Nesting %DO Loops

Nesting %DO loops allows for more complex iterative processing. This can be useful for processing multi-dimensional data or performing operations that require multiple nested iterations. Here is an example of nested %DO loops:

```
%macro nested_do_loops;
   %do i = 1 %to 3;
      %do j = 1 %to 2;
         %put Outer loop &i, Inner loop &j;
      %end;
   %end;
%mend nested_do_loops;

%nested_do_loops;
```

```
Outer loop 1, Inner loop 1
Outer loop 1, Inner loop 2
Outer loop 2, Inner loop 1
Outer loop 2, Inner loop 2
Outer loop 3, Inner loop 1
Outer loop 3, Inner loop 2
```

This example demonstrates how the outer loop runs three times with i ranging from 1 to 3, and for each iteration of the outer loop, the inner loop runs twice with j ranging from 1 to 2.

Conditional Execution within %DO Loops

It is possible to include conditional statements within %DO loops to control the flow of execution based on specific conditions. This can be achieved using %IF and %THEN statements. For example:

```
%macro conditional_do_loop;
    %do i = 1 %to 5;
        %if &i = 3 %then %put Special Case for i = 3;
        %else %put Iteration: &i;
    %end;
%mend conditional_do_loop;

%conditional_do_loop;
```

```
Iteration: 1
Iteration: 2
Special Case for i = 3
Iteration: 4
Iteration: 5
```

In this macro, the iteration message is outputted for each value of i, except when i equals 3. In that case, a special message is printed.

Iterative Processing with Dataset Contents

For scenarios involving iterative processing based on dataset contents, %DO loops can be used in combination with SAS data steps. A common approach involves using call routines to create macro variables dynamically from dataset observations and then iterating through these variables. Consider the following example that processes a dataset named mydata:

```
* Sample dataset;
data mydata;
    input ID $ Name $ Age;
    datalines;
    001 John 30
    002 Jane 25
    003 Alice 27
    004 Bob 22
    ;
run;

* Create macro variables from the dataset;
data _null_;
    set mydata;
    call symputx(cats('id',_n_), ID);
    call symputx(cats('name',_n_), Name);
    call symputx(cats('age',_n_), Age);
    call symputx('obs_count', _n_);
run;

%macro process_dataset;
    %do i = 1 %to &obs_count;
        %put ID: &&id&i Name: &&name&i Age: &&age&i;
    %end;
%mend process_dataset;
```

```
%process_dataset;
```

```
ID: 001 Name: John Age: 30
ID: 002 Name: Jane Age: 25
ID: 003 Name: Alice Age: 27
ID: 004 Name: Bob Age: 22
```

In this example, the dataset mydata is processed to create macro variables dynamically for each observation. The process_dataset macro then iterates through the observations, printing the values of ID, Name, and Age for each row.

By integrating %DO loops with other macro functionalities, complex data manipulations, and iterative operations can be performed efficiently within SAS macros, significantly enhancing the capability for dynamic coding and automation.

10.9 Debugging Macros with MLOGIC, MPRINT, and SYMBOLGEN

Effective debugging is essential for the efficient development and maintenance of SAS macros. SAS provides several macro system options that facilitate debugging by offering insight into the execution of macros and the resolution of macro variables. The primary options for debugging macros are MLOGIC, MPRINT, and SYMBOLGEN. These options can be activated to output detailed messages in the SAS log, aiding in the identification and resolution of macro issues.

MLOGIC displays messages about macro execution. It shows when a macro is called, how the parameters are resolved, and when the macro execution completes. This option is useful to trace the flow of macro execution. Activating MLOGIC can be accomplished by using the options statement:

```
options mlogic;
```

MPRINT outputs the SAS code generated by macro execution. This is particularly helpful to verify that the macro is generating the correct SAS code. To enable MPRINT, include the following statement:

```
options mprint;
```

SYMBOLGEN shows resolution of macro variables. This option provides detailed information on how macro variables are resolved, which can help identify issues with variable assignment or unexpected values. Enable SYMBOLGEN with:

```
options symbolgen;
```

Consider a simple example macro:

```
%macro example(data);
    proc print data=&data;
    run;
%mend example;

%example(sashelp.class);
```

If we enable MLOGIC, MPRINT, and SYMBOLGEN, the SAS log will provide detailed information about the macro's execution process:

```
options mlogic mprint symbolgen;
%example(sashelp.class);
```

The resulting SAS log would include:

```
MLOGIC(EXAMPLE): Beginning execution.
SYMBOLGEN: Macro variable DATA resolves to sashelp.class
MPRINT(EXAMPLE): proc print data=sashelp.class;
MPRINT(EXAMPLE): run;

NOTE: There were 19 observations read from the data set SASHELP.CLASS.
```

Analyzing each component of the log:

- MLOGIC(EXAMPLE): Beginning execution. indicates that the example macro has started executing. - SYMBOLGEN: Macro variable DATA resolves to sashelp.class signifies that the macro variable data was resolved to sashelp.class. - MPRINT(EXAMPLE): proc print data=sashelp.class; outputs the SAS code generated by the macro. - MPRINT(EXAMPLE): run; completes the generated code. - Finally, a standard SAS note confirms that the procedure ran and processed 19 observations from the dataset SASHELP.CLASS.

For more complex macros involving conditional execution and loops, these debugging options become even more valuable. Consider a macro that includes conditional logic:

```
%macro conditional(data);
    %if &data=class %then %do;
        proc print data=sashelp.class;
        run;
    %end;
    %else %do;
        proc print data=sashelp.iris;
```

```
        run;
    %end;
%mend conditional;

%conditional(class);
```

With MLOGIC, MPRINT, and SYMBOLGEN enabled, the SAS log output would be:

```
MLOGIC(CONDITIONAL):  Beginning execution.
SYMBOLGEN:  Macro variable DATA resolves to class
MLOGIC(CONDITIONAL):  %IF condition &data=class  is TRUE
MPRINT(CONDITIONAL):   proc print data=sashelp.class;
MPRINT(CONDITIONAL):  run;

NOTE: There were 19 observations read from the data set SASHELP.CLASS.
```

- The log shows that the conditional macro begins execution. - The macro variable data resolves to class. - The %IF condition is evaluated and found true. - The generated code for printing sashelp.class is displayed. - Finally, the note confirms the procedure's execution.

Debugging macros leveraging conditional execution and loops:

```
%macro loop;
    %do i=1 %to 3;
        %put Loop iteration: &i;
    %end;
%mend loop;

%loop;
```

Enabling MLOGIC, MPRINT, and SYMBOLGEN provides insights as follows:

```
MLOGIC(LOOP):  Beginning execution.
MLOGIC(LOOP):  %DO loop beginning; index variable I; start value 1; stop value 3; by value 1.
MPRINT(LOOP):   Loop iteration: 1
MLOGIC(LOOP):  %DO loop iteration 2; index variable I=2;
MPRINT(LOOP):   Loop iteration: 2
MLOGIC(LOOP):  %DO loop iteration 3; index variable I=3;
MPRINT(LOOP):   Loop iteration: 3
MLOGIC(LOOP):  %DO loop ending; index variable I=3.
```

- The log captures the macro loop starting. - The %DO loop initiates, iterates, and concludes. - Each iteration produces a %PUT statement output showing the current iteration.

Using these debugging techniques significantly enhances the capability to precisely track macro execution and resolve errors efficiently.

10.10 Best Practices for Writing Macros

The effectiveness of your macros in SAS can significantly affect the overall performance, maintainability, and readability of your SAS programs. Here, we outline important best practices to follow when writing macros.

1. Use Meaningful and Descriptive Names: Ensure that the names of your macro variables and macros are clear and indicative of their function. This practice not only makes the code more self-explanatory but also aids in debugging and future maintenance.

2. Comment Extensively: Commenting is crucial in understanding the macro's purpose and logic. Add comments to describe the overall purpose of the macro, explain complex expressions, and note the purpose of key macro variables. For example:

```
%let file_path = /data_source/data_set; /* Define the path to the dataset */
```

3. Avoid Global Macro Variables: Restrict the scope of macro variables where possible. Use local macro variables within macros using the %LOCAL statement to prevent unintended side effects on other parts of the program.

```
%macro example;
  %local counter;
  %let counter = 1;
  /* Rest of the macro */
%mend example;
```

4. Modularize Code: Break down complex macros into smaller, more manageable pieces. Write smaller macros that perform specific tasks and then invoke these smaller macros from a higher-level macro. This approach enhances readability and reusability.

5. Use Argument Lists: Clearly define input parameters to macros using argument lists. This practice improves the flexibility and reusability of the macro functions.

```
%macro example(input_data, output_data);
  /* Macro code utilizing input_data and output_data */
%mend example;
```

6. Validate Parameters: Validate input parameters using conditional statements within macros to avoid errors and ensure that the macro receives appropriate arguments.

```
%macro validate_example(param);
```

```
  %if &param. = %then %do;
    %put ERROR: Parameter cannot be empty!;
    %abort cancel;
  %end;
%mend validate_example;
```

7. Optimize Macro Performance: Be mindful of the performance implications of your macros. Avoid repetitive and unnecessary computations by calculating results once and storing them in macro variables. Also, consider the efficiency of the underlying SAS code the macro generates.

8. Use System Options for Macro Debugging: Utilize system options like MLOGIC, MPRINT, and SYMBOLGEN to debug macro executions. Enabling these options will print valuable debugging information in the SAS log.

```
options mlogic mprint symbolgen;
```

9. Include Error Handling: Incorporate error handling to gracefully manage unexpected conditions. Use %PUT statements to display informative messages to the log and handle errors with %ABORT or by setting return codes that the calling program can check.

```
%macro safe_divide(numerator, denominator);
  %if &denominator = 0 %then %do;
    %put ERROR: Division by zero!;
    %abort cancel;
  %end;
  %else %do;
    %let result = %sysevalf(&numerator / &denominator);
    %put The result is &result;
  %end;
%mend safe_divide;
```

10. Test Macros Thoroughly: Thoroughly test macros with various input scenarios to ensure correctness. Testing should cover common use cases, boundary conditions, and potential error cases.

11. Document Macro Usage: Maintain comprehensive documentation for each macro. Documentation should include the macro's purpose, the input parameters, expected output, and an example of its usage.

```
Macro: safe_divide
Purpose: Safely divide two numbers
Parameters:
  numerator - the numerator of the division
  denominator - the denominator of the division (must not be zero)
Example usage:
  %safe_divide(10, 2);
```

By adhering to these practices, you can ensure that your SAS macros are robust, efficient, and maintainable. These strategies not only streamline the macro development process but also simplify future debugging and enhancements. Employing these best practices will significantly enhance the quality of your macro-driven SAS programs.

10.11 Advanced Macro Techniques

Mastery of basic macro constructs opens the door to advanced techniques that further enhance SAS macro programming. These advanced techniques encompass macro quoting, indirect referencing, and macro arrays. Each technique provides a powerful toolset for sophisticated and dynamic code generation, which can optimize complex data-driven tasks.

Macro Quoting

Macro quoting resolves issues surrounding special characters and text strings that contain macro triggers or symbols. There are two primary types of macro quoting: compile-time and execution-time quoting. Compile-time quoting functions include %STR and %NRSTR, while execution-time quoting functions include %QUOTE, %NRQUOTE, %BQUOTE, and %NRBQUOTE.

```
%let special_char_macro = %str(This %inside% will &not trigger any error!);
%let resolved_value = %quote(This &inside will not trigger any error!);
```

The difference between compile-time (e.g., %STR, %NRSTR) and execution-time quoting (e.g., %QUOTE, %NRQUOTE) resides in their application phase. %STR and %NRSTR mask significant characters such as ampersands and percent signs during the macro compilation, while %QUOTE and %NRQUOTE mask them at execution time. Here, %NR signifies non-resolvable items, thus extending to macro expressions that must remain unchanged until invoked.

Indirect Referencing

Indirect referencing, or "double ampersand" referencing, allows the dynamic utilization of macro variable names. This technique is pivotal for scenarios requiring variable macro names that are constructed during program execution.

```
%let day1 = Monday;
%let day2 = Tuesday;
%let i = 1;
```

```
%put &&day&i;
```

The output will resolve into the value of day1 (i.e., Monday). The double ampersand (&&) resolves in two stages: firstly, &i resolves to 1, and subsequently, &day1 resolves to Monday. This flexibility extends the utility of macro variables by accommodating constructed names dynamically.

```
Monday
```

Macro Arrays

Macro arrays facilitate handling lists within macros, leveraging the %DO loop alongside a systematic approach to variable naming.

```
%let days = 7;
%do i = 1 %to &days;
  %let day&i = %scan(Monday Tuesday Wednesday Thursday Friday Saturday Sunday,
      &i);
  %put The &i day is &&day&i;
%end;
```

In this scenario, %SCAN function dynamically assigns the names of the days of the week to macro variables. The %DO loop iterates over these names, creating macro variables day1 through day7.

```
The 1 day is Monday
The 2 day is Tuesday
The 3 day is Wednesday
The 4 day is Thursday
The 5 day is Friday
The 6 day is Saturday
The 7 day is Sunday
```

Dynamic Code Generation

Combining the advanced macro techniques can lead to highly dynamic code generation. Consider a scenario where data tables are dynamically processed based on the period defined by the user.

```
%macro dynamic_proc(periods);
  %do p = 1 %to &periods;
    data period&p;
      set master_data;
      where period = &p;
    run;
  %end;
%mend;

%dynamic_proc(4);
```

Here, the dynamic_proc macro generates a distinct data set for each period specified by the periods parameter, dynamically creating datasets period1 through period4.

Including External Code with %INCLUDE

Sophisticated applications might involve modular code stored externally, callable through the %INCLUDE statement. This facility enables code reuse and maintains a clean and organized code base.

```
%include '/path/to/external_macro.sas';
```

Integrating these modular code snippets through %INCLUDE allows a seamless and maintainable approach to augment SAS macros, especially when dealing with extensive and detailed processes.

Macro Autocall Libraries

For persistent and reusable macro definitions, macro autocall libraries provide an efficient mechanism. By storing and referencing macros in specified libraries, the SAS system can automatically compile them when invoked.

```
options mstored sasmstore=macrolib;

/* Define the macro and store it */
libname macrolib '/path/to/macro/library';

%macro sample_macro / store source;
   %put This is a stored macro example;
%mend sample_macro;

/* Invoke the stored macro */
%sample_macro;
```

When establishing autocall libraries, the options statement enables the storage and referencing of macros from predefined libraries, thus ensuring that macros are only compiled when called, optimizing resource utilization and expanding reuse capabilities.

Subsequent to understanding these advanced techniques, practitioners can create advanced, optimized, and sophisticated SAS macro applications that drive high efficiency and robustness in dynamic SAS environments.

10.12 Storing and Reusing Macro Code

Storing and reusing macro code is an essential practice that enhances efficiency, maintainability, and consistency in SAS programming. By modularizing and centralizing macro definitions, programmers can ensure that macros are readily available across different programs and sessions, thereby eliminating redundancy and promoting code reuse. This section delves into techniques and strategies for effectively storing and reusing macro code in SAS.

Using Autocall Libraries:

An autocall library is a collection of macro definitions stored in external files that SAS can automatically compile and execute when a macro is invoked. To leverage this feature, you must specify the library path using the MAUTOSOURCE system option and the SASAUTOS option.

```
%let path_to_macros = C:\my_macros\;
options mautocource sasautos = ("&path_to_macros");
```

In the above snippet, the MAUTOSOURCE option allows SAS to automatically access the macros stored in the specified directory, C: my_macros. Each macro should be stored in a separate file named after the macro itself, with a .sas extension. For example, a macro called macro1 should be saved in a file named macro1.sas.

The content of macro1.sas might look like this:

```
%macro macro1(param1, param2);
  /* Macro definition */
  %put This is macro1 with &param1 and &param2.;
%mend macro1;
```

Once the autocall library path is set, you can call the macro anywhere in your SAS session as shown below:

```
%macro1(value1, value2);
```

Storing Macros in SAS Catalogs:

Macros can also be stored in SAS catalogs, which enables encapsulation within the SAS environment. A SAS catalog is a type of SAS file that contains entries representing various kinds of SAS objects, such as macros. Use the STORE option with %MACRO to save a macro in a catalog.

First, enable the storage system option:

```
options mstored sasmstore=mymacros;

libname mymacros 'C:\my_sas_catalog';
```

Then define and store a macro in the mymacros library:

```
%macro macro2(param1) / store source des='Example of stored macro';
  %put This is macro2 with &param1;
%mend macro2;
```

The / store option tells SAS to save the compiled macro in the specified library. Subsequently, you can invoke the stored macro as follows:

```
%macro2(test_value);
```

Including Macros from External Files:

Another method to store and reuse macros involves including macro definitions from external files directly in your SAS program using the %INCLUDE statement. This approach is straightforward and useful for sharing macros across different programs.

Assume a macro is defined in an external file named macro3.sas located at C:
my_macro_files:

```
%macro macro3;
  %put This is macro3;
%mend macro3;
```

You can include and execute this macro in your program with the following code:

```
%include 'C:\my_macro_files\macro3.sas';

%macro3;
```

Best Practices for Storing and Reusing Macros:

To maximize the benefits of storing and reusing macros, consider the following best practices:

- **Modularity**: Design macros to accomplish a single, well-defined task. This promotes reusability and simplifies testing and debugging.
- **Documentation**: Always document macro parameters, functionality, and side effects within the macro definition. This aids in understanding and reusability.

- **Naming Conventions**: Use consistent and descriptive naming conventions for macro files and macros. This reduces confusion and enhances clarity.
- **Version Control**: Maintain version control for macro files, especially when multiple users or projects depend on them. This helps in tracking changes and ensures consistency.
- **Test and Debug**: Rigorously test macros in isolation before deploying them in larger SAS programs. Use the debugging tools provided by SAS such as MLOGIC, MPRINT, and SYMBOLGEN.

Effective storage and reuse of macro code significantly enhance productivity and code maintainability in SAS programming. By leveraging autocall libraries, SAS catalogs, and the %INCLUDE statement, and by adhering to best practices, you can ensure that your macro codebase is robust, reusable, and easy to manage.

Made in the USA
Monee, IL
05 November 2026

67845319R00184